*When two cultures collide is the only time
when true suffering exists*
Hermann Hesse (1877–1962)

UNBROKEN SPIRIT

UNBROKEN SPIRIT

Ferzanna Riley

A true story of a girl's struggle
to escape from abuse

HODDER

First published in Great Britain in 2007

This paperback edition first published in 2008

3

British Library Cataloguing in Publication Data
A record for this book is available from the British Library

ISBN 978 0340 94349 6

Typeset in Sabon by Avon DataSet Ltd,
Bidford on Avon, Warwickshire

Printed and bound in Great Britain by
Clays Ltd, St Ives plc

The paper and board used in this paperback are natural recyclable products made
from wood grown in sustainable forests. The manufacturing processes conform to
the environmental regulations of the country of origin.

Hodder & Stoughton
A Division of Hodder Headline Ltd
338 Euston Road
London NW1 3BH
www.hodder.co.uk

For Ion and Sophie

My home is not a place, it is people
Lois McMaster Bujold (1949–)

Contents

Prologue

Prisoners!

Locked in the airless heat of a dark, dingy room, the girl and her younger sister waited with dread, comforted by the fact that, whatever happened, at least they were together.

The older girl's hair was damp with perspiration and the humidity made her cotton *kameez* cling to her body. It was early evening but outside it was already dark. For in the East there is no transitional period of dusk where the day lingers lazily into evening; in this part of the world the sun gathers up her golden skirts and makes a hasty retreat and night falls swiftly. The crickets started to sing their familiar night-song as the blistering heat of day gave way to a welcome evening breeze, breathing the scent of orange blossom and jasmine across the courtyard.

But no soft breeze reached the claustrophobia of this small, stifling room, where the heat made it difficult to breathe. Elsewhere in the house there were cool tiled floors and open windows where brightly coloured curtains danced beneath the humming *punkhas* (fans). But in this room, the door was shut and the one small window was shuttered and barred. Here, there was a bare concrete floor and an old pedestal fan, which had been turned off earlier that evening as punishment.

The room was located in the main body of the *bungla* (house), built by the girls' Dadda, paternal grandfather, for his wife and young family. Years later when the children had grown up, the girls' mother had come to this room as a new bride.

After their parents left, the room was taken over by other members of the family as, one by one, the rest of the sons were married off and their brides were brought in turn to live here. Then, as the third generation of the family expanded, Dadda had built outward and upward, adding more rooms and another storey. The house had now been changed beyond recognition since their parents last lived here. Now, this room was considered too insignificant to be used as anything other than a store room. For the past few months it had also been a prison.

'They're going to murder us, aren't they?' the younger sister whispered. It was more of a statement than a question, but the thought of being killed here suddenly brought the reality of their situation home. To die here in this room would indeed be ironic because it was in this very room that the older girl had been born, twenty-four years ago.

'I think so,' the older sister replied, no longer having any comfort to offer. Perhaps it was better that they should admit the unspeakable and prepare themselves for the unthinkable. For months the girls had clung to the hope that there would be a miraculous change of heart and they'd be released, or that they might be able to escape to the British Embassy and demand their right as British citizens to be given sanctuary and returned home to England. But now, even this dream was fading. There was no hope left. A wave of homesickness caused an involuntary sob to catch in the older girl's throat as she remembered how they'd been told that they'd never see England again. She knew she'd either die here or go insane.

'Do you think they'll come tonight?'

She didn't know. Maybe. It depended on whether their family's *izzat*, their respect, could be salvaged by killing them. For this was an Islamic state and in Pakistan honour killings happened every day. They'd been told in great detail that people could do anything to them here, told of girls who'd been murdered for dishonouring their families by 'immoral conduct'. The nature of that 'immorality' was a very subjective test, with the killer being judge, jury and executioner. What's more, instead of being punished, family members were given sympathy because, to some Muslims, honour killings are construed not as murder but as justified execution. And what Muslim would not do the same? To a Pakistani, what else comes above honour? A person cannot live without *izzat*. It is better to die. Or to put to death a daughter who brings shame and dishonour. Indeed, does not the Koran demand it?

She didn't know how long they could both go on. They were losing the will to fight. And yet, incredibly, that prospect in itself gave her the will and determination to survive. While she breathed, she would keep fighting – and she shuddered suddenly at the memory of when she'd first fought back, quite literally.

'*Haramzadi!* Bitch!' the woman had cried at her younger sister. 'You live like a whore with your Western ways and shame me. I'd rather you were dead!'

And snatching the old man's heavy walking stick, she raised it to strike the girl, who cowered as the blow fell.

'No! Don't you *dare* hurt her!' the older girl yelled, lunging at the weapon in order to shield her sister and wincing with pain as her own body took the blow. 'Run!' she cried, grabbing the walking stick with both hands before it was raised again.

'*Shaitan ki aulad!* Spawn of Satan!' the woman spat, turning on her, eyes blazing with hatred. '*Haramin!* This is all *your* doing! She does whatever you brainwash her to do! You should have been strangled the day you were born!'

'You're mad!' the girl cried. Something inside her suddenly snapped, all reason gone as hatred for this woman consumed her. She no longer cared what else they'd do to her. This was insanity born of anguish and despair. She felt she could take no more.

'Let go!' she cried, tugging at the stick. 'I *said*, let *go*!'

'What are you going to do?' the woman demanded, suddenly afraid. Some instinct told her that she must not let go of the stick, and holding on for dear life she screamed for someone to come and help her. Feet came running, and the girl was seized and flung to the floor in disgust while the woman was pulled to safety and collapsed into her rescuer's arms, weeping with relief. Yet still she refused to unfasten her terrified grip. Because she, the girls' mother, knew, as they both did, that if she had lost control of that weapon, her daughter would have smashed her skull.

These events had taken place some weeks ago. Tonight, the girls had dragged the bed across the room to face the door so that they could be alerted should anyone try to enter the room. The unfamiliar positioning of the bed made the girls even more uneasy and they both knew sleep would not come easily. As they lay in bed, sleep was the last thing they wanted, too terrified to close their eyes, afraid that they'd never wake up again. For this could be the night – the night a silent executioner crept into the room and murdered them.

The older girl sat up in bed, and a sudden chill gripped her heart as she heard footsteps approaching . . .

Part 1

A turbulent beginning

I

An abusive start

What we remember from childhood we remember forever.
Cynthia Ozick (1928–)

I grew up being called a bitch, a bastard and an idiot.

From an early age I answered to a whole variety of names that roughly translated into the same thing. *Sali, haramin, haramzadi, kameeni* were just the ones I was most familiar with, but other names of various unspeakable sexual acts and perversions were flung at me long before I was old enough to understand what they actually meant.

My father could terrorise me simply by looking at me and using a range of these profanities that conveyed illegitimacy, promiscuity or sexual depravity. *Bhahenchode* (sisterf***er) and *Maaderchode* (motherf***er) were ones I heard frequently but only understood many years later. When I was young I recognised them simply as words that my father used when he was angry. It was only when I grew up and acquired a more adult vocabulary that I realised, with horror and shame, exactly what he had meant. For this reason I never swore in Urdu, for even the worst English expletives I uttered could not match the ones I heard at home for utter baseness.

My mother rarely disciplined me, but if need be she would administer a reprimand or slap. A slap, however, would be the furthest thing from my father's mind. A punch with a closed fist, a hard male fist, inflicted far more pain. Slaps and slippers were for amateurs, especially when the beating was not to discipline but to vent frustration or anger at some unrelated cause.

He'd drag me around the room by my hair, punching me and battering my head against hard objects. Sometimes he'd choke me, releasing his grip just before I lost consciousness. Or he'd hurl my body against a wall, a door, a hard floor. I'd be knocked to the floor, kicked and punched. He'd drive his fists into my face, my head, my ribs. No part of my body would be spared. He'd use his fists and feet, and anything he could lay his hands on – a belt, a boot, the flexible orange plastic tracks of a toy car racing set; any implement so long as it hurt me. And didn't hurt him. My screams just made him beat me more and he stopped only when his strength was spent. Sometimes he'd pant from the sheer physical exertion and needed time to recover his breath.

My distraught mother would silently remove me from his presence, check my bones were intact and then clean up my battered face, split lips and broken skin. Later I'd suffer the humiliation of swollen eyes and multi-coloured bruises that drew gasps of pity from my siblings. I'd be excused chores while my wounds healed: damaged joints and limbs, crushed fingers, an arm where I'd landed badly, a limp where he'd smashed my hip against the table. It was my duty to keep out of his way and spare his feelings when he was 'good Dad' again.

It didn't take much to trigger my father's outbursts. Any excuse would justify giving me a good beating, such as not putting enough salt in his dinner. Or whistling!

The 'whistling' incident happened when I was about seven years old. He came home one night vexed about something that had happened at work. His grumblings gathered momentum as his voice became louder, waking me as I slept upstairs. As his language became more profane I lay trembling, knowing from past experience what was to come. Sure enough, as I'd dreaded, his angry footsteps thundered up the stairs and he burst into the bedroom. My head hit the floor first as he flung back the covers and dragged me out of bed by my legs and shook me, demanding to know why I'd been whistling the day before, the week before, or was it the month before? It was immaterial, really, what the crime was or when it was committed: the point is that it gave him justification for beating me. Crying was forbidden, and I lay on the ground as he left me, not daring to move or make a sound, face averted, hot tears silently spilling over. Only when he'd gone back downstairs and had sat down to eat his dinner did I dare to move my frozen limbs, hoist myself back into bed and quietly sob myself back to sleep, in the knowledge that I had served my purpose.

I remember all too clearly the first time I was in fear for my life.

My father was visiting my mother and the new baby in hospital, leaving my ten-year-old sister and me at home taking care of the younger children. As it was late, we assumed he'd stopped off at the place where he acquired that strange smell on his breath. The two other babies, aged one and two, were asleep and the original black-and-white *Godzilla* film was on television. By today's standards that plastic model monster seems primitive, but in the late 1960s it was deliciously scary. We were riveted and so absorbed that we didn't hear my father come in.

Hearing my baby sister Farah grizzling in the cot, he strode over to discover her nappy had leaked and her clothes and bedding were a mess (to this day, the colour of Coronation Chicken makes me gag). The room shrank as my father loomed, more terrifying than Godzilla, very real and very angry. Predictably, the verbal and physical abuse was directed solely at me, but this night, although I was used to his assaults, the violence was about to take a terrifyingly new turn.

To my horror and disbelief he grabbed a big knife from the kitchen and, roaring that he was going to butcher me like an animal, he pulled my head back by my hair, exposing my neck, and held the knife across my throat. I was barely conscious, aware only that these were the final moments of my life.

My sister fell to her knees, hands clasped, weeping and imploring my father not to kill me. Only then did his fury subside and he released me. Then he went out, leaving us both cleaning up the mess, sobbing from the fright of what had just happened.

My father had almost murdered me by cutting my throat. I was six years old.

2

A new life in England

There are only two lasting bequests we can give our children. One is roots, the other is wings.
William Hodding Carter II (1907–72)

Perhaps things might have been different for me if, like my sister (older than me by four years), I'd been able to form a relationship with my father before he emigrated. I was only a few months old when he left Pakistan to make a new life in England.

In 1947 my father had been one of Midnight's Children. Born in Allahabad, he was Indian by nationality until the stroke of midnight on 14 August 1947, when he and millions of Muslims like him suddenly stopped being Indian, took on a new nationality and became Pakistani. The days of British occupation had ended after almost two hundred years; and in the aftermath of Independence, after Lord Louis Mountbatten, the last Viceroy of India, and the rest of the British had departed, a new nation was born in the western portion of the country that had been India. This was the Islamic state negotiated and campaigned for by the founding father, Mohammed Ali Jinnah, the brilliant English-educated lawyer revered by this new nation as the *Quaid-e-Azam* or 'Great Leader': Pakistan, the land of the *Pak* (pure), stretching from Karachi in the south, a thriving port by the coast of the Arabian Sea, to the forbidding borders of Afghanistan in the northwest, to the foothills of the Himalayas in the north.

Dadda, our paternal grandfather, and Nanna, our maternal grandfather, who were yet to meet, each took their wives and young families and made the long hazardous journey west along the now famous Grand Trunk Road, crossing the newly defined borders to make a new home in Karachi, having survived a bloody trail of massacre and misery. Muslims were crossing into Pakistan while Hindus were making an exodus the other way to reach India, and all along the route both Muslims and Hindus were slaughtering one another – men, women and children – for no other reason than that they were of the other faith. Muslim independence from India was purchased at the cost of much Hindu and Muslim blood. Millions died in the aftermath of Partition. The atrocities perpetrated by both sides were burned into the memories of all who witnessed them, and my parents, who were young children at that time, never forgot.

Having lived through the experience, Dadda, a strong-willed and forceful man, was determined to be prosperous. In India he'd had an uncanny ability to make money and coming to Pakistan was no different. The political upheavals happening on the Indian subcontinent had meant leaving everything behind in Allahabad, loading up a bullock cart with his young family and taking whatever possessions they could carry. Once in the new country, he settled on the plot of land given to them by the government, built the family home and established a new business. The nature of that business changed frequently but his ability to make money did not. He had a daughter and six sons, and by the time they were old enough to take over, Dadda had established a large family home and a prosperous, thriving business. My father told us that Dadda always carried a rolled-up wad of money secreted in an inside pocket of his *kurta* because having ready money always at hand gave him a sense of security.

More importantly, it also bought status and respect. The family had achieved a name for itself in the community. The sons took on the businesses and the only daughter, Zainab, was put through college and qualified as a lawyer. They worked hard and achieved the one thing all Pakistanis believe is worth living and dying for: they had *izzat*, honour.

It was easy to see why my father was his parents' favourite. He was the most handsome and cultured of his brothers, with film-star good looks. And even more unusually, in a country where the majority of the population have brown eyes, my father had pale, blue-grey eyes, inherited from Dadda who had piercing blue eyes. All of this made my father stand out from the rest.

My father proved early on that here was a son who'd make them proud. He brought *izzat* to his parents by doing everything expected of him. He went through college, got a good job, married a suitable girl and became a father. He was the perfect son, brother and husband; indeed, he was so beloved of the whole family that his pet name was Acha Bhai (Good Brother). My Dadda and Daddi (my paternal grandmother) never concealed their pride and overwhelming love for this son, calling him simply Acha.

However, he also inherited his determination and adventurous spirit from Dadda, and it was apparent he'd always do things differently from his brothers. Therefore, while it was a huge blow to his parents and brothers, it came as no surprise to anyone when he announced he was emigrating to start a new life with his own young family in England.

In the 1960s, England was in a state of economic boom. Almost two decades after the war had ended, the country was busy rebuilding its economy, and employment prospects were excellent. Indeed, the problem for the country was the abundance of jobs, which allowed the indigenous workforce to pick and choose and left unfilled those jobs that were classed as dirty, lowly or badly paid. There was, in particular, a need for cheap labour in the heavy manufacturing industries in the West Midlands, in cities such as Birmingham and Coventry, and with the thriving textile manufacturers of Lancashire and Yorkshire.

Hence, an invitation was issued to Commonwealth countries such as Pakistan (and the West Indies, where England was still known as the 'mother country' by people who'd never yet set foot on its soil). The word went out for men to come and work as bus conductors, factory hands, cleaners and any other jobs the British didn't want to do. To this day, northern towns and cities such as Bradford, Preston, Blackburn, Manchester and Birmingham are associated with the large Pakistani communities that came over during the 1960s. My father was one who took up the challenge.

In retrospect, I believe that a great deal of his frustration came from doing a job and living a lifestyle that he and his family would have considered beneath him. He arrived with £6 in his pocket to take up a job in the Courtaulds factory on the outskirts of Preston, Lancashire, in the North West of England. This was a social come-down for him. He exchanged a shirt and tie in an office for a pair of overalls in a factory in order that his children would have access to opportunities that would not have been possible back in Pakistan.

Anyone unfamiliar with Pakistani culture may wonder why a man would leave behind the security of a large extended family, comfortable home, servants, status and position in order to embrace the bottom rung of the social ladder on the other side of the world. But to understand that, you have to understand the kind of man my father was.

The challenge of bringing up his family in a new country,

with a different culture and different opportunities, would have been irresistible to a man who was never comfortable in his comfort zone. My father wanted to push boundaries, to do something no one in his family had done and achieve what no one else had achieved. He respected his father for his ability to start all over again in another country and go on to do well for himself. When his time came, the fruits of all that Dadda had achieved in his lifetime would be my father's for the taking, should he choose to step into his inheritance. However, the responsibility of being the head of the family would never challenge him. What did challenge him was the prospect of becoming a success in England on his own terms and without his extended family to help or hinder him. Back in Pakistan, my father had not even been able to choose names for his own children.

This was not unusual. A young couple begin their married lives living with the husband's parents and usually have little say in the naming, educating and upbringing of their own children, with the grandparents claiming the prominent role. By imposing his own will, the son can risk upsetting his parents and rocking the domestic boat. Or he can take the easy way out and allow them their own way. The young wife's opinions and wishes regarding her own offspring barely register as far as her mother-in-law is concerned. My Daddi was no different from other Pakistani mothers-in-law. She was a very forceful woman who'd have created a storm had she not been given a free hand with her grandchildren in every aspect of their lives, from how they were dressed to what they were called.

When I was born my grandparents named me after the Mogul emperor who'd built the Taj Mahal. Exactly why they chose to bestow a male (albeit royal) name on me was a mystery. Nevertheless, whether my parents liked the name or not, the decision was made on their behalf and they had to accept it. However, while he allowed them their grandparents' prerogative in Pakistan, one of the first things my father did when I arrived in England was to change the name I'd been given at birth. In Pakistan I'd been called Shah Jahan. In England my father renamed me Ferzanna.

When my father pursued his dreams and came to England, he initially left behind his young wife and two daughters in the care of his parents. During this time he sent money regularly to support the three of us back in Pakistan. It wasn't an easy life for the first generation of Pakistani men who came to England. While they were tolerated in the factories where their cheap labour was needed, they were not made welcome in the society where they'd been invited to live and work. My father told us stories of those early days, when Pakistanis had to help each other to survive.

Finding somewhere to live was a problem, for a start. *Angrezis* – the English people – were suspicious of the 'coloureds'. They were even more suspicious of a people and culture they'd hitherto never encountered. Furthermore, they had never experienced such cooking before, and to people who were more used to the smell of boiled ham and stewed cabbage, the spicy aromas of a cuisine that was to captivate the British nation within the next decade or so were decidedly alien – and therefore offensive. What they didn't know they disliked. To them, Pakistanis carried with them this strange pungent smell that pervaded their homes and clung to their clothes. This made them reluctant to rent out their houses or let rooms to these smelly 'Pakis'. As a result, Pakistan men had to help each other.

In a culture where *biraderi* (brotherhood) comes naturally, during those early years the men would of necessity buy a house together and rent rooms out to other Pakistanis. This *biraderi* benefited the men enormously. It offered companionship in their loneliness and separation from their families, and also offered financial benefits. Rooms and even beds were rented on a shift basis in order to maximise accommodation and save as much money as possible to send back home. And in their own houses the men had the freedom to come and go as they pleased without being monitored by curious landladies, ever watchful for the suspicious or deviant behaviour they half-expected from these foreigners.

More importantly, in their own homes the men were free to cook the *desi* (native) food that seemed to offend the *Angrezis* but which for them evoked memories of the lives and families they'd left back home.

Even in these early days, the first enterprising Asians, quick to spot an increasing demand in the market, had set up businesses importing and supplying authentic Asian ingredients hitherto unheard of in this country – spices such as chilli, turmeric, coriander and cumin, and exotic vegetables such as okra and aubergines. These shops were also the only places where the men were able to purchase halal or kosher meat required by their religion. At first these specialist Asian shops were few and far between, but they increased in number as demand grew.

Like other men in his situation, my father rented a room in the house of a friend. He worked hard to establish himself in this suspicious, unfriendly society that required his over-qualified labour but gave him no help or encouragement in return. It was the drive and determination he inherited from his own father that helped him to succeed. Within three years, he'd saved enough to buy his own property, obtained an English driving licence and purchased his first car, a brown Morris Minor.

However, even in those days he was different from the other Pakistanis. They had sought out areas already inhabited by Pakistanis, where they could feel secure by being surrounded by their own kin. As more Pakistani immigrants moved in, the *Angrezis* started moving out, thus increasingly creating almost exclusively Pakistani areas which happened to be located in the more affordable or otherwise poorer parts of town. I clearly recall one such area of Preston where there were, and still are, streets of terraced houses all named after birds and nicknamed the 'Canary Isles'. This extended into the area called Deepdale, which was one of the first areas where there was a purpose-built mosque and specialist Pakistani shops, and where it was quite normal to see people walking around dressed in traditional *shalwar kameez*.

However, my father wanted a decent house in a better area and, eschewing the areas where other Pakistanis had begun to settle, purchased a house in Morgan Street, which was an all-*Angrezi* street. His belief was that integration, not segregation, was the way to live in a new country.

Thus, having prepared a home for his family and saved for three airfares, he was finally able to send for his family.

This came as an enormous relief to my mother. Like so many other Pakistani wives in the same position, she had been given little choice but to wait behind with her children as her husband departed to the other side of the world to make a new life for the family. She lived with her in-laws, waiting for the day when he would send for her, resigned to the fact that it would take some time to work hard and save for somewhere to live and, just as important, save for the airfares.

Worryingly, from time to time stories came back to Pakistan of certain men who'd left behind wives and children with the intention of making a better life in the West. It was said that, once in England, they took up with *goris* (white women). Some did eventually send for their families but carried on doing what they'd been doing, secure in the knowledge that here in England they were far removed from the disapproval and censorship of the extended family. Isolated in a new and alien culture, the wives were helpless to do anything about it. A few others were even less fortunate. My father told us of some men of his acquaintance who actually married their English mistresses and settled down to have second families in England, leaving the first families languishing in Pakistan.

I was just a baby when my father left Pakistan to come to England, and therefore had no memories of him. It was, however, a very different story with my elder sister. A tragedy had occurred prior to her birth that shaped the nature of her relationship with my father: my parents had lost their eighteen-month-old baby son. In a patriarchal society where the birth of a son is regarded as a blessing to the parents, the death of their first-born son doubly devastated the young couple. The birth of another baby soon after had been the balm to my father's inconsolable grief; according to my mother, my sister's feet never touched the ground as she rode everywhere on my father's shoulders. They adored each other and were inseparable. When the time came for him to leave, again according to my mother, my sister grew thin and almost wasted away with grief, living only for the time when she would be reunited with her beloved Abba-Ji.

I was three when I saw my father again, so I had no such anticipation. Having no memory of him, travelling to England was less of a reunion and more of an adventure for me. It had been a long flight from Pakistan via Switzerland and the journey was very emotional because of my mother's quiet anticipation and my sister's irrepressible joy at being reunited with her father. The strange new Western food can't have agreed with me as I do recall throwing up all over the elegant feet of the stewardess.

My meeting with my father was equally inauspicious. I observed my mother receiving a discreet pat (Pakistani couples don't do public affection) and my sister running to him, crying, 'Abba-Ji! Abba-Ji!' But I felt totally overawed by this man who was presented to me as being the far-away father everyone loved. All my life I'd been told about him by Dadda and Daddi; been told how clever and handsome he was, what a good son, brother and husband he was. He was always the topic of grown-up conversation. Everyone loved him, Acha Bhai was a legend in the family – and suddenly here he was, stooping down to greet me, arms outstretched.

If he'd been overjoyed that his elder daughter lived up to the memories he'd cherished of her, he was to be very disappointed in whatever expectations he may have had of his youngest. I remember feeling a pang of wanting the same rapturous welcome I'd just witnessed between him and my sister, but there was quite simply no history between us for that to happen.

While I knew about 'Abba-Ji in England', he was simply a name on everyone's lips and a face on a photograph. I'd been only a baby when he'd left. My Dadda, *chachas* (father's brothers) and *mamoos* (mother's brothers) had been the men in my life. It was my *chachas* and *mamoos* who'd carried me on their shoulders, bought me sweets and played with me. To the infant that I was, this man before me was no more than a stranger and I hid behind the voluminous folds of my mother's *shalwar* and cried. My father was displeased but laughed it off, saying I'd get used to him in time.

Unfortunately, things didn't get any better after we arrived at our new home. My shyness of this stranger-father must have felt like a rejection to him, and it wasn't long before my cowering irritated and angered him. He'd shout at my mother to keep me out of his way and, either by choice or default, turned all his attention and affection to my sister.

From the very beginning he'd bring home little presents for her. She'd squeal with delight as she played with these toys, basking in the glow of being the Loved One. That was a state of affairs I accepted and had always accepted. Even before I met my father, I could not avoid her memory of him, because during the years of separation, when the family spoke of my father, she'd been able to share in their memories of him, claiming him as her own.

However, my father had kept his promise to my mother and had sent for us. Once here, there was much for us to learn about this new society. For instance, there was a new language, and as young children my sister and I were unable to speak a word of English. In the beginning I didn't understand that there was any language other than the one we'd always spoken.

Away from my father, I was a happy, sociable child and would stand outside our front door chatting to neighbours and passers-by. To eyes that had known only dark-skinned, dark-haired people, *goras* (white people) were strange but beautiful to look at with their pale, translucent skin and hair of shades that I'd never seen before: blonde hair in particular fascinated me. I'd always let blonde *gori* ladies pick me up so I could stroke their hair because it never failed to amaze me that this golden hair was real.

This was the late 1960s, when people like us were still a novelty. *Angrezis* would smile at me indulgently as I chattered away. I didn't understand what they were saying and they quite clearly had no idea what I was babbling on about in Urdu baby talk. There were huge differences between us in terms of race, language and culture. But despite that, I think we understood that we liked each other.

3

Home life under siege

*It does not matter who my father was: it matters
who I remember he was.*

Anne Sexton (1928–72)

Ironically, of all of his children, I was the one most like my father.

I was aware that I infuriated my father, exasperated him and made him feel uneasy. The fact that I was a female version of him in so many ways always disturbed me because I grew up anxious that I would turn out like him in temperament. Many times as I was growing up, I'd ask myself whether, if I had children, I would beat them as my father beat me. This gave rise in my mind to the age-old question concerning human behaviour: would it be nature or nurture? Until I was a mother myself I could not answer that question.

I always had a strong sense of what was just and unjust, and I felt it was my right to say so. I never lost an opportunity to deliver scathing opinions of my father's treatment of me. As an obedient Asian daughter I should have held my tongue, but that went against my nature, something that does not go down well in an Asian household where absolute obedience is demanded by the parents.

Nevertheless, despite his treatment of me, my father was first and foremost a home-loving man. When he wasn't at work, he preferred to be at home with his family around him – sitting on the sofa next to him, on his lap, eating from his plate, drinking from his cup. He used to take the family on days trips out to Knowsley Safari Park, Chester Zoo, Blackpool and Morecombe. He'd tell my mother to pack a picnic and we'd all pile into the back of the car (which was now a Morris Minor van) and spend the day out. I clearly remember one incident that illustrates the paradox that was my father.

One summer evening, he announced that, because it was so nice, we were all going to drive to Morecombe Bay. We hadn't been there very long when my mother began frantically searching for something in her handbag, eventually emptying everything out onto the car seat.

'Where is it?' she wailed fearfully, 'I know I put it in here. How could I be so careless?' Because it had been a last-minute trip, my mother had quickly counted up the day's takings from the shop and put the money in her handbag intending to bank it first thing in the morning. The money had now disappeared and I could sense from the tremble in her voice that she was dreading my father's reaction. I think she had lost at least a few hundred pounds. To everyone's dismay, my mother was overcome with distress and burst into tears. Perhaps moved by my mother's uncharacteristic tears, my father did not get angry, as we expected, but put his arms around her, comforting her and telling her that it was only money and although we would miss it, the most important thing was that the family was safe. This was not a tragedy he assured her, a tragedy would be losing a member of the family.

Incidents like this show that, beyond any doubt, the family was the most important thing for my father – the centre of his universe, without which he could not function.

In fact, the main objective in his life was to provide for the financial security of his family, and the reason he left Pakistan in the first place was to make a better life for his wife and two daughters (five more children came later). My father simply didn't handle rage very well, and when he was under stress he'd look around for someone to be the butt of his frustration. Once that emotion had subsided I'm certain he felt remorse.

Perhaps he might have felt differently about me if I hadn't been so nervous of him and responded more positively when he was trying to be 'good Dad' (and he did try, very hard). I'd freeze at the very suggestion of cuddling up to him on the sofa. While I dared not refuse, I'd sit rigid, avoiding eye contact, responding to his conversation in monosyllables until I could make an excuse to check on the dinner, the babies, anything that gave me a reason to flee. I think I spent my whole life trying to avoid being in the same room as him.

In Pakistan, Dadda was feared for his temper and my *chachas* were also hot-tempered. My father similarly inherited the *khandani* (family) temperament and it affected his relationship not only with me but also with the rest of the family. One moment he'd be laughing and joking, the next he'd become exasperated from stress in other areas of his life and begin shouting. No one wanted to be the one who got him started. We all wanted a normal home life instead of being hostage to his mood swings. He was unpredictable – it could happen at any time, sparked off by something totally insignificant or unexpected, like shoes left on the landing or a Muslim acquaintance casually questioning why his daughters wore English clothes instead of *shalwar kameez*.

The criticism and cussing would start, with all his comments being addressed to my mother regarding his lazy, ungrateful offspring whose sole purpose in life was to cause him problems or embarrass him. A heavy atmosphere of anxiety and foreboding would descend on the household with everyone speaking in hushed voices, treading around the house quietly, taking care not to let doors bang or plates and cutlery clatter too loudly, avoiding getting in my father's way. If he walked into a room, within minutes there would be an exodus as one by one we'd all find an excuse to get up and go, leaving him sitting on his own.

Paradoxically, if he was in a good mood, my father rarely used physical punishment, instead administering a carefully worded reprimand, pointing out the misdemeanour and its possible consequences. Solomon-like, he would dispense justice, appeal to our sense of right and wrong and leave us feeling fairly treated and justly chastised.

However, when he was not in a good mood, he'd complain, curse and criticise loudly, working himself up into a passion, by which time the verbal abuse would have escalated to the next stage. Then he'd begin to focus on one unfortunate individual who would be summoned and ordered to stand to attention before him, back straight, chest out, arms by the side while he, the sergeant-major, remained seated, barking questions. How he dealt with that offending party depended entirely upon who it was. If it was my elder sister, for example, whom he never hit, he'd redirect his anger on to me, the scapegoat, finding any excuse to vent his frustration and give me a good hiding.

However, it was not simply physical abuse I endured, but emotional. My father used to take great delight in playing games with my younger siblings to torment me. It was quite simple; two or more of them would be called to sit with him and watch me work, taking bets on how long it would be before I dropped or broke something. My brothers and sisters had little choice but to go along with my father's games and they were too young to understand the hurt and humiliation I endured. While I was washing up, for example, he'd do a running commentary.

'She's picked up a plate now, she's washing it, will she, won't she drop it? . . . no, she's managed to keep it in one piece. Well, there's always a first time for everything. Now it's a cup. Whoops, almost slipped! Will she, won't she? Yes! Yes, she's done it!' and a big cheer would go up, my father whooping with laughter as he played to his uncomfortable audience, encouraging them to mock me.

He said it was only a game, but it always left me feeling utterly crushed and wishing I was dead. Being told every day of my life that I was stupid, fat, clumsy and, above all else, that I had no *akal* (common sense) left me with a fragile emotional disposition. From a very young age any confidence I might have had was mocked and bullied out of me, leaving me a nervous and timid child. I felt worthless and never believed that I was worth a look or gesture of kindness, or indeed that my life was of any value at all. I accepted his treatment of me as my *kismet*.

Even away from my father's presence I could not escape. He told me his eyes were everywhere and he'd encourage – even bribe – my siblings to spy on me; grass me up for the slightest thing.

When I was thirteen, I bought a birthday card to send to a famous pop star, but before I had a chance to send it my sister discovered it under the mattress and took it straight to my father. The first I knew about it was when my father made me stand in front of my siblings and read it out loud, before he ordered me to tear it up into small pieces. I burned with shame and embarrassment, wishing that I could crawl into a hole and die as my mind raced with ways by which I could leave everything behind and run away, somewhere far away from these people.

Not that I had much to leave behind. In terms of possessions, I simply didn't own anything. I just took it for granted that nice things were for other children to own. I remember finding a silver coin on the street one day. Suddenly owning this money made me feel rich, and whooping with happiness I skipped inside to show it to everyone. My bubble was burst when my father told me to hand it to my brother Mohammed. I was devastated.

'But it's mine!' I protested, tears welling up as I stood frozen in disbelief that my father could issue such an unfair command. 'I've just found it.'

'Give it to him,' he ordered. 'He's saving up.' And that was that. Heartbroken, I did as I was told to do and ran weeping from the house, wishing I could keep running and never return.

I always thought that my father's treatment of me was due to his need for a scapegoat; someone to bear the brunt of his temper when he was angry. Strangely, in a way, it gave me my identity and prescribed role within the family, and I accepted it. When my father wasn't in a temper, he was actually very funny. He was only horrible when he was angry, but this all changed one Sunday when he asked me to come and sit with him. Heart pounding with dread, my mind raced as I tried hard to think of something I had done wrong.

'Come and talk to me,' he said gently. It was the voice he used for the others, not one he used for me. My mother sat next to him, knitting. I looked from one to the other, puzzled.

'Tell me, do you think I'm fair to you?'

'I – I don't know,' I stammered, sensing a trap.

'Do you think I should treat you differently?' My mind went into overdrive trying to recall whether I'd complained to my older sister, who I assumed must have reported it back to my father.

'No,' I faltered. 'No, I don't mind.'

'But I've just bought your sister a guitar. Do you think I should have bought you one too?'

'No,' I replied, looking from my father to my mother and trying to understand where this was going. My mother continued knitting, without looking up.

'But you hate your sister, don't you, because I favour her?'

'I don't hate her,' I replied unhappily. 'I don't hate anybody.'

'Do you know what justice means?' he asked, taking my hand gently. I was used to him being angry with me. He was being nice and using a tone of voice that I wasn't used to, and I was confused.

'Y-yes. It means being fair,' I faltered.

'Do you think I'm *just* to you?' Tears began to well up in my eyes. It began to dawn on me exactly what response he was looking for and I was determined not to give him the satisfaction of seeing me cry. I looked at my mother, who continued to knit. Her expression never changed.

'Was it justice to buy a guitar for your sister and not for you?' he persisted kindly. It was no use; my heart felt as though it would burst and a huge tell-tale tear escaped, rolling gleefully down my face, declaring my inner anguish.

'No,' I hiccupped, wishing he would stop. But he was relentless.

'Tell me,' he ordered smoothly, 'tell me how you feel about how I treat you.'

It was no use. I was a child and my fragile emotional state was no match for him. The first disloyal tear was joined by another and another, until the floodgates opened and I could no longer hold back the rush of tears spilling over.

'I don't like how you treat me,' I wept. 'You've always favoured her and let her be mean to me.' There was no point stopping now. 'I wish you'd be nicer to me and buy things for me but you're never nice to me and I wish you were!' I ended, sobbing, with my face in my hands. He looked satisfied.

My mother slammed down her knitting and cried, '*Bas! Bas ho gaya!* (Enough! That's enough!) You ought to be ashamed of yourself!'

'What do you mean?' my father asked, eyes opened wide in innocence. 'I was only having a conversation with one of my children.' He wasn't used to my mother criticising him and suddenly looked almost sheepish.

'I know exactly what kind of conversation you were having!' she replied crossly. 'Why do you torment her like this? You're determined to break her heart. You carry one of them on your head and trample the other beneath your feet. It isn't right!'

'Go and wash your face and go outside and play,' she ordered me. Then, turning again to my father, she continued, 'It's a miracle she doesn't hate the pair of you, the way you both tease and torment her. That's down to her nature, nothing to do with you. When she grows up you'll both see exactly what she thinks of you!'

She was right. As I grew up he definitely came to know exactly what I thought of him. Things didn't get better at home. In fact, matters became much worse; as by the time I turned fourteen I'd begun to answer back.

The terror he inspired in me as a child had matured into a deep resentment towards his ill treatment of me. My father was wrong to treat me the way he did and I let him know how I felt, through either words or defiant looks.

From a very young age I had begun to fantasise that when I grew up, I'd marry a big, strong man who'd protect me from my father. For years I carried an image of this future husband in my head, and in the aftermath of yet another beating would comfort myself by imagining my father cowering before this tall, green-eyed, square-jawed hero of a husband whose very presence would be enough to intimidate him and warn him against raising a hand to me again. Meanwhile, until he came, I had to stand up to him alone.

It was the contemptuous look that he hated most and which always provoked him to administer a fresh assault against me. On one occasion he was so angry that I had dared to stand up for myself that he gave me a beating, flinging me against a wall with such force that I was knocked unconscious and spent several days in bed recovering.

Incidents like this deeply affected the whole family. The atmosphere would be tense for days as my mother would be the only one speaking to him. Everyone else would scarcely dare to breathe too loudly in case it set him off again.

I remember a singularly joyless and unhappy childhood of crockery hurled against walls, smashed windows, verbal abuse, screams of terror and deathly silence in the aftermath.

It was like living in a state of siege.

4

Abba's favourite

*If you can't understand how a woman could both
love her sister dearly and want to wring her neck at the
same time, then you were probably an only child.*
Linda Sunshine

After we came to England, my father and sister's relationship
continued as if they had never been separated by those three
years and that alone gave her superiority over me: she was the
one he'd waited for and whose memory he'd cherished.

Despite being a witness to the brutality against me, she never
ran away to hide. In situations where most children would
cower in terror in case the violence was turned on them, she
instinctively knew she was never in any danger of being beaten.
Thus she was able to plead with my father for my life the night
he was about to murder me.

It did not occur to me that my father should perhaps have
given me an equal measure of his affection.

Once he brought her a small toy washing machine with a
handle that you turned and which actually washed little items of
dolls' clothes. As usual I was allowed to look but not touch, but
it was the first time I remember being so unhappy at being left
out again. I wanted to make her cry so I grabbed the small
handkerchief she'd just washed and rubbed it furiously into the
ground to dirty it. She howled in dismay and my father whipped
me soundly.

But it was the new bicycle that I'll never forget. He proudly wheeled it in and watched her eyes sparkle with joy. As he took her outside to teach her to ride it, I felt as if my ten-year-old heart would break. That was the day that I discovered I was a means of measuring my father's love for my sister. Treating me so badly proved how much he loved and cherished her. He kept looking up at me to see my reactions, as if he were only able to enjoy the giving of the new bicycle if he could at the same time witness my unhappiness from the sidelines.

'Touch it, Fatso, and I'll tell!' she threatened, gesturing towards my father, who beamed proudly at her as she polished the shiny new frame.

'Mean, spiteful cow!' I bristled, resentment and indignation oozing from every pore. I never understood why she was so horrible to me when she was the loved one. I took her threat as a challenge and determined to do exactly what she warned me not to do, knowing how much it would enrage her. I came home from school at lunchtime especially to ride her precious bike and couldn't believe my luck when my mother, who always kept out of these disputes, became co-conspirator against them both. The first day she hesitated, looking at me doubtfully, saying there would be trouble if my sister found out.

But: '*Inki aisi ki taisi!*' she said suddenly (this has no literal English translation, but conveys the sentiment of 'Up theirs!'). Then she helped me to drag the bike out on to the street. From that day, I'd come home at lunchtime in order to ride the hateful thing until it was time to return to school. Then I'd run all the way to school in a blaze of happiness because I'd had half an hour of my mum's undivided attention with no other children around to compete with.

One day disaster struck when I fell off the bike and saw to my horror that the frame was slightly damaged. I was terrified my sister would guess that I was to blame and tell my father. I wasn't wrong.

'Admit it, Fatso!' she demanded angrily, eyes filling up with tears. 'It was you, wasn't it? You've been stealing my bike!'

She'd already given me a slap but looked tearfully at Mum to corroborate her accusation that I'd been riding it while she was at school, which of course I had. I'm afraid to say that, despite the slap, I thoroughly enjoyed the sight of my sister in tears. It made it well worth the hiding I anticipated receiving from my father when he came home from work. I could picture the scene now, in my mind's eye. She'd be standing by the door, watching the clock, every so often reminding me, 'Just you wait, Fatso, wait till I tell him!'

Fortunately however, that day my father was in a good mood, and this was one of those extremely rare times when he announced that he would listen to both sides and make a just decision based on evidence. He needed proof that it was indeed I who had damaged the bike, and for that they looked to my mother for confirmation.

I held my breath. As far as I was concerned, Mum was good and honest and never told lies, so why would she lie for me? Also, with seven children she always stayed out of her children's disputes and never took sides, and not in a million years did I expect her to say anything other than what had actually happened. Therefore it was to my utter astonishment that I heard Mum say that my sister must have damaged it herself at some time because I hadn't been near her bike.

Mum was sticking up for me! It was more than I could have dared to hope for – much, much more! Thoroughly enjoying my sister's howl of outrage and disbelief, I threw her a malicious look of triumph and skipped away, with her abuse ringing like music in my ears. My father had the bike fixed but it was never the same for her, a fact that gave me great satisfaction. My point had been made, the scores were evened up somewhat and after that I wasn't interested in the bike any more.

By the time she was in her mid teens, we were locked in hostilities. As young children we played together, but it was never as equals. She always had to have the upper hand and pull rank on me in order to win. She once suggested a game of leapfrog, announcing she'd go first because she was the eldest. I duly bent over so she could leapfrog me.

'Let's have two goes each,' she said, and I let her leapfrog me again.

'Let's have three goes each,' she suggested. Then four, then five, then six. When she had had thirteen goes, she announced she didn't want to play any more and without so much as a backward glance went indoors chuckling, leaving me standing outside feeling cheated, knowing she'd conned me.

She was always competing against me, which was unnecessary. What stands out in my mind is the fact that she could never bear me to have anything she didn't have. Should I ever acquire anything she deemed worth having, it would torment her day and night; in fact she'd lose sleep over it and think of little else until she was able to relieve me of it. She usually did this by suggesting a game of 'swapses' whereby she would offer me something of hers (carefully chosen for its lesser value) in return for whatever it was she coveted from me, persuading me it was for my own benefit and that she was doing me a favour by taking it off my hands. I'd be left feeling disappointed and dejected because, once again, she'd relieved me of something I had, simply because she didn't want me to have it.

If she was not exactly the ideal older sister, then in all fairness I must take responsibility for being the younger sister from hell. She owned make-up and had secrets that sisters should share, and yet shared none with me. And I dealt with it by taking perverse pleasure in stealing her things just to spite her. Like the time she brought home a box of chocolates. She claimed she'd bought them herself but had been decidedly shifty, and I reckoned someone, maybe a boy, had given them to her. Now she was searching for them frantically.

'I know it was you!' she shrieked. 'I know *you* took them, Fatso!'

Of course I took them! I was at that very moment upstairs, hiding under the bed, stuffing myself with the stolen chocolates and chuckling with glee as she furiously turned the house upside down.

I emerged only when I heard the rest of the family returning home, guessing rightly that she wouldn't create too much of a scene if it involved her explaining to my parents where the chocolates had come from. At that time, while I was still the punch-bag, my father's outbursts had become more frequent and unpredictable. No one felt comfortable around him and the whole family did everything to avoid arousing his temper. Even my sister had stopped grassing me up because it risked unleashing my father's increasingly violent temper and sending the entire household into turmoil.

My sister and I didn't get any closer as we got older. One day when I was in my teens we were having a catfight at the top of the stairs, screaming abuse at each other. My mother came running up to separate us, shouting that we could have caused a serious injury if one of us had fallen down the stairs.

'That was the whole point!' I thought, scathingly, taking satisfaction in the defeat that I'd seen in my sister's eyes before my mother had intervened. I felt she now realised I wouldn't hold back from punching her.

By this time it had ceased to hurt me if my father bought her things. She could get anything out of him just by sidling up to him and telling him it was for educational purposes. If I wanted something, I considered it beneath me to beg, flatter and cajole him, which is what he expected. It had to be given freely or not at all, and I refused to compromise. The consequences were that I was seen as the angry, belligerent one while my sister was seen as charming and ladylike, not just by the family but by outsiders as well. They never bothered to look beneath the surface.

This was really brought home to me when my mother visited Pakistan. It was the first time she'd returned since leaving fourteen years previously. It was also the first time my father had been parted from her in all those years and he took it badly. His attachment and emotional dependence on her was now great. While he was the head of the family, her strength had become his rock, and increasingly she had more of a say in how the family home and finances were run.

My elder sister had already left home to go to teacher training college in a north Nottinghamshire market town called Retford that none of us had ever heard of. I thought she was daft to go somewhere my parents could drive to in just over two hours. It was a seriously missed opportunity – had it been my choice, I'd have gone much further.

With my sister gone and my mother abroad, it fell on me to run the home, take care of the younger children, who were now aged between nine and thirteen, shop and prepare all the family meals. It was not easy. I had to wake early to get the children up, dressed, breakfasted and off to school, then walk the two miles to my own school. In class, my mind was distracted by the need to get out early in order to shop for the evening meal, then rush home before the children got back from school and begin the evening routine. By the time I'd cooked dinner, fed the family, cleared away, got the children into bed and tidied the house, it was late and I was exhausted. I simply wanted to fall into bed before the whole routine began again.

I was getting further and further behind with my studies and increasingly in trouble for failing to live up to the high standards expected of me. It was a very difficult time. My sixth form teachers were encouraging me to try for a place at Oxford or Cambridge to study law. It had been hard enough studying while I helped my mother. Now that I was left to carry the burden alone, it became impossible to even contemplate the Oxbridge exams.

'Fat chance of that now,' I thought bitterly, 'not while I have to skivvy and play cook, housekeeper and nanny to *him*!'

In theory, looking after the family was meant to be my father's job, but he spent most of his time under my feet and getting on my nerves. Instead of taking control he spent his time on the sofa grieving for my mother, pitifully calling out her name.

'Oh, for heaven's sake!' I thought crossly. 'She hasn't died, she's only gone to Pakistan!' wishing he'd jolly well gone too, for all the use he was to me.

That gave me the idea to persuade him to go. How much more difficult could it be? I was already coping with everything on my own. He was more hindrance than help. With him gone, I could arrange my routine to suit myself and leave enough time to study. I hadn't realised just how much my mother fetched and carried for him and now he expected me to do the same. If his meals were late or the children needed anything, he made me feel guilty, especially if I was trying to study at the time. So I'd wearily put my books down and attend to it.

The night before, he'd been displeased at something and picked up his dinner and flung it against the wall. My mother would simply have cleaned up the mess and then given him more food, regardless of whether it was spare or her own. Well, *she* might be submissive and self-sacrificing but I was not! I'd been reprimanded at college that day for being late again and was trying to get all the chores finished so I could put the children to bed and study. Being so tired had made me as ill-tempered as he was, and I wasn't afraid to show it. He was really getting on my nerves!

'I spent ages cooking that!' I cried belligerently, hands on hips, wishing I could shove his petulant face into it. 'That was your dinner. Don't think I'm going to do what Mum does and give you mine. *You* threw it, *you* clean it up!'

I knew he'd get angry and hit me for shouting at him and being disrespectful, but I was past caring. I was exhausted and weary of his tantrums.

'That does it!' I thought venomously. 'He's going to Pakistan!'

The next day I ventured a casual suggestion that perhaps he could go out and join my mother in Pakistan. They never had any time away from us kids and perhaps they might even have a second honeymoon (not that I was aware they'd actually had a first honeymoon). Guilt and paternal duty saw my father putting up a feeble resistance, but he was clearly overjoyed, and as I expected he seized the opportunity.

'Of course,' he assured me, 'your older sister will come back from Retford and help you out as well.'

'Yeah right,' I thought sardonically, 'right after I'm crowned Miss World!'

'Of course,' I said to my father, taking a page out of her book and smiling sweetly.

My sister came down for the weekend to see my father off. A friend of my father's, a Mr Khan, was also there to lend his support and get under my feet.

'What a tender-hearted daughter you have,' remarked Mr Khan, indicating my elder sister, who was weeping. 'Not like the other one, eh?' he said, nodding towards me as I was busy packing up the kebabs I'd made for my father's five-hour journey down to Heathrow airport and checking his passport and tickets.

'*Pattar ka dil* (heart of stone),' he finished, casting me a disapproving look.

'Drop dead, Creep!' I hissed under my breath, throwing my sister a poisonous look. Now the reality was hitting home, I was trying my best to keep my emotions together, anxiety setting in as to how I'd actually cope being left alone to care for the younger children, run the house and go to college. My father might have been useless parted from my mother but at least I had the reassurance of having a grown-up in the house. It was a punishing routine and a heavy enough responsibility for an adult, whereas I'd only just turned seventeen. Suddenly I was overcome with anxiety about my ability to hold it all together and felt tears well up. Angrily I forced them back. I couldn't afford to fall apart now because, unlike my elder sister, I didn't have the luxury of sitting in a corner crying. If I similarly chose to be just as selfish and gave in to the way I was really feeling, it would distress the younger ones, who were upset enough already.

'Nothing gets past you, eh, Mr Khan?' I breezed lightly. 'That's me, no heart, all mouth. I couldn't care less about anyone or anything!'

'*Bas! Chup!* Be quiet!' warned my father, appalled at my lack of respect to a guest and an elder. Then, totally ignoring me, he addressed all his instructions and advice about running the home, security, finances and such to my sister. He was over-whelmed by the anticipation of returning to Pakistan for the first time and of being reunited with my mother, and thanked my sister for coming down and making it all possible. Giving her a grateful embrace, he departed. Twenty-four hours later so did she, only reappearing weeks later when my parents returned with cases full of gifts and hearts full of gratitude. My father gave an emotional public speech in front of family and friends about what a wonderful job she'd done taking care of the family to enable her parents to go back to Pakistan for a second honeymoon.

No one bothered thanking me.

5

My mother

Bitter are the tears of a child: sweeten them.
Deep are the thoughts of a child: quiet them.
Sharp is the grief of a child: take it from her.
Soft is the heart of a child: do not harden it.
Adapted from a quote by Pamela Wyndham Tennant,
Lady Glenconner (1903–83)

My childhood memories of Ammi were of an angel.

Married in her early teens, she was beautiful and sweet-natured. It is not the Eastern way to show affection through hugs and kisses or overt expressions of love as Westerners do and my mother was no different. Where my mother was concerned, her feelings for her family were expressed through the fabulous meals she created for her husband and children.

Because he was the head of the family, and a loud one at that, we all assumed my father was the strong one in the marriage. His drive and ambition certainly played a huge part in the family finances. However, it was my mother who really kept the family going. Silently and through steely unacknowledged determination, she worked hard for us all, running the home, managing the clothes shop he'd purchased for her and cooking those wonderful meals. Unlike my father, she treated all seven children equally and had no favourites. But as far as I was concerned, in the turbulence of an increasingly violent domestic life, my mother was sanctuary.

As a dutiful and obedient young Muslim wife, my mother was torn between her loyalty towards her husband who was her lord and master and her maternal instinct to protect her child who had the misfortune to fail to win her father's affection. When I was little, she was a refuge: the place to which I would run, burying myself within the folds of her *shalwar*, a fragile barrier standing between my father's wrath and me. When he was angry, she'd push me behind her or hastily thrust me into another room, out of his reach, to stop him from hitting me. However, most of the time sanctuary was short-lived as he simply dragged me out from behind her to beat me, and at times her efforts to protect me sometimes served only to bring his wrath on to her own head.

One of the most vivid memories I have of her is when I was about four or five and my parents were getting ready to go to a wedding. In those days, before all the other children came along, she had more time to spend on herself and we chatted as she sat at the dressing table getting ready. I watched in fascination as she applied her make-up, put on her jewellery and piled her hair up in the fashionable Sixties style. My mother had a good sense of style and always knew what suited her. She said she liked to look nice. While, like most Pakistani women, she normally wore the traditional *shalwar kameez*, that day she was dressed in a sari. As she stood up, allowing the folds of fabric to fall into place, I recall looking up at her spellbound, in awe of her beauty, not sure whether my mother was a film star or a queen, but absolutely certain that no one else's mother was as beautiful as mine.

I can't recall exactly what upset my father, but as they were getting ready to leave he began to yell and hit me. My mother drew me protectively to her.

'Why?' she cried. 'Why do you dislike her so much? She's

only a child!' Begging him not to hurt me any more, she braved my father's anger and stood steadfastly between us, shielding me with her slender frame as I wept and clung to her sari, screaming in terror. My father was furious at being thwarted by her, or perhaps peeved because she chose to protect me against him, and he turned his fury on her for interfering and gave her such a hiding that she was laid up in bed for several days.

A great cloud of sorrow descended on the house. My father left the house as my mother took refuge in the bedroom. I learned years later that the primary reason for this was that, as a Muslim wife, it was her duty to safeguard her husband's *izzat* from reproach and criticism from outsiders and it would have dishonoured him if people had known what he had done. Therefore, as it was to be kept secret from everyone, she remained out of public gaze. Whatever happened at home had to be suffered in silence for the sake of his dignity. However, for him personally, without her uttering even a single word of reproach, every mark and bruise on her face condemned him; it was not something he could easily bear, so he stayed away, out of the house and away from her, only returning at night when he had to.

I was quite happy for him to do so because, with him temporarily out of the way, it left the coast clear for me. I simply wanted to be near my mother, burying myself in the bed next to her, breathing in her fragrance and letting her know how much I loved her.

'Ammi,' I whispered, 'why does Abba-Ji get mad?'

'I don't know, *beta*, darling,' she replied sadly.

Although she assured me that she was all right, she winced as she tried to sit up in bed. I took in the horror of the ugly purple bruises on her beautiful face and recall how guilty I felt that she was suffering on my behalf. I felt responsible for the sadness she tried to conceal from me and my heart almost burst with love for her. She never told us she loved us – Asian parents rarely do. But I took those bruises on her face as evidence of her love for me. She was willing to suffer to protect me and I loved her for it. How could anyone not love her?

My siblings and I had been told the story of how my father fell in love with her from the beginning. Despite the fact that his family were moneyed and therefore socially superior, my father's family brought a proposal of marriage to her family. It was easy to see why he wanted to marry her. As well as being a fabulous cook (always an excellent selling point when considering a potential bride for a cherished son) she was petite, beautiful and very, very fair skinned.

Angrezis, or *goras* as they are more generally known by Asians, usually think of skin colour only in terms of a general racial description; Africans are black, Chinese are yellow, Native Americans are red, Asians are brown. For *goras* the differences of colour are in many cases a political statement, not merely a description of racial category.

Take the case of African Americans. A man may have pale skin and Caucasian features, but if he has any black blood in his genes from past generations, he is politically and socially classed as being 'black'. The different shades of black or brown are immaterial.

However, when Pakistanis are judging other Pakistanis, the varying shades of brown are paramount and very often the deciding factor of what is aesthetically pleasing. A lighter-skinned complexion carries a higher premium on the marriage market than a darker complexion. A dark complexion implies a lower social class: a class that toils outdoors under an unrelenting sun that turns skin dark. Conversely, a person of a higher social class has the time and money to choose a lifestyle that keeps them out of the sun. The darker the skin, the implication is, the less desirable they are and the lower down the social scale. This way of thinking is not entirely alien to Western culture, as these same attitudes to skin tones were prevalent in England up until the twentieth century.

For Asians, therefore, dark complexions are not considered desirable in a wife, on the basis that her dark genes will manifest themselves in dark-skinned offspring. Indeed, on the serious question of choosing a daughter-in-law, most Pakistanis will reject a dark-skinned beauty in favour of her plainer but lighter-skinned sister: genes that produced her fairer complexion will be more desirable to join their own *khandani* genetic pool, which will produce the next generation of fair-skinned children. No one wants a *kali* (black) so the *gori*-skinned daughter-in-law will be preferred every time.

My mother, having a beautiful bone structure as well as an unusually white complexion, was regarded as an outstanding beauty and therefore to be prized as a trophy and brood mare. (As an unrelated aside, there is a popular skin-whitening product widely available for purchase in Pakistan called 'Fair and Lovely'. If light skin implies beauty, I've often wondered whether that renders the rest of the population 'dark and ugly'; if the product was marketed by a Western company, would they be allowed to get away with such blatant discrimination?)

My mother had little say in the decision to come to England. In Pakistan husband and wife did not sit down to discuss the pros and cons of emigration in an equal manner. It was a decision that my father, as the husband and man of the house, made unilaterally on behalf of his wife, who was told only after the decision was made. Had any discussion taken place, my father was more likely to have consulted his parents and family first. In the early years, the quality and direction of my mother's life would have been totally dependent upon the will and nature of her husband. The decision was made for him to go to England and my mother would continue to live with her in-laws until the day my father sent her a one-way ticket to join him.

She was always called *dhoolan* (bride) in my grandparents' house but it was no honeymoon living there. While Daddi, my grandmother, was happy enough to bring this beautiful and very useful domesticated bride into the family, she was nevertheless a very domineering woman who was used to having her own way and she would not have entertained the remotest possibility that she could be supplanted in her son's affections by a mere slip of a girl who was his new wife.

Daddi blamed my mother for her precious son's defection to the other side of the world – it never occurred to her that she herself might have been part of the real reason for him going. My mother would tell us how Daddi, ever the drama queen, rarely missed an opportunity to loudly declare her grief to anyone within earshot, bewailing the tragedy of how '*Inglaaand*' had stolen her favourite son and she'd never see him again. (Poignantly, Daddi's theatrics aside, this was what actually happened. It was to be seventeen years before my father made his first return visit to Pakistan, by which time Daddi had died without ever seeing him again.)

Meanwhile, my mother meekly and uncomplainingly did her duty as a daughter-in-law, cooking, cleaning, taking care of her husband's younger unmarried brothers and her demanding in-laws as she waited for my father to send for her.

When he did, she left Pakistan, her parents, family, friends and everything she'd ever known, to follow her husband to the other side of the world where everything was different. She told us what a culture shock it was to come to this cold climate, with its alien language and a society where women dressed and behaved immodestly.

In Pakistan, she'd been an only daughter with five brothers. She'd later been married to a man who had five younger unmarried siblings and therefore, while the burden of housework and cooking had fallen on her, she'd always been surrounded by people and work was spiced with gossip and camaraderie. There wasn't any question of seclusion: solitude and physical space are not commodities that are in great supply in large Pakistani households, where noise, bustle and activity are the norm and, with the constant stream of friends, relatives, neighbours and servants around, a person is never alone. Indeed, solitude and privacy was not something my mother had much experience of.

In England, by contrast, the isolation was overwhelming. In those early years, she had no one to talk to until her husband returned from work, having only an increasing brood of young children for company during the day. With little or no English, she and so many other Pakistani wives like her were tied to the house, shy of the *Angrezis*, unable to make friends unless they had been vetted and approved by her husband and able to go out only when taken by him. The babies started coming within nine months of her landing, and she delivered five babies within five years.

I can only speculate on how hard it must have been for my mother to cope during those years. I remember when I was eight or nine, being woken by unfamiliar noises in the kitchen. My father was on night shift so the coast was clear, and as I crept downstairs in the dark I could hear my mother weeping softly. I was alarmed.

'Ammi?' I whispered fearfully. 'Why are you standing in the dark?'

She straightened suddenly, wiping her face and forcing a smile, 'It's all right, *beta*. I just trapped my fingers in the washing machine. I'm all right now.'

Because I was a child and because I was afraid to see my mother cry about something I could not make better, I believed her. It's only with the benefit of hindsight, when recalling that poignant scene as an adult, that I now understand why she was standing alone in an unlit kitchen in the middle of the night, weeping. And now I understand the pain of her loneliness, isolation and homesickness, I weep for her.

A Pakistani bride comes to her new home a shy timid young creature, totally under the rule of her new husband. Her will is subservient to his. His likes, dislikes, hopes and aspirations become hers. He maintains the power during the years of their marriage as the children are growing up. That was certainly the case in my family, and for many years my father ruled the home with an autocratic will, with my mother silently, unquestioningly doing her duty.

As I grew up, I have no memories of ever going shopping or sharing meaningful mother-and-daughter conversations. Indeed, the word 'conversation' is misleading as it implies a two-way exchange of communication, a sharing of thoughts and ideas, when in reality it scarcely moved beyond instructions of the day's menus or reminders of my duties as a daughter, sister and Muslim. In short, after about the age of eight, my relationship with my mother did not exist outside of the kitchen and household chores.

From a very young age I knew that my worth as a good Muslim was measured in terms of my domestic usefulness. Girls existed only to cook, clean and take care of babies. Therefore, cooking, care of younger children and housework were the only skills I was taught at home. As far as my mother was concerned, they were the only skills a girl needed to know. A wife had to be able to get on with her in-laws and not shame her family. She needed to be able to produce acceptable meals on the table for her husband, run his home and bring up his children. Beyond that, I don't think my mother was really ever interested in getting to know her children, their likes, dislikes, hopes or aspirations. She certainly knew very little about me. Perhaps this was because she did not expect to be known or understood by anyone, herself. She was a closed book.

It's true, therefore, to say that as far as my own relationship with my mother was concerned, I never really knew her, and in turn she certainly never tried to know or understand me. After I left infancy behind, I have memories of other children being treated with affection, being met at the school gates by their parents, being greeted with hugs and kisses while I looked on. I have no memories of being cuddled on my parents' laps or being tucked into bed and kissed goodnight. As I grew older, I was never asked my opinion or consulted on my feeling on any subject. I was merely given a command and expected to comply without question or hesitation. As a daughter, that was my prescribed role within the family. My duty, like that of any Asian son or daughter, was not to love or understand but simply to obey.

Part 2

East is East . . .

6

The best days . . .

Collective fear stimulates herd instinct and tends
to produce ferocity towards those who are not
regarded as members of the herd.

Bertrand Russell (1872–1970)

'Yer've killed 'er, yer murderin' Paki! Yer gonna get fookin' battered!'

I stared in disbelief at the body lying crumpled and motionless at my feet.

'She can't be dead!' I thought. 'She's only pretending!' I couldn't see her face, just a mass of black clothes and long dyed-black hair. She'd sunk down on to her knees before collapsing at my feet. Repulsed, I pulled my foot away. She dressed like a vampire and behind her back her victims called her 'Morticia'. Her cronies called her whatever flattered her the most. Male and female alike were afraid of her. The teachers were wary of her. And I'd just launched a violent assault on her.

Mary Harker and her cronies had made my life a misery since infant school. They'd made fun of me from the very beginning because I couldn't speak English. That hurt. But because I was my father's daughter, I worked harder at school than my *Angrezi* peers who did not have to learn a new language, a new culture or new social etiquettes in order to belong.

I was always aware that my father had brought us here with high hopes and aspirations of making a new life and of

49

belonging in this new society. He'd stepped down in the world in order that we might step up. I owed it to him, and to myself, to work as hard as I could to fit in and, above all, to succeed. My parents came from a society where schooling came at a high price. My grandfather had already purchased an expensive education for his favourite children. In Pakistan, no one took schooling for granted.

By contrast, English education was free, and what people do not pay for becomes no longer a privilege but something they take for granted. *Angrezi* kids were complacent. They didn't need to work hard in order to secure what they already possessed. They already belonged. Unlike me, they had nothing to prove and neither knew nor cared how many sacrifices my parents had made in order for us to have an English education. And why should they?

But the daughter of an ambitious first-generation immigrant takes nothing for granted. Therefore, not only did I learn to speak English, but I spoke English with perfect grammar and perfect diction. In fact, like many people who overcome the challenge of learning a new language in order to fit in, I spoke better English than the English, mercifully by-passing the stage where a thick local dialect became part of my speech. Furthermore, having mastered the language I read every book I could lay my hands on, working my way during my early years at school, through every class library and eventually borrowing from the years above me. By the time I was in my second year at primary, I'd read every book in the school. To my utter delight, the school wanted to encourage the children to read and took us all down to the town library to get membership. I didn't need telling twice about reading. Visiting the library every week was one thing I knew my father would allow me to do on my own, and once I had access to the extensive and diverse collection of books at the town's Harris library, there was no stopping me.

I adored the ancient Norse legends about Hrothgar, King of the Danes, and the warrior Beowulf who defeated the monster Grendel. I was captivated by the chronicles of Narnia by C.S. Lewis, and by the time I was twelve I'd read Homer and Virgil because I was enthralled by Greek myths and the stories about the sack of Troy and the flight of Aeneas in the *Iliad*. Books were the one all-consuming joy of my childhood, because through their pages I could leave behind my own unhappy life and, for hours, escape to any time and place in history and to worlds beyond, restricted only by my own imagination. There was very little I could not or would not read.

It was not just reading. With the exception of maths, I was a good all-rounder. By the age of nine I was easily top of the class in most subjects, and by the time I was doing O levels I'd firmly established myself as one of the top three in the year. If I was hoping my hard work meant my contemporaries would accept me as a friend however, I was to be bitterly disappointed. Being a 'Paki' was bad enough. Having the audacity to be a 'clever Paki' sealed my fate and I continued to be picked on and bullied.

The bullying began from the age of eight, with them poking, prodding and calling me names. Any girl trying to be nice to me soon learned it made her the target of bullying, so I became used to sitting by myself and never having a best friend. Loneliness was punishment in itself. Being unfairly targeted was almost unbearable. There was a small group of girls led by Mary Harker and her friend Dora Truman who instigated most of the bullying.

Truman considered herself superior to everyone else, despite the fact that her father was only a window cleaner and she lived in an ordinary house in a very ordinary area. And yet her favourite game was to go through the entire class naming everyone in order of how well off they were. She'd point her way around the class, always starting with herself as being the richest, and to my indignation would always name me last, as the poorest, simply because I was Asian.

I don't believe these two girls even liked each other. Truman considered herself socially superior to Harker, who lived in a terraced house and had an absent father. Of the two, Truman was more physically abusive towards me. She was a hefty girl and ruled by threatening to thump anyone who disagreed with her. I didn't need to do that because she thumped me anyway. I recall some years later, when we were all in our teens, seeing her walking arm in arm across the school yard with Darren Coleman, one of the boys who hovered on the periphery of their circle. Everyone assumed they were doing it as a dare to make people laugh. She was taller and a good deal wider than him and the sight of them striding purposefully across the school yard, arms clasped around each other, his barely making it all the way around her stout waist, was a huge joke. Until someone whispered, 'They're going out together.' Huge silence.

'Are you sure?'

'Yeah. Since the weekend.'

'Whose idea was it, do you think?'

'Dunno. But I'll bet it wasn't his!'

If everyone was scared of Truman, they were terrified of Harker. She was considered really weird. These days she'd have been called a Goth, but when she first dyed her brown hair jet black at the age of eleven, painted her long nails black and started wearing black clothes, she established herself as a freak. Especially when she bragged about having a boyfriend who was much older. Rumour had it that she'd had her first sexual experience at the age of ten. As she grew into her teens she attended school less and less and eventually dropped out altogether. But while she was at school, no one dared to cross or contradict her because she was known to have a vicious temper.

Both Harker and Truman made my life a misery, but most of their dirty work was done by their cronies and hangers on. These girls (and a few boys) could have been nice people if they'd had the courage to stand on their own. But they sought safety in numbers, afraid of being on the outside if they did not stay within the group. So they all hunted with the pack. And I was their main prey.

I don't know what offended them more, that I was a 'Paki' or that I was a 'Paki' who always got better marks than they did. Whatever the reason, they did their utmost to make my life a misery. It wasn't difficult, as one timid girl was no match for them all. I didn't mind the poking, jabbing and pushing as much as the isolation. Almost every break time someone or other was trying to prove how tough they were by slapping me and threatening to batter me, knowing I could never retaliate and confident in the knowledge that it would make them popular with the Cronies.

In Year 4 at primary school, a new French teacher was appointed. Being already bilingual, I found that learning another language came easily to me. I really loved French and always looked forward to our weekly classes. Because the new French lessons were a first-time experiment for the school, Miss Barton did not hold back in showing her appreciation of having a receptive pupil in her class and the bullying spilled over into the classroom. I'd be poked and pushed from behind at every opportunity, with sniggers and snorting every time I opened my mouth. Sometimes, they didn't even wait until break time or after school and began tormenting me during class. They'd sit immediately behind me, stabbing me with pencils and hissing 'Paki Blue Eyes!' into my ear.

Most of the time I'd ignore them and with a heavy heart pretend nothing was wrong, but over the months I became more and more unhappy as my spirit was crushed. One day it became too much for me and I broke down, covering my face with my hands and sobbing as though my heart would break. The normally sweet-tempered Miss Barton angrily told the whole class that she was ashamed of them for behaving like a pack of animals, then, as it was almost lunch time, she threw everyone out, closing the door and coming over to kneel down beside me.

I don't recall what she said, but instead of being comforted I became even more distressed. I was used to people ignoring me, calling me names and hitting me. I wasn't used to anyone being nice to me, and I felt as though my heart would burst with grief.

Miss Barton asked how long this had been going on. When I told her it had always been like that but had got worse during French, she replied that they picked on me because they were jealous. Then she told me something she said she wasn't supposed to.

It was about the annual prizes that the school gave to the most outstanding pupil. There was a class prize and also a year prize. This year there was to be an additional one, for French. However, because I'd already been nominated for both the year and class prizes, the school wouldn't let Miss Barton award me the French prize and she'd been told to nominate another pupil.

'You are the best pupil in the class and I didn't want you to think that someone else was better than you because they got the prize. I tried to tell them that no one deserved it as much as you but they wouldn't change their minds. I'm so sorry,' she ended, looking genuinely upset.

The tears had finally stopped and I was able to smile back at her and tell her it didn't matter. It was true. It didn't matter. I didn't care about any prize. It meant much more to me that someone as pretty and clever as her cared enough about me to stick up for me. Ironically, by doing so she'd probably guaranteed me another good pasting after school, but I didn't tell her that.

When I started secondary school, just having an elder sister in the fifth year meant that the bullies left me alone for most of my first year. The biggest surprise, however, was the reception I had from my sister's teachers and friends who seemed to know about me. They'd heard what a character I was and how clever I was. That surprised me because my sister never said those things to me and I certainly didn't know that was how she saw me. I began to see her in a different light and hoped that maybe she'd let me join her and her friends and that we could do sisterly things together. Unfortunately she still kept me at arm's length, but at least I felt safe with her being there to watch out for me. She warned me about one of the teachers, Mr Taylor in the science labs, because apparently he had quite a reputation for being a bit of a creep with the girls.

One morning during my second week at the school, she introduced me to her friend Sarah. Sarah seemed very interested in knowing about my new timetable and which teachers I had for certain subjects, asking me who I had for science. When I told her that Mr Taylor was my new science teacher, she asked me what I thought of him. Now that was a question I was most happy to answer, and I launched into an animated account of all the stories I'd heard about him since arriving. I told her how he stood unnecessarily close to the girls to look down their bras and told rude jokes, and how he'd been in trouble for putting his hand up one girl's skirt. In the midst of this outpouring, I suddenly noticed my sister had stepped back out of Sarah's eye-line and was furiously signalling me to shut up. But it wasn't often I was the centre of attention and I was only just warming up. Ignoring her frantic signalling, I gleefully told Sarah that everyone said Mr Taylor was a real pervert.

'Why did you want to know?' I asked, finally stopping to draw breath. 'Is he your teacher too?'

'No,' came the reply. 'He's my dad.'

In Year 2 of secondary school, we were all put into streams according to academic ability. I'd made some friends by now, but there was no one I could call my best friend for the simple reason that all the best-friend positions seemed to be taken. No one was inclined to break up an existing best-friend relationship to become the target of bullying simply to be my friend. The Cronies were into boys by now and looked down on me because I didn't have a boyfriend.

I didn't have a boyfriend for two reasons. First, I was a Muslim girl and not allowed to date boys, but the second reason was simpler: I wasn't a pretty child and had failed to blossom into a pretty teenager. Unkind as it was, my elder sister was right when she called me 'Frog Face' and 'Bugs Bunny'. My eyes were too big, and so were my front teeth. Even my mother called me *habri* (buck-toothed). As far as school kids go, loneliness and unpopularity are catching and ugliness is downright offensive, so they all gave me a very wide berth. In fact, to add insult to injury, the boys used to threaten each other by saying, 'Watch it or I'll tell the Paki bird you fancy her!'

But the fact remained that my home life was totally different from that of my peers. While they went to pubs and parties, I'd go home to domestic chores. And without the distractions of boys and a teenage social life, apart from housework there was only schoolwork left.

Although I was the only Asian girl, there were two Hindi boys in the 'A' stream and the three of us always competed for the top place in exams. This didn't go unnoticed and I overheard one of the Cronies remarking, 'These Pakis have always got to come first, don't they?'

'You'd come first too if you didn't spend all your time skiving school and trying to get off with boys,' I retorted indignantly.

The bullying had started again and was becoming increasingly more vicious. In my second and third year at secondary school, scarcely a week went by when I didn't come home with my clothes torn or my face bloodied. They always laid in wait for me and ambushed me as I left the school premises. As I came home having had yet another battering, my mother turned on my father.

'Is this what you brought us to this country for?' she demanded angrily as she cleaned me up. 'So these *goras* can beat up your children? Why don't you do something to protect her?'

I expected my father to go up to the school and demand that my teachers did something to punish the bullies whom I'd have no problem in naming. But I discovered that my father, like most immigrants of his generation, hated confrontation with authority. However, he did come to pick me up from school in the car, which only served to invite open derision from the bullies.

'What's the matter, Paki? Can't fight yer own battles? Got yer dad t'pick you up after school? Chicken shit, we'll get you anyway!' they'd threaten. The verbal abuse didn't stop, but at least for a week or so I was not attacked after school. After a while however, my father announced he'd sorted the problem and to my dismay stopped picking me up. As soon as his car stopped appearing outside the school gates, the violence picked up again.

It escalated to a new level when I was almost put into hospital after the most horrific beating so far. This happened during the cross-country run in my fourth year.

I loved the cross-country run. I was away from home and away from school and had the novelty of being outdoors dressed in trainers and a short PE skirt, legs uncovered. At home I was never allowed to go anywhere unchaperoned or to take part in outside activities, and this was a truly rare moment of fresh air, exercise and freedom. Ever since I was about ten years old, one of my favourite pastimes had been to stand where I could catch sight of the Pennines to the east, and even more exciting was the M6 motorway which ran beneath the bridge in the park. I always felt a thrill knowing that this road would one day take me far away from this place. It was the road to freedom.

I enjoyed feeling the wind in my face as the run took me away from the school, through the park, across fields, through the woods on the outskirts of the town and towards the flood plains of the River Ribble, from where I could see the motorway stretching away for miles. It was one of the rare times that I felt free and untroubled. Little did I know that it wouldn't last long.

On the way back through the park there they were, waiting for me: Truman and Harker, hands on hips, bravely flanked by all their cronies and a great many others from the year, some curious to see what was going on, others in gleeful anticipation of what was to come.

They circled round me menacingly, gloating as they blocked me in. There was no way I could outrun all of them even if there was a way out. There was no one to stop them, and I knew I was in trouble. To my horror I saw Harker and Truman casting glances at the bridge, just yards away. I tried to edge away from it, terrified that they intended to throw me off it on to the M6 motorway below. I was in no doubt they were capable of it, particularly if they were being egged on by their followers. There were between fifteen and twenty of them closing in – I didn't stand a chance against so many.

Then it started. Harker and Truman threw the first punches, knocking me down. Once I was down, they let fly with their feet, viciously kicking me, as more feet joined in the assault. I could hardly feel what part of my body was being kicked because there were so many feet attacking me. Every angry kick was punctuated with an expletive.

'Fookin' black bitch!' or 'Friggin' cow! I 'ate Pakis!'

I could hardly see through the tears and the tangled mass of hair that had been pulled loose from my hair band, and I could taste the mud in my mouth as I cowered, face down in a foetal position, trying to protect my head. It seemed to go on for ever, but I was determined that I would not give them the satisfaction of losing consciousness or even letting them see me cry. I don't recall how long it went on for, except I was afraid they wouldn't stop until they'd killed me.

'Oi! What are you lot up to?' Above the din, I heard a voice yelling out. It was a woman out walking her dog in the park. She shouted that they should be ashamed of themselves, so many against one girl, and she was going to call the police. As the crowd suddenly broke up and they began to run away, she called out that she knew which school they were from and would be reporting them.

She helped wipe my eyes free of the mud, tears and hair so I could see, and pulled my torn clothing around me so I'd at least be decent. I was caked in mud and hurt everywhere; my head, my limbs, my ribs ached terribly and I could barely walk. But she helped me limp back to school as my emotions broke free and I wept inconsolably.

School had ended by now, so most people had already left. The first person we met happened to be my form teacher, a brusque, dumpy little woman called Banfield. Instead of calling an ambulance or getting me medical attention, her first words when she saw me were 'Look at the state of you! What have you been up to?' And despite being told in no uncertain terms by my rescuer about what had just happened to me, she abruptly dispatched me home, on my own, making me feel as if I was in disgrace. The matter was never mentioned again and no one was ever punished. In fact, I remember how Banfield always treated me as if I was a troublemaker and she wrote on my report that I was inclined to be a 'fusspot', getting me into further trouble with my father.

I was fifteen by now and sorely tired of being battered all the time. One afternoon, heartily sick of being picked on, I told Mary Harker she was a dog, knowing I'd really get it after school, but I pretended I didn't care. The school bell signalled home-time, and with a heart heavy with dread I slowly walked to the cloakroom to get my coat, aware of the buzz of excitement as the Cronies smelled blood and gathered to wait for the show to begin. There was no point running as there was only one exit. Sure enough, they were all waiting for me when I got outside. One of the Cronies stepped up to face me, shaking her fist at me.

'Yer gonna get fookin' battered for calling her names!' she squeaked.

I was in no mood for this and laughed in her face.

'Get lost, Midget,' I replied scornfully, enjoying her momentary look of panic as she hastily retreated into the safety of the gang. Away from the Cronies I knew for a fact she was a nice girl who came from a good family. She was one of the smallest girls in the year and even a kid in the year below could have flattened her, but she was hunting with the pack and right now the pack leader was after my blood.

Then it began.

'Don't talk to her like that!' ordered Harker.

'I'd rather she didn't talk to me at all,' I retorted

'Think yer better than everyone, don't you?' Harker demanded, hands on hips, playing to her audience. 'Don't yer, Paki?' she spat.

'Better than being a slag!' I replied defiantly. They all gasped with shock. No one ever spoke to her like that. Neither did I, normally, but I knew I was going to get it whatever I said, so I really didn't care any more. Like all bullies, she had an aversion to receiving what she dished out and turned purple with fury.

'What did you call me?' she screamed. 'What did you just call me?'

'You deaf as well as being a slag?' I asked wearily.

She came at me. But something inside me snapped. I didn't deserve this. I'd suffered years of bullying and torment when all I'd wanted to do was to be friends. How dare they? How dare they subject me to this abuse? For as long as I could remember they'd tormented me. And for what? For being different? For not being aggressive? I'd always put up with whatever treatment was handed out to me, accepting it as my lot. No one ever gave me any credit for being nice because everyone was too busy calling me names and picking on me.

'Not any more,' I fumed. 'Not this time!'

So I turned on her, suddenly realising that I wasn't afraid of her. Knowing that, in fact, I'd never been afraid of her. I also realised that, having spent years being battered, I knew exactly what to do when it came to doing the battering: I knew what hurt the most and where it hurt. And now all I wanted to do was hurt this girl who took such delight in hurting me. I couldn't see clearly through the red film covering my eyes. I didn't hear and I didn't feel because I was totally consumed with rage and indignation at being forced into this kind of ugliness. My temper had been unleashed, and now my one and only objective was to hurt her badly. To kill her. To beat her nasty, ugly, spiteful face to a pulp until she was dead.

I knocked her to the ground again and again, pummelling her face with clenched fists. She didn't stand a chance. I heard something crunch in her face but didn't stop battering her until my rage subsided. She tried several times to get up, but she never got the chance to do more than scream and try to protect her battered and bloodied face with her hands.

'Get up!' I snarled. 'Fight back, you bitch!'

When she didn't get up, I grabbed her long hair, twisting it around my hand, dragging her screaming to her feet. As soon as I released her hair, her legs buckled beneath her and she sank to the ground with a moan. Only as she collapsed at my feet did I become aware of what was happening around me.

I heard threats being hurled at me but no one came to help her. Screams of anguish had turned to deathly silence as she sank to the ground and failed to get up again. I stepped back from her, eyes blazing with fury, fists still clenched, hissing, glaring, snarling at them, daring anyone else to try. I hated them for this, and right now I was ready to kill anyone who tried to take me on. No one did.

'Murderer!' called a voice from the crowd. I looked at the crumpled mass at my feet with horror and disbelief. Was she dead? It wasn't possible, I reasoned. I wasn't capable of doing this. I felt the bile rising and knew I was going to be sick. Suddenly, seeing one of the teachers pushing their way through the crowd, I came to my senses as the awful realisation of what I'd done hit home. Then I turned and fled.

I ran all the way home, expecting to find the police already there waiting to charge me with murder, but to my relief only my mother was home. Carefully avoiding her, I went straight up to the bathroom and cleaned myself up. I was badly shaken and still in shock, but I said nothing to anyone, trying to calm my rapidly beating heart, keeping the horror of what had just happened to myself as I changed out of my school skirt into trousers, swept back my hair into a pony tail and went downstairs. For once I was grateful for my mother being too busy to take any notice of me, and I picked up the sweeping brush and started my domestic chores.

In the event, Mary Harker was not dead. But I suffered nightmares after that day. Fighting was unladylike and undignified – I never wanted to do it. But I had fought back, and in doing so I was forced to confront the question of violence that had haunted me all my life. Was it nature or was it nurture? I didn't know.

By beating my tormentor unconscious, had I just proved that I was indeed my father's daughter?

7

The food of love . . .

*Do not forget to entertain strangers, for by so doing some
people have entertained angels without knowing it.*

Hebrews 13:2

Food and hospitality played an important part of our upbringing, and this significance is something I've carried with me into
adult life. It's not just what we eat but how we eat and with
whom we make it that is such an essential part of Asian culture.

Mealtimes form a bond that ties an Asian family together,
and when I was growing up they were central to family life and
our daily routine gravitated around them. Large pots of meat,
rice and vegetables were prepared every day, dispensed into
large dishes and platters which were then placed centrally so
that everyone could help themselves to as little or as much as
they wished.

One of the first things I learned as a Muslim daughter was
that the giving and receiving of hospitality is an intrinsic part of
Pakistani culture. Indeed, the Koran goes further and
commands a host to make available only the best food and
accommodation to any visitor or guest. Hospitality is taken for
granted in Asian homes and would be extended to anyone who
visited our house. Regardless of the time of the day, should any
visitor drop in unexpectedly, my mother would simply
disappear into the kitchen and produce something delicious to
place in front of the guest, be it a simple snack such as pakoras

(gram flour fritters that *Angrezis* call bhajis) or a plate of cut fruit such as oranges or melon. Friends, neighbours or acquaintances alike would be urged to stay to join us for the next meal and share curry, rotis and rice with the family even. Casual visitors dropping by for a few minutes would not be allowed to leave without being urged to take a seat and offered tea, coffee and a plate of biscuits.

In English society, tea or coffee will usually be offered once and a refusal is generally accepted without question (sometimes, I suspect, with relief). In Asian homes, however, it could not be more different. There are two protocols at work here: a guest will be practically force-fed with the best food and drink available, as a host will not wish to appear ungenerous or stingy, while for the guest there is an unspoken obligation to accept the hospitality being so generously offered. To refuse is to risk giving offence to a host who could feel that his home, family and offerings have been spurned. This is why the *izzat* of the host is at stake if there are guests in the house and there is nothing to offer. In these situations, my parents would thrust some money into the hands of one of the children and discreetly despatch them to the local shop to purchase something for the guest.

No distinction would be made between the visitors whose company was enjoyed and the ones we were glad to get rid of. I remember one such incident when, to my dismay, even the busybody who went from home to home carrying tales of people's private lives was given respect.

'Aw! Ammi!' I pleaded, 'Don't be a spoilsport. She's such an old cow! Let me spit into her drink just once!'

But barely suppressing her amusement and despite the fact that she herself couldn't stand this woman, my mother would adamantly refuse to let me hock up into her coffee cup, reprimanding me for being disrespectful and I'd be despatched to the living room with a tray, bristling with disappointment. What I learned from this was that, regardless of how much I disliked someone, contaminating a guest's food and drink was sinful, and failure to offer hospitality to any guest would have been dishonourable and shameful.

Food and hospitality had another significant role in my life because they were the basis of the only relationship I had with my mother. When my father first began to hit me, my mother would usher me out of his way into the kitchen, where she would comfort me and soothe my tears by giving me something nice to eat. For many years after, I associated food with refuge from emotional upset and this set a pattern for my becoming a classic comfort eater.

However, where my relationship with my mother was concerned, the only times I was able to break through the silent, impenetrable aura that usually surrounded her and enjoy any sense of closeness with her was when I stood beside her in the kitchen, helping her to peel, chop and stir as we prepared the family meals. Sometimes my efforts would be rewarded when her brusque manner relaxed and there was a thawing of the blank expression on her lovely face. On rare occasions when she wasn't rushed off her feet, she'd even share little anecdotes about her childhood, relating to the meal we were preparing. She'd tell me stories about when she first cooked such and such a meal or how she used to make it in Pakistan, using ingredients I'd never heard of. She'd magically produce these exotic ingredients from her cupboards and show me what they looked and smelled like and how they were used.

I learned to recognise the bright yellow colour of *haldi* (turmeric) and the vivid red of sweet paprika powder. I knew that *dhania* (coriander) came in three forms: the seed, which looks like a small brown peppercorn and which, when ground up, becomes *dhania* powder, and my favourite, the bright green *dhania* herb whose stalks and leaves were chopped and sprinkled over most finished dishes for colour and flavour.

I knew that my father never purchased *garam masala* (literally 'hot spices', but actually a blend) and other spices in the *Angrezi* supermarkets because they were flat, flavourless and usually adulterated with cheaper ingredients, and did not have the proper scent and same depth of flavour as spices bought from the Asian stores.

I learned that there was no such spice as 'curry powder' and that the yellow, pungent-smelling powder used by *Angrezis* to make 'curries' was a blended concoction for the benefit of those who didn't know any better. Curry powder as the *Angrezis* understood it was never used in our home and was in fact banned by my father for being so disgusting.

Learning to cook was one-to-one quality time that only happened because I was a girl and had a duty to help my mother in the kitchen. I wasn't being told off or ordered around, but being taught and sharing my mother's all too scarce time. This did not happen very often, which made these moments all the more precious.

I recall how the kitchen would buzz with activity and be filled with the most intoxicating aromas on special festival days such as Eid, which followed Ramzaan, the month of fasting. Mum always made *biriyani* on Eid. This was a special rice dish made with plenty of lamb or chicken, spiced with cardamom, cloves and cinnamon for flavour, infused with saffron soaked in milk for colour and finally garnished with soaked almonds and butter-fried onions to keep it moist.

Then there was *haleem*, which my father insisted was made with generous amounts of lamb.

'You can't skimp on the meat in *haleem*,' he'd declare, before handing over a huge parcel of mutton that he'd just bought specially. Pakistanis prefer to eat mutton rather than lamb for the depth of flavour. But in England lambs are slaughtered before they get a chance to mature, so mutton is something generally only available in the halal meat shops.

In my father's house meat was not negotiable. Dhal and vegetables were merely side dishes and poor people's options. What the men in our house demanded was meat, usually chicken and mutton or goat, and plenty of it, so as far as my father was concerned meat couldn't be skimped on.

A spicy meat sauce was made and then thickened with a variety of yellow, green, white and brown lentils and pearl barley. After simmering for hours until the meat fell apart, the mixture was pounded until the meat fibres broke down and blended with the lentils and barley to produce an incredibly thick meat stew that you could almost stand a spoon in.

It was served in bowls sprinkled with *garam masala* and garnished with fried onions, shredded ginger and chopped coriander leaves. We'd all compete to see who could eat the most bowlfuls, then spend the night with stomach ache because we'd eaten too much! As nourishing as all those beans and pulses in *haleem* were, they did in fact have an unfortunate side effect and one which would cause the house to resound with shrieks of protest from the women and guffaws of male laughter, as the men in the family not only competed to eat the most but, later in the evening, held contests to see who could out-fart the others.

On Fridays we often had our family favourite, spicy grilled chicken. My father always bought chicken despite the fact that this was before chicken was mass produced and it was therefore quite expensive. Two chickens were cut into portions and rubbed with oil, paprika, chilli and seasoning, then placed under the grill. The half-cooked chicken was smothered with a paste of onions, ginger, garlic and green chillies and grilled to golden perfection. This was served with roast potatoes, vegetables and gravy. My father never particularly liked chicken but he would eat this dish. I don't recall us ever serving this meal to anyone who didn't demand the recipe.

On special occasions, Mum made *nehari*, a traditional Pakistani dish. *Nehari* was a rich stew made with enormous chunks of beef simmered in a special blend of fennel seeds and spices for many hours until the meat was tender and falling apart in a thick, flavoursome sauce. At the table it was served sprinkled with shredded ginger, chopped coriander and *garam masala* and eaten with delicious tandoori roti, puffed up and hot from the grill.

My favourite meal of all was *kofta*: lamb meatballs and potatoes in a thick spicy fenugreek-flavoured sauce. Sometimes Mum made special *nargisi koftas*, which were koftas stuffed with half a hard-boiled egg. We mopped this up with rotis and fluffy basmati rice.

Rotis were eaten every day and with every meal. They were made from wholemeal flour and water, left to prove and then rolled out thinly to the size of dinner plates. There is a skill in rolling them out so that they are thin and perfectly round, something achieved only through practice and experience. Then they were cooked on a *tawa* (flat griddle) and finished over a naked flame, where a skilled cook like my mother could make them swell and puff up with steam. With each adult person eating between two and three each, that meant a whole basinful of dough to knead and roll out daily. Rotis are best eaten fresh and hot, so the men would be seated and began their meal while being waited on by the women. The one rolling out and cooking the rotis was always the last to sit down to eat.

It is not simply what and how it is eaten that makes Asian food different from English meals, it is also the order in which particular food is eaten. There are no 'courses'. All the food – rotis, meat, dhal, vegetables, salad and pickle – is served at the same time, and following a silent prayer of *bismillah* the meal begins with everyone helping themselves, taking as much or little of each dish as they desire, passing around what cannot be reached by others. This is totally different from the Western way of being presented with a full plateful of food already dished out, something I have never been comfortable with. Being Asian, I have always been used to selecting particular dishes as my appetite and tastes dictate, without someone deciding for me; for example, I usually prefer less meat and more lentils and vegetables.

The meal is eaten in two parts. After rotis, rice will be eaten with the same dishes. *Angrezis* will eat curry with bread (naan or rotis) and rice on the same plate. Pakistanis would never eat this way. Bread and rice are eaten separately. Jugs of water would always be served with the meal.

Pudding or dessert would normally only be served on special festive occasions, or if there were guests. On these occasions my mother would make *zaarda*, a sweet saffron rice dish with plump raisins, almonds and pistachio nuts. Or *gulab jamun*, sweetmeats soaked in sugar syrup, *keer*, a creamy pudding made with ground rice, or *supenni*, a milky vermicelli pudding with raisins and nuts.

However, after everyday meals, pudding, if pudding were required, would simply be a plate of cut fruit such as oranges, watermelon, honeydew melon or mangoes, depending on the season. But even this would have a typically Eastern kick to it.

The food of love . . .

In the West, ground black pepper is used only as a savoury seasoning. Pakistanis are far more adventurous, knowing how freshly ground pepper brings fresh fruit to life. I never believed the English would go for it until I read of Nigella Lawson enthusing about her discovery that black pepper brings out the flavour of strawberries. This was nothing new – my parents had been using black pepper as a fruit seasoning for years.

The preparation, cooking, serving and clearing of the main evening meal was the major chore in our home. The midday meal could be the previous night's meal heated up, or a simpler version. The evening meal, however, always had to be fresh. There were five men in the household, all with big appetites, so an early start needed to be made on dinner, with onions, ginger and garlic needing to be peeled and chopped. Everything was cooked in large amounts. After I left home, for years I always made too much because I'd grown up in a large family and cooking for a family of nine was a habit that took years to unlearn.

My mother was always experimenting to produce the food she remembered from Pakistan, as these were the meals that my father liked best. Like most Pakistani husbands of their generation, he'd do the shopping and bring home the ingredients for her where she worked her magic in the kitchen to produce the fabulous meals and snacks that her family came to expect. It was not just Pakistani food; Mum could turn her hand to English meals too, regularly making batches of bread rolls, family-sized meat and potato pies and fish cakes. Any time she came across something new and interesting, she'd disappear into the kitchen and proudly reproduce it with admirable results.

Although I did not know it then, her skills in the kitchen made a lasting impression upon me. My father was extremely fussy, refusing any food that was not made by my mother's hands, so I was permitted only the mundane jobs in the kitchen like making rotis, peeling, chopping and stirring, as well as doing the inevitable clearing up afterwards. I was however, allowed to experiment with the food my father was not going to eat and became accomplished at cooking the dhals and vegetables more preferred by the women in our family. I'd also use leftovers to make things like *pooris* stuffed with spicy potatoes or minced lamb and peas. It was praise indeed when I'd turn these dishes out and the men of the family would gingerly have a taste, then, unexpectedly liking it, help themselves to a large portion. One of the biggest compliments my father ever paid me was to announce that my *paranthas* and stuffed *pooris* surpassed even those made by my mother. Huge praise considering she was a fabulous cook.

I also acquired a detailed knowledge of the different cuts of meat, learned how to recognise the infinite variety of lentils, spices and herbs and acquired an instinct for successfully throwing them all together, without needing to use recipes.

Having sampled Pakistani food in a large variety of homes and restaurants as well as in my own kitchen, I can honestly say that even after all these years I can still appreciate the skill of my mother's cooking. Rarely, very rarely, do I come across Pakistani cuisine that comes anywhere close to the meals we grew up eating.

My father considered himself a connoisseur of good food, having been brought up on meals made with the best quality cuts of meat, basmati rice, vegetables and spices available at the bazaar. Daddi's children were raised with high expectation of family mealtimes. These were expectations that featured high on the list of qualities desired in future daughters-in-law. When he was married with a family of his own, it was inevitable that my father too would insist on the very best ingredients. But it was not enough simply to buy good quality ingredients at the bazaar, as skilful hands were essential in putting it all together. My mother did not disappoint. Her skills in the kitchen impressed her critical in-laws as she turned out wonderful dishes that rivalled her mother-in-law's cooking and won her husband's heart.

Looking back, I realise how fortunate we were to have a mother who was so adventurous and creative in the kitchen. Our family life revolved around food and mealtimes as the topic of food dominated most discussions; indeed, I used to wonder whether there would have been any conversation at all between my father and the rest of the family if the topic of food had been banned in our house. Perusing modern Asian cookery books, I recognise most of the dishes featured and realise exactly how well and adventurously we ate.

Now, years later, my sister Farah and I will reflect on the food that featured so significantly in our lives as we were growing up and the meals that we ate together as a family. Having lived through a home life such as ours, there is very little we can comfortably reminisce about among the turmoil of suppressed or uncomfortable memories of the turbulent childhood that was ours. Now, as adults, cooking and eating those meals together provides us with a safe haven, a culinary sanctuary and our only path to painless nostalgia.

8

Oh brother!

Seniority is very important in an Asian family, and *izzat* for authority and elders is bred into Asian children from the outset. This training begins in the family home with respect towards elder siblings, whose authority in the eyes of younger brothers and sisters is second only to that of parents.

One fact not generally known by many Westerners is that Asians do not address their elders by their first names. This is not just restricted to natural elders such as grandparents, aunts and uncles but applies equally to cousins, friends or older brothers and sisters. In the same way as a child would call parents Ammi or Abba (sometimes with a *-ji* added on for extra respect) a younger sibling would similarly never use an elder sibling's first name, but would use a title of respect. In this case, an older brother is addressed as Bhai (brother) and an older sister is Apa (sis).

Because of the age gap between us and the younger children, my elder sister and I were Burri Apa (Elder Sis) and Choti Apa (Younger Sis). When my brothers reached their teens, and particularly after they married, they did once or twice chance their luck with both my elder sister and me by using our first names. They were rewarded with either a sharp rebuke or a slap for disrespect.

The exception to this was with Farah. Because the younger children were so close in age and were at school together, where they'd be embarrassed to be heard calling their sibling by a strange name not understood by their English friends, Shoukat, Lee and Jo, who were younger than Farah, were allowed by my parents to call her by her first name.

Oh brother!

As second eldest, I was changing nappies not long after I was out of them myself. With five younger siblings I had no need for dolls when I had real babies to care for. This is not unusual – in large Asian families it is perfectly normal for older siblings to help bring up and care for younger children, and it is simply an extension of parental responsibility filtering down the hierarchy of the family, from oldest to youngest.

My father was nothing if not brutally honest about his prejudices and favouritisms towards his children. As very young children, if there were differences in the way we were treated, it had little to do with personalities and more to do with partiality being shown to particular individuals over others for a variety of reasons. As well as showing favouritism towards my elder sister, my father had other reasons to single out his children for special treatment: for example, simply being born the eldest son, something dear to the hearts of most Pakistanis like my father.

As children, our birthdays were never celebrated and the only time I recall any of us having a birthday was when my father organised a party for Mohammed, his eldest son and heir, when he was little. My mother was ordered to provide a birthday tea with jelly, sandwiches and a cake with candles, and to our mortification my older sister and I were ordered to play an accompaniment on toy trumpets while the rest of the family sang 'Happy Birthday'. It was only the thought of getting a hiding from my father that prevented us from braining the smug little brat with his own plastic trumpet.

Another thing I remember is the Weetabix episode. Weetabix were doing a special promotion, with some toy or other to collect inside the box. As with a lot of things, Eldest-son-and-heir always had first refusal on anything inside a cereal box. Only if he didn't want it were any of the other children allowed to take it, which rarely happened as usually the most thrilling thing about the plastic toy inside a cereal box was the excitement of ripping open a new box and extracting it. After that it simply became an uninteresting plastic toy.

Most parents would be content with simply buying the cereal with their weekly shopping, but when it came to keeping Eldest-son-and-heir happy, my father went the extra mile and purchased an entire case from the cash and carry. I recall watching my brother rip open box after box, extracting the prized toy within, promising he'd never eat anything but Weetabix from now on and quite unaware of the mounting indignation of the rest of the family. We knew exactly who'd be eating that cereal. As I'd guessed, after about a week Mohammed announced that he was tired of Weetabix and didn't want to eat it any more. He gleefully tucked into the other cereals my father purchased just for him, totally oblivious to the murderous looks of the rest of us forcing down bloody Weetabix for months after.

Shoukat was the second son of the family. From a very young age, he was prone to headaches and dizzy spells and was generally considered delicate. His intolerance to pain stayed my father's hand against him on most occasions because he had a tendency to dissolve into floods of tears, and as a result, we'd all call him a cissy and sing rude songs at him, making him cry even more.

The nurturing of the younger children by the older ones was evident from the special relationships that existed within the family unit itself, such as that between Shoukat and my older sister: the eldest and the second youngest. There was an age gap of ten years between them, and since he was very young he was her special favourite. He craved affection and she was the one who gave him that affection, petting him, taking his side in sibling disputes and mothering him when he was ill or upset, taking him with her everywhere and buying him special presents.

None of the other children received as much attention from her, and in turn she was always the one he sought for affection.

Shoukat was a pretty child who grew into a man possessed of an innate charm that endeared people to him, and his sense of humour and ability to make people laugh made him popular among his peers. Long after my sister had left home, and even after she was married with children of her own, the two still had a special bond.

As far as my father was concerned, there were two children with whom he could never get along; I was one and the other was my brother Lee. We were both strong, wilful characters who refused to accept that my father's treatment of us was justified parental discipline, and felt instead a deep sense of wrong and injustice towards us.

The principal difference between Lee and me was that I was desperate to escape, to put myself out of my father's reach and simply have the chance to make a life of my own, independent of the family. However, when Lee grew up, his main objective was not to escape but to be accepted, and his rebellion was the need of a son to be noticed and accepted by his father, who saw him as an academic failure. Lee was a likeable little rogue, always in trouble for being cheeky to teachers and (even while in infant school) flirting with the girls. He was always up to mischief.

I recall one Saturday afternoon when Farah answered a knock on the door to find two extremely smartly dressed children standing expectantly on the doorstep, armed with a brightly wrapped package.

'We've come for Lee's birthday party,' they announced, to learn that not only was there no party but it wasn't even Lee's birthday. The prankster, of course, having orchestrated this hoax, had long since disappeared and was nowhere to be found.

I believe what really shaped Lee's character was the fact that while he was streetwise and bright as a button, during his first years at school he was put into remedial classes and my father and brothers rarely let him forget it.

'Yaa! Who's an ex-remedial?' they'd taunt.

'I'm *not* an ex-remedial!' he'd protest indignantly. 'I used to be, but I'm not now!' To his dismay, even Farah, his favourite sister and ally, would collapse into a quivering, hysterical heap with the rest of his siblings, leaving him perplexed as to what he'd just said to cause this collective sibling fit.

There was an episode when Farah was being bullied at school. Lee dealt with these older girls in his own inimitable way.

'Oi! Slag!' he called to the ringleader. 'Touch our kid again and I'll forget yer a girl an' I'll fookin' nut yer!'

There was no subtlety about the way he said or did anything. He was loud, brash and incorrigible and always in trouble for disdaining authority, which was something my father thoroughly disapproved of. However, despite all his bravado, Lee never stopped trying to win my father's approval and went to great lengths to achieve it. To his Asian way of thinking, the most obvious way to achieve this was by being financially successful. After he'd left school and had spent a few years working for other people, Lee set up his own finance company and became one of the original 1980s Porsche-driving, twenty-something yuppies: fast, flash, loud and bound by few rules other than his own. Ironically, his determination to succeed only served to set Lee and my father even further apart.

By contrast Mohammed, the first-born son and heir, and Jo, the youngest and baby of the family, strolled through their childhood and early adult years, reaping the benefits of my father's affection and finances with very little conscious effort on their part. But then, being male, they never had to prove anything.

9

Being female

*Education makes a people easy to lead, but difficult to
drive; easy to govern, but impossible to enslave.*

Henry Peter, Lord Brougham (1778–1868)

Many Muslims are against education for females.

I understood why my mother was against educating females.
As a girl, my role was solely to provide for the comfort of the
men in my family – a female could serve no higher purpose. My
mother believed that education spoilt a girl's nature. A girl
overburdened with education becomes dissatisfied, develops
opinions and starts to think for herself, none of which are
desirable characteristics in a potential wife.

As far as my mother was concerned, education teaches a girl
disrespectful Western ways and encourages her to argue with
her elders and rebel against what is best for her. What is best for
her, of course, is to be safely married off at sixteen, virginity
intact, before she has a chance to shame her parents. For me, as
a Muslim female, education provided possibly one of the
greatest challenges of growing up caught between two cultures.

To my mother's consternation, my father did not hold the
same views on education. He'd brought his family to England to
give the children access to British education and was entirely of
the opinion that it was important for females to be educated,
more so than males. He used to say, 'A man will always be able
to make his way in life, but a woman is dependent on a man.

You only know what kind of husband a man will be to your daughters after it's too late and they are already married. That's why a woman needs to be able to look after herself!'

What my father was alluding to was the example of certain Pakistani families with whom he was acquainted. Most Pakistani men are devoted husbands and fathers. But, just as in any other community, there were the men who pushed the boundaries of acceptable behaviour.

There was one married Pakistani who carried on with his *Angrezi* girlfriend despite having a wife and four children. His wife complained to relatives but remained powerless to do anything about her errant husband, who'd give her a slap for daring to complain. Another gambled away a thriving grocery business and, eventually, the family home. His wife's tears were useless.

It was not that these women were unwilling to help themselves. They simply did not know how. Most were first-generation immigrants who did not speak English and depended on their husbands or children to translate for them while out shopping, in hospital or dealing with callers. Back in Pakistan they would have had a large network of relations from both sides of the family to draw on. Asian marriages are made not simply between couples but between both families, and therefore it's acceptable for these families to intervene when a marriage is in crisis. For a husband to publicly flaunt a mistress or gamble away his family's livelihood would bring shame upon the entire *khandan*, so members of his family would censure his behaviour. However, if the family is thousands of miles away, there is no one for a wife to turn to.

I knew of women who did not even know how to use a telephone. For these women, their lives were lived in isolation and were utterly locked into dependency upon their husbands. If he was a good husband, she counted herself as blessed. If he was not, she would consider it was her bad *kismet* and something she must endure for the sake of her children and family *izzat*. To complain would be to bring shame. Men who battered their wives were confident of unflinching loyalty from them because these women would protect the husband's *izzat* at all costs. Society's judgement would always be against her shortcomings as a wife rather than his failings as a husband, and the onus would always be on her to protect the family honour.

My father declared that if a girl was educated she could at least provide for herself and her children if she was treated badly. I listened to my father and learned my lesson well. His wise words about education would be prophetic in that, via the route of education, I would make my own escape years later.

Nevertheless, I have to give my father credit for being very forward thinking and advancing the cause of the women in his family. In Pakistan, his own father put his sons into business and purchased an expensive education for his only daughter. Dadda had sent his daughter to college to become a lawyer so it was not surprising that my father similarly felt it was important to educate the females, contrary to general Muslim thinking. Provided, of course, the house was kept well run and his meals appeared on time. On the serious issue of having his needs taken care of and being well fed, as far as my father was concerned theory and practice were two different things.

However, there were other ways in which he differed from Pakistani men. To his credit, my father never followed the Pakistani practice of sauntering several yards ahead of his wife, leaving her trailing behind. He used to say that in Pakistan he'd seen situations where a woman had passed out in the heat and the husband strolled on ahead, in happy ignorance of what had happened to his wife behind him.

I recall travelling to town in the car with my father one

afternoon. It was one of those rare occasions when I had him to myself and we were having a laugh.

'See him?' asked my father, pointing to an Asian man walking by, hands in his pockets, oblivious of the frail young creature walking several yards behind struggling with shopping bags, pram, toddler and baby.

'Idiot!' pronounced my father. 'Watch this!' he chuckled mischievously as he slowed down the car, wound down his window and, sticking his head out of the window, yelled out, 'Hey! *Bewakuf!* Idiot! She's your *biwi*, not your *bakri* – your wife, not your goat!'

He ended with a rude expletive and we drove away, howling with laughter, leaving the startled husband wondering who on earth had just driven past shouting insults at him.

However, as I already knew, theory and practice were two very different things. My father was full of contradictions, and while half of the time he chose to empower the girls in the family, where important decision-making was concerned there was a strict male–female divide. Despite being older and far cleverer than my brothers, as a female I had no voice in our house. The males made all the important decisions, and any attempt to add my voice was in vain. My brothers would simply talk over me and show no sign that they'd heard me at all. If I made a valid comment, it would be acknowledged only if endorsed by another male, who'd receive the credit for having come up with such a good idea in the first place. Quite simply, I was a girl and my place was in the kitchen. My voice was silent. I was invisible. According to an English translation I once read, the Koran states that one man's testimony is worth the testimony of two women. The reason for this, I was told, is that in the Islamic world, women are considered to be of lesser intelligence, with smaller brains.

'Huh! Not in my family!' I thought indignantly, thinking of my grade As in English, French, Law and Journalism. I was cleverer academically than any of my brothers, having achieved better qualifications while they were building their muscles doing kickboxing and weight-training. But I lived in a man's world where I was inferior for no better reason than gender. As a female, I had to work twice as hard to prove I was half as good. Or, where my own brothers were concerned, I had to be twice as clever to get away with being half as stupid.

This was really brought home to me when Mohammed, Eldest-son-and-heir, left school. My father purchased him a shop and flat. The deeds were in Mohammed's name and the business was duly handed over to him ready to run. I was livid: my father had never offered to set me up in life with so much as a dowry, as was his Muslim duty. What's more, he added insult to injury by suggesting that I stack shelves for Mohammed. I was mortified at the suggestion that I should work as my brother's shop assistant! It didn't take long to wipe the hopeful look off Mohammed's face.

'Get stuffed, Daddy's boy!' I informed him sweetly. 'I've cleaned your arse at one end and wiped your snotty nose at the other. I'm buggered if I'll stack your shelves as well!'

The men in my family assumed their superiority from what they learned at home. Women were there to serve the men. Mother and sisters waited on father and brothers because that was the way it had always been done. The women make the lives of the men comfortable and must always display submission and deference to them, for no other reason than because they are male.

Yes, I admit I had an attitude. And yes, I can understand why my mother would be suspicious of allowing us girls to be educated. She was absolutely right. I had begun to think for myself and question the status quo of a woman in a Muslim world. I was growing increasingly discontented and frustrated at the inequality of my life as a Muslim female and was beginning to resent the disparity of the opportunities given to the boys. Even as young children, the boys had more freedom to run around outside and stay out most of the day, coming home only for mealtimes. As they grew older, this freedom increased as they were allowed to come and go as they pleased, sometimes late into the night, free to pursue friendships, hobbies, go to the cinema, invite friends back to the house and have girlfriends.

By contrast, Farah and I were tied to our chores, with no life outside school or home. In a Pakistani home, as soon as a girl is old enough to wield a dustpan and brush she is required to help her mother to run the home and begin to earn her keep. While our *Angrezi* peers were out playing with roller skates and going swimming on Saturday mornings, we girls were slaves to the never-ending cycle of doing housework and preparing meals. With seven children and a demanding husband, my mother was overwhelmed by her domestic duties, so it was of necessity that her daughters helped. Of course, it was totally out of the question for a son to be expected to share any of this workload and my mother would sooner have collapsed with fatigue than have a male wield a vacuum cleaner when there was someone of the female gender in the vicinity. She seemed almost to regard it as a great sin and failing if a situation arose whereby a male in the house had to do any housework.

My father, on the other hand, used to shout at the boys to clean up after themselves and take responsibility for their own coffee cups and plates used after we girls had already cooked and cleaned up. As a result, while they were useless then, my brothers did grow up being useful around the house for their own wives, not because of my mother but in spite of her –

something for which their wives have my father to thank. However, as we were growing up, the burden of housework fell largely on us girls, with my brothers playing no part.

We knew a Muslim family of six sisters and envied the sharing of domestic chores between so many girls with only one very spoilt little son-and-heir to look after. To our minds the most pitiable creature possible is the unfortunate female reckless enough to allow herself to be born into a house of men, where she is the lone daughter in a family of many sons and where the domestic burden is destined to fall squarely on her lonely female shoulders.

Our routine was simple. Come back from school, get changed out of school skirt and cover up with trousers. Tidy up the house and start on evening meal. After the men had eaten, they'd depart for whatever plans they had made for that evening. The women would hastily finish their own meal and begin clearing up the dishes and sorting out the kitchen. By mid-evening we'd be finished and would have perhaps an hour or so to attend to our own studies, read a book or watch a television programme. Unless, of course any of the boys had been absent from the meal owing to a prior appointment in the gym or with mates. In that case one of us would wearily get back into the kitchen, heat up the meal and serve it to him.

'What's wrong with him doing it for himself?' we'd protest loudly to my mother, bristling with indignation and resentment. 'Is he so lazy or stupid that he can't put it in a microwave and heat it up for himself?'

'It's a sister's duty to take care of her brothers,' she explained. 'Later, they'll take care of you.'

Somehow that was a very high price: a pay-off that might or might not happen. And had we known then what we know now, my sister and I would quite happily have fed my brothers

Pedigree Chum! Meanwhile, we had no choice but to do as we were told. If Farah and I wanted time off to go into town on a Saturday for an hour or so, we had to make sure the chores were done and the meals were on time, or there was trouble. And apart from college, we were never allowed out without a chaperone.

'Don't see *him* taking a chaperone!' we'd comment resentfully. We knew that, without exception, all four of them had *Angrezi* girlfriends. On Saturday nights, one by one the boys flew out of the door in a waft of expensive aftershave, which was quite obviously not intended to impress the unshaven, unwashed Neanderthals who went weight-training with them.

'Huh! Typical!' I muttered sourly, 'For the first sixteen years we can't get the filthy beasts into a bathroom. Now we can't get them out!'

In our household, it was far better to be male than female. My brothers remained blissfully detached from the inconvenience of domestic responsibility. That was women's work. My sister and I deeply resented the monotony and inequality of our lives compared to those of our brothers, and there was little by way of compensation. To add insult to injury, when they brought their friends home we girls had to make ourselves scarce or else we'd be labelled 'fast' or 'immodest'. So if they arrived while we were watching television in the living room, we'd have to leave and sit in the kitchen or up in the bedroom until they'd gone. We didn't like it but we had no choice, as our opinions and feelings on the matter did not enter into the equation.

My mother, seeing this as our duty, did not seem to care how unfulfilled or unhappy we were. The important thing was to keep the household running and serve the men. Interestingly, this was supposedly done in the name of 'protection'. If we wanted to go out or to do things that other teenage girls did, like going to see a film or meeting in a coffee bar, we'd be made to feel guilty, as if we were abandoning my mother or, even worse, that we were behaving like Awara (loose) females, wanting to go out and mix with boys and shame our parents. As far as my family were concerned, we were denied any freedom in order to safeguard us from anything bad that could happen to us, or from gossip that would give us a bad reputation with other Muslims.

Gossip! That is the ultimate weapon wielded by all Muslim parents to keep their daughters under control. It is the fear of being the subject of gossip and being criticised by other members of the Muslim community that makes even a liberal-minded parent, such as my father, think twice and hold fast to the belief that daughters should be kept under lock and key.

This kind of pressure to conform served only to make me rebel against my home life even more. I learned to be devious and resourceful and to lie in order to steal that extra hour or so of time away from home, after school and college, in order to meet up with friends or go round the shops on my own without a chaperone. I would invent all kinds of excuses to come home late, such as extra classes, educational trips out of town or library study. It never occurred to me to consider the rights or wrongs of being deceitful, as I never knew any other life except the one where I juggled the two halves of my East–West existence just to belong.

I envied my brothers because they never had to do this. They wore what they wanted to wear, went where they wanted to go and did more or less what they wanted to do without the fear of gossip or scandal. They did not have these things because they were more deserving or clever, but simply because they had been born male.

It simply did not occur to my mother that we girls might have had every right to feel aggrieved and resentful. She never understood that liberating the men was only made possible by the enslavement of the females. What I found most difficult to comprehend was the fact that this system has only been allowed to continue through the complicity of women. My mother told us it was our Islamic duty, impressing upon us that it was ordained in the Koran. I was not so sure. I used to wonder why, in order to be deemed respectable and therefore acceptable, a woman must be silent and invisible. If, like me, she doesn't accept this, she is seen as a social deviant and shunned for being immoral or labelled a troublemaker.

Being female in the culture I was brought up in was being made to feel you were a burden. When a girl crosses that divide where she becomes a woman able to bear children, she is perceived to be a dangerous creature, capable of bringing shame and calamity on herself and her family unless she is watched closely and kept under control. Usually she is not told the facts of life and is made to feel unclean and guilty about something she does not really understand.

Generally, however, in our house the male offspring had fewer parental expectations foisted upon them and certainly fewer social pressures to conform to a lifestyle far removed from the society in which they now lived. This was because as males they were not subjected to the same strict social demands made of Muslim females in terms of dress, attitudes to modesty and restrictions in freedom. Their virginity is not guarded like the crown jewels; the loss of it, should it become public knowledge, is not a catastrophe that renders them unmarriageable and the rest of the family social outcasts. They are not expected to stay at home, tied down and enslaved by domestic duties.

I do not feel that my brothers were unusual in this because I saw that males, whether they were in England or Pakistan, were comparatively free to come and go where and when they pleased, with no question of being chaperoned. In short, they had a life. Where my brothers were concerned, I observed very little evidence of an East–West culture clash. If there was conflict it was more a clash of personalities between my brothers, who wanted to run things their way, and my father, who demanded they were done his way.

We girls could only look on with resentment and envy as we saw how very different their lives were compared to ours. They had no need to rebel against the restrictions of a Pakistani culture and religion and, unlike us girls, my brothers were able to transcend the East–West divide that oppressed the lives of their sisters, brought up in the same society yet dictated to by very different standards and rules. As far as I could see, our brothers had the best of both worlds. It wasn't something they had to fight for or earn. It wasn't a measure of character or intelligence or merit. It was simply a matter of gender.

It is believed by Muslims that hell – *jahanum* – is largely inhabited by females possessing blatant sexuality and deviant intent, seen as the potential bringers of calamity upon innocent unsuspecting males. From a very young age I got the impression that Allah didn't like us females very much. As a case in point; the Koran promises men that, when they die, they will go to a Paradise where beautiful young virgins will wait on them, offering food, drink and sensual pleasures. There is no mention of what females can expect. One cannot help but be left with the distinct impression that perhaps Paradise is, like everything else in the Muslim world, an essentially male preserve.

Questions in a spiritual wilderness

*Too often children get answers to remember rather
than problems to solve.*
Roger Lewin (1946–present)

'She has an active enquiring mind' my school report read.

A good report was no surprise because I loved learning and liked nothing better than to be given the opportunity by a teacher to challenge current academic thinking and present my own perspective on a topic. The English education system gave me scope to do that because, in my experience, its primary objective was to advise and inform while problems were to be thought through logically and solved. Furthermore, students were encouraged to debate, think around a subject, question and push boundaries. It was only in the classroom that I felt free to be an individual in my own right, free to hold opinions and free to express them.

However, once at home, the standards of the English society in which I was being educated became secondary to the culture of absolute obedience to authority. In this environment, I'd be told what to do, what to say and what to think. I was no longer an individual but an extension of my parents, an entity that served only to represent to the rest of the world their values, thoughts and opinions. I no longer belonged to myself. There was absolutely no scope whatsoever for argument, questioning or debate – no middle ground at all. At school my 'active, enquiring mind' earned me praise and good grades. At home, it simply got me into trouble.

This was because, as an Asian daughter, I was merely required to submit and obey. Asking questions was beyond the pale – and there were so many questions I wanted answered. I wanted to know, for example, why *sharab* (alcohol) was not permitted to Muslims.

'Because when men are *sharabi* they do bad things,' my mother replied. I thought about that. I'd witnessed the *sharabis* leaving the local pub and staggering past our house as I sat on the wide sill of my bedroom window. Most evenings I recognised the same characters with the same red-flushed faces as they paused to relieve themselves in whichever garden or against whichever wall was handy. They repulsed me. My parents had warned me to stay away from the pub and from the men who frequented it. I didn't need telling twice. What my mother told me about alcohol made sense so I accepted it without further question. Common sense told me that it was best not to push my luck and ask how come, if alcohol is forbidden, I'd seen familiar Muslim acquaintances coming out of the same pub, or why my father kept a bottle of that stuff hidden at the back of the cupboard. I was well aware that asking would only get me a good slap.

Another very pressing question that I wanted an answer to concerned the issue of pork. I wanted to know why Muslims are not allowed to eat pig. My mother told me that the Koran says they are dirty animals and if you eat pig meat your breath and body will stink for forty days and you will die unclean.

'Why are pigs any different to sheep or cows?' I asked.

'We are not allowed to eat animals with cloven hooves,' my mother replied.

'But we eat goat meat and goats have hooves!' I persisted. 'Why does eating pig make you unclean?'

At this point my irritated mother would rebuke me sharply for being argumentative and tell me to accept what I was told.

I received the same answer when I asked about the Islamic rules on halal meat. I wanted to know why it was necessary to slit the animal's throat and let it slowly bleed to death when there were quicker, more humane ways of killing it.

'That's the way halal meat is killed,' came the reply. 'It's better.'

'Not for the animal it's not!' I retorted, still not convinced.

There was something else I'd been trying to work out. I was told that the animal's head is pointed in the direction of Mecca while prayers are said over it and the knife is applied to its throat. In the case of halal chickens, where hundreds of birds were facing slaughter at once, I wanted to know whether prayers were said over each individual chicken with its beak pointing towards Mecca. Or was it a wholesale prayer chanted over a roomful of birds? How did they get them *all* to point towards Mecca at the same time while a prayer was being said over them? Or, if they were all over the place, did it still count as halal?

But whenever I tried to get answers I always ended up getting into trouble. At best I'd be reprimanded for being argumentative; at worst I'd receive a slap for being insolent and insubordinate. It therefore became clear to me very early on that the qualities that marked me out as a good student at school, and earned me high marks, were best left at school. An enquiring mind that challenged, reasoned and debated did not sit well on the shoulders of an obedient Pakistani daughter, because at home these very same qualities labelled me as being quarrelsome and disobedient and always got me into trouble. Self-preservation taught me that once I left the school gates and set off for home, it was prudent to re-adjust my brain eastward, metaphorically speaking. Experience taught me that the best way to stay out of trouble was to accept everything without question and leave my brain on the doorstep on the way in.

However, while I accepted that the answers to my questions would not be found at home, they did nevertheless still demand investigating so I tried to discover those answers for myself. The 'pig' question was one of the first I ever experimented with.

I was seventeen when I succumbed to the intriguing aroma of bacon. It had tantalised me for years. If it was so vile and unclean, why did *Angrezis*, a fairly sensible lot in my opinion, go into such raptures over it? I determined to find out. I was always being told I was going to hell anyway, so it wasn't as if I was risking anything I hadn't lost already. Nevertheless, putting my spiritual and physical wellbeing on the line, this intrepid reporter decided to investigate.

'May as well be hung for a sheep as a lamb,' I chuckled to myself. 'Or a bacon buttie!'

I went into one of those old-fashioned grocery shops run by a very amiable middle-aged couple. It smelled of coffee, sandwiches and pies, and at lunchtime their regulars queued patiently as each order was taken and prepared. All the girls at our sixth form college went there.

As I entered the shop, I felt as if I'd come to commit some dreadful misdemeanour with an imaginary handgun hidden beneath my coat. I felt unbelievably guilty as I placed my order, hesitating as the unfamiliar words took shape and were uttered by a voice unused to asking for a bacon sandwich, please.

I kept looking over my shoulder, anxious that at any moment someone who knew my family would come in and drag me off home by the scruff of the neck and haul me up before my outraged parents, flinging me to the floor as I confessed my sin.

'Hurry! Hurry!' I urged the shopkeeper in my head, as he took my order and disappeared into the back to make up my sandwich. He'd been gone almost ten seconds. It was taking far too long! I was starting to lose my nerve and was finding it increasingly hard to resist the urge to snatch my bag off the counter and leg it out of the shop to a safe place in the park, where I could retreat with my spiritual integrity intact.

'Of course!' I thought with dismay. It suddenly became perfectly obvious to me why he was taking so long. 'He's in the back telephoning my dad.' Right at this very moment, Shopkeeper-man was on the telephone grassing me up to my father! My father was always spying on me and had probably given him our telephone number ages ago, telling him to keep an eye on me and call him the moment I ordered bacon. Shopkeeper-man was telling my father he knew we Muslims weren't allowed to eat pork and he was certain my father would want to know that his daughter was at this instant in the shop, waiting for the sandwich to be made up. Yes, she'd brazenly walked in and shamelessly ordered a vile, despicable bacon sandwich, in full public view and with no consideration to her parents' *izzat* at all. No, it wasn't a problem. Yes, of course he'd keep her waiting until my father arrived.

'Here we are, dear!' he beamed as he emerged from the back, carrying a white paper bag containing the forbidden sandwich. I was jolted out of my day-dream and my heart jumped into my mouth as I instinctively tried to make a run for it.

'Can't say I remember you ordering one of these before, love,' he commented.

'What?' I cried, 'Issnotforme! It's for, er . . . a friend. Thassright a friend. Thanks! Bye!' Then, snatching the sandwich from his hand, I flung the money on the counter and fled.

Five minutes later my heart had finally stopped trying to beat its way out of my body and I was sitting on the grass beside the lake within the sanctuary of the college grounds, well out of sight of any passing Muslims, about to sink my teeth into the forbidden bacon sandwich. I threw a quick glance down at the grass as if expecting the ground to open up, revealing a slide chute straight to hell. There was no change. No helter-skelter ride to the fiery pits of the underworld. Only green grass.

I bit into the sandwich, looking heavenward this time, waiting for an angry bolt of lightning to come out of the heavens and strike me dead. But no, the sky was still very clear and blue and manifesting no signs of divine outrage. I took another bite as I looked anxiously down, then upwards again.

'Surely one of them would have something to say about it,' I thought in disbelief. 'Such blatant porcine consumption must surely offend *one* of them.'

Still nothing. No thunderbolt, no lightning, no road to hell. I didn't choke on a piece of piggy and drop down dead. Nor did I suddenly sprout bat wings and fly off, destined to spend eternity hanging upside down in a belfry. Absolutely nothing happened.

'Huh!' I sniffed scornfully, 'What a load of flippin' rubbish they talk!'

Then carried on eating.

I knew so little about my Muslim faith, and this was unfortunate because I had so many questions to ask and nowhere to go for answers. Experience had taught me that it was futile to look to my mother. Everything I wanted to know about the Muslim faith and Pakistani traditions came under the general heading of things she'd been taught to accept without question, and it didn't take a genius to work out that half the time my mother didn't know the answers herself. Like all Muslim children, she'd chanted her way through all 114 chapters of the

Koran and had thus accomplished her Islamic duty. However, as the Koran is written entirely in Arabic she didn't actually know what it all meant, because she had learned her lessons parrot fashion, as had her mother and her mother before her. No one had ever thought or dared to question anything.

However, I had been brought up in the West and given a Western education: being told to believe something for the sole reason that this was how it had always been was not enough for me. I needed to know and to understand. Unfortunately, I had not been taught the very basic things about Islam.

For example, doing *namaz* (prayers) is something all Muslims are taught to do from a very young age. Even before a child is taught to read and write, he or she is instructed in the performance of *wazu* (ritual washing) and *namaz*. Children begin by copying the adults and are usually proficient in going through the motions and chanting the verses and prayers before the teaching of the actual Koran begins. I asked why I was not allowed to go to the mosque and was informed that females over the age of twelve stayed at home and were taught by the women, which begged the question (not asked) of why I'd never been sent to study the Koran at the mosque with all the other kids when I was younger. Going to the mosque was a part of almost every Muslim kid's life. At teatime, straight after school, I'd hear the familiar cry of 'Mosque van's here!' then watch as the younger kids in the street dutifully piled into the back, boys wearing their white skull caps, little girls in *shalwar kameez* with *dupattas* wrapped modestly around their faces. My brothers and younger sister complained loudly and frequently about being forced to go. Every day the stomach aches and headaches, together with an assortment of undiagnosed complaints and illnesses, would mysteriously and conveniently begin to manifest themselves as the four o'clock mosque van time approached. My mother, who was usually easy to break when faced with persistent whinging from her offspring, was unusually stubborn and unyielding over the matter of religious education and was totally deaf to their protests.

''S not fair! We hate going!' they'd complain, pushing Lee, who was the most vocal one, to the front to be their spokesperson. 'The mullahs shout at you and hit you with a stick if you get it wrong!' they'd wail.

My mother, however, remained unmoved and stood firm, insisting it was their Islamic duty to learn the Koran, and said the mullahs were well within their rights to punish them if they didn't pay attention.

My father, who had an intense aversion to contention and discord within the family home (unless he was causing it), usually managed to avoid being drawn into these arguments. He'd never made any secret of his intense dislike of mullahs and was inclined to be fairly indifferent, even dismissive, about religion, only getting involved and putting a half-hearted foot down just to keep my mother from nagging him about their Islamic duty as parents. However, he was inclined to assert his parental duty more forcefully if his lenient Western ideas drew criticism from others regarding any neglect of his Muslim duty. On these occasions he'd bellow at the kids to get in the van and not shame him. So they had to go.

I sometimes watched them go with a feeling that I was missing out. Aside from a few lessons at home when we were younger, my elder sister and I had no religious schooling.

The task of teaching children to read the Koran generally falls on the mother, as does the day-to-day care and upbringing of her offspring. In a large extended Pakistani family, this job would naturally be shared between various aunts, cousins and older females. However, with seven children and no extended family in this country, together with a husband who was simply not interested in his cultural or Islamic duties where his children were concerned, my mother did not have time to teach me much. I was therefore completely illiterate in reading and writing Urdu and never progressed beyond the first few chapters of the Koran.

With my mother too busy to teach me herself and my father indifferent, I was sent to the wife of a mullah who was meant to teach me the Koran, but that was short-lived. I didn't like going there because her house was dingy, messy and smelt of dirty nappies. She had too many distractions to concentrate on teaching me properly and seemed just as busy and burdened down with domestic duties as my own mother; as well as four children of her own, she took care of her husband's nephew, who'd come to live with them from Pakistan. Some time after, she was charged with disciplining her nephew with a poker and sent to prison. That was the end of my Islamic schooling and there were no more lessons after that.

Nevertheless, the fact remained that I wanted to know more about my Islamic faith but there was simply no one to ask. I imagined the consternation I'd cause if I marched into the mosque and asked to speak to a mullah. I'd most likely be asked to leave, with the prospect of a good hiding from my father for venturing into a male domain and giving him a bad reputation for bringing up a promiscuous and wayward daughter.

What I had a problem with was the fact that, somewhere along the line, customs and traditions had become intermingled with teachings from the Koran to the point where many people didn't actually know where one ended and the other began. I'd lost count of the number of times I'd heard Muslim girls say, 'I'm not allowed to wear a dress', or 'I'm not allowed to go out on my own', or even 'I'm not allowed to cut my hair because it's against my religion'. Whether it concerned what they had to wear or what they could eat, these declarations came out so easily, yet these girls did not have a clue as to which rule or custom they were breaking. It never seemed to occur to them that there might be a difference between religion, culture and tradition. Due to extremist interpretation of the core religion, culture and religion had become so intertwined as to have become virtually inseparable. The question of dress – or, more to the point, the matter of covering up – was a good example of this. The Koran states that women should dress modestly, yet because so much religion had crept into the Pakistani culture, many Muslims believe that unless women are covered from head to foot, hidden behind a black veil, seeing only through eye slits, they are 'unIslamic'. It frustrated me so much because I worked out that most people who called themselves Muslims had no idea where religion ended and culture and tradition began.

I began to realise there were very few people in my life who did know what was actually in the Koran. There certainly wasn't anyone who could give me the impartial advice and guidance I craved so much. Most Muslims are remote from Orthodox teachings of the Koran, learning it as children by heart, parrot fashion, as my mother had done. But because the Koran is written in Arabic, most ordinary people do not under-stand what it is they are reciting, relying upon the Imams or priests who translate and interpret its teachings. Any interpre-tation of its teachings is therefore subjective and a reflection of the personal attitudes and beliefs of the translator. In any case, I was in no position to study any translation, as the mosque was out of the question because I was female.

With no one else to turn to for help and guidance, I was floundering, lost in a spiritual wilderness.

11

Trapped in a cultural void

To bring up a child in the way he should go,
travel that way yourself once in a while.

Josh Billings (1818–85)

According to my mother, the Koran decrees that it is the duty of all Muslim parents to ensure their daughters are respectably married. She told us that on Judgement Day, parents will be commanded to stand before Allah to give an account of how they've discharged their parental obligations. Or explain why they have failed in their duty and go to hell. That is what would happen if we girls were not married off.

Once a Muslim daughter is married, she becomes her husband's responsibility. What she gets up to after that is his business and down to him; it is his *izzat*, not theirs, at stake, as they will have fulfilled their parental duty. However, until she is married, the daughter's physical and moral welfare remain the parents' responsibility. It seemed to me that Muslim parents can't wait to get rid of their daughters, because my mother certainly never made any secret of the fact that an unmarried daughter is a liability.

For years we girls assumed the burden of guilt about being unmarried. We were made to feel it was our fault that our parents were denied the joy of seeing any of their three daughters respectably married off into good Pakistani families, and our fault that they were denied the joy of welcoming a respectable son-in-law into their home and of being able to do the social rounds with the newly married couple. Instead, they lived with the burden and shame of daughters who were married to an *Angrezi* or, even worse, *not* married to him.

But after years of carrying this guilt I hand that responsibility firmly back to my parents. It was not our fault. We were the product of an upbringing that did not teach and guide children through the trials and traumas of living between two different cultures. Being a Muslim child growing up in a Western society was like being two people trapped in one skin. Outside the home, I dressed and spoke like everyone else. I had the same hopes, dreams and aspirations as any young girl brought up in the West. I wanted to style my hair, wear fashionable clothes, listen to music and mix with both sexes. However, unlike most Western girls, I also had this other 'life'. There was the Eastern part of me where I was required to be a dutiful daughter and give my parents absolute obedience, help run the home and, when the time was right, accept the man they had chosen for me to marry, with very little say in the matter.

I was aware that I was fortunate in being allowed more freedom than other Muslim girls and preferred making friends with the English, Hindu and Sikh girls. They, in contrast, seemed less uptight about things like dress codes and talking to members of the opposite sex.

Muslim society segregates the two sexes from an early age. Male and female children are permitted to run around and play together. Then, from the age of about eight, little girls are subjected to the same stultifying decorum as adults and made to cover up. They are taught that the onus is on the female to cover up and not invite unwelcome male attention. Should that happen, the sin is hers for enticing him rather than his for lack of self-restraint.

As the girl gets older, increasing restrictions are placed upon her freedom, ranging from who she is permitted to speak to to what she is expected to wear. As long as I could remember, my mother had desperately tried (and failed) to make us wear *shalwar kameez*. In contrast to Western clothes that permit – indeed, encourage – the flaunting of parts of the body deemed sexual, such as breasts and buttocks, Pakistani clothes are designed for modesty. The *shalwar* forms the lower half of the outfit and is made of several yards of fabric that falls into voluminous folds. The upper half, the *kameez*, is usually long, with a fitted bodice. The whole outfit is loose and designed to permit the wearer to sit cross-legged on the floor with modesty and propriety.

The *dupatta* is an essential part of this outfit. It is worn to preserve a woman's modesty by covering her head in the presence of elders or non-family members. Generally, it is worn thrown across the chest, from shoulder to shoulder, to conceal the swell of her female curves. To be seen without this essential item of clothing is to be seen as immodest.

My sisters and I vigorously resisted our mother's attempts to make us wear traditional Pakistani clothes. If she'd been given her way, we'd never have been allowed to wear English clothes at all, as she considered them unfeminine and immodest.

Much to her chagrin, our father took our side. Having chosen to live here, he believed that it was only right that we should behave in a way that respected the society that we'd opted to join. He added that it was not an Islamic requirement to wear traditional dress, and wearing Western clothes would not compromise our Muslim faith, so long as we dressed modestly. He told my mother that the important thing was for his children to fit in so that they could take advantage of all the opportunities that were being offered. He said that this society had many advantages and it was important to integrate and not to invite undue criticism. He said he did not believe that women should be put behind *purdah*, unlike other Muslim men who thought that women should be hidden away, unseen and unheard.

However, it was one of the few issues where my parents were not united and my mother would vehemently disagree with him. Once a year, at Eid, amid much protesting from us, my mother determinedly put her foot down and forced us to abandon our English clothes and wear that 'hateful fancy dress', as we called it. But other than that, my sisters and I never wore *shalwar kameez* and my father didn't support my mother in her desire to force us to.

Unless it directly affected his day-to-day comfort, mealtimes or social standing, my father showed little interest in domestic matters such as the question of his daughters being made to wear traditional dress or the need to get his daughters married off. To my mother's frustration, he always over-ruled her on the issue of traditional dress, allowing us to wear Western clothes as long as they were decent and didn't accentuate the obvious bits.

We knew for years how badly my mother had wanted my father to help her arrange marriages for us. If she'd had her way, all three girls would have been married off as soon as we left school at sixteen. This is what had happened to several girls of our acquaintance, including one of Farah's best friends.

On the question of a potential marriage partner, Pakistanis rarely consider looking outside the family if there is anyone remotely eligible within it, and a first cousin is always first port of call. There are various reasons for this. Dowries are kept within the family and, with the couple being of the same blood, both bride and groom's family are tied by a mutual interest in preserving family stability and honour.

However, with our Western aversion for marriage between close cousins, my sisters and I refused point blank to even consider marrying a cousin, close or distant. We'd known that a particular first cousin had been mooted years ago for my older sister. He was the eldest son of Burra Mamoo (mother's oldest brother). This marriage would have strengthened the family ties between my mother and her eldest brother and would also have given Mamoo the foothold he longed for into this country. My father was not happy for any of his daughters to be wedded into Mamoo's house, as he and Mamoo didn't get on. Mamoo ruled his family with an iron will and his son would do exactly as he was told. If it suited him, Mamoo could order his son to make things difficult for his cousin-wife in order to manipulate her father, whom Mamoo hated.

As far as we girls knew, the problem with marrying us off had been the lack of *rishtas* (proposals of marriage) from suitable families. Quite simply, to our knowledge, there hadn't been any. Our lack of proposals was nothing to do with looks or eligibility. On the contrary; I would assert with some degree of confidence that, from a Western point of view, we were actually very eligible indeed. Had we been allowed the freedom to place ourselves on the marriage market and been judged by what we could offer a husband, any English Mama would have been happy to have us marry her son. No son of hers would have come home to a house with a basketful of dirty laundry, an empty larder or a suspiciously unfamiliar aftershave on his wife's clothes. We were intelligent and had been trained to run a home and care for a family. We knew our duty. As far as we were concerned, we were as eligible as the next unmarried Pakistani girl – even more so, because we were educated and also able to earn our own living.

Unfortunately, no amount of beauty, domesticity or earning power was going to attract *rishtas* for our hands in marriage if our eligibility was not in circulation on the Pakistani marital grapevine. This was not very likely, given the fact that our family did not really move in Pakistani circles.

Most Pakistanis are part of an ever increasing extended family of brothers, sisters, aunts, uncles, cousins, second cousins and so on. Everyone knows everyone else and everyone knows someone with a son or daughter of marriageable age. These links are forged over a lifetime; in many cases families will have possibilities lined up while the children are still in nappies and nurture these links until they come to fruition or other more suitable candidates appear later on.

My father had always been reluctant to facilitate demands to bring relatives over once he was established in England. He wanted the freedom to bring up his family away from the demands and constraints of a large extended family with relatives telling him how he should do things, demanding help setting up a business, being drawn into petty squabbles, disapproving of the amount of freedom he gave his children or dealing with envy and resentment if he had a bigger house or better car than someone else. He always said Pakistani people consider it a neglect of their duty not to pass on the benefit of their opinion and involve themselves in other aspects of their relatives' lives.

My family, therefore, was fairly unusual in not being part of an extended family. Instead, like most *Angrezi* families, we knew only our immediate nuclear family of parents and siblings. Furthermore, while my parents had Pakistani acquaintances, they never allowed anyone to get close. My family never really moved in Asian circles so my acquaintances were all English.

My father always believed that, in order to integrate into any society, it was important not to dress and behave differently. He believed in integration, not segregation, and used to say that if you look or behave differently, people don't understand you; what they don't understand they begin to fear, and that is where prejudice begins. He also taught us never to speak Urdu in front of *Angrezis*, saying, 'They know you speak their language and will misunderstand your reasons for speaking a language they don't understand in front of them. They will think the only reason you are not speaking in English is because you are talking about them, and they will resent you for it.'

So we were brought up to keep our Pakistani and Western sides separate. We spoke English with each other and spoke Urdu at home with our parents. In the same way as our brains were able to switch from one language to another without thinking about it, so we were able to switch mentally from our East and West sides. The seams hardly showed at all. We knew other Muslim families but were never really a part of their circle. Thus isolated, my sisters and I were not put into circulation where marriage was concerned.

We knew many Pakistani parents returned to the 'homeland' to find spouses for their offspring. In the case of an imported bride, the transition from Pakistan was easy. A bride comes to her husband's home and becomes a part of his family, adapting to his ways and needs.

However, finding a groom for a daughter raised in the West throws up problems of a different nature. We girls refused to even contemplate living in Pakistan after marriage, giving up everything we had ever known. Furthermore, given the fact that most potential bridegrooms would be lured by the prospect of a wife with a British passport anyway, that situation would be rare, as in most cases the bridegroom's family would insist on his coming to England to live. This was one of the first lessons we learned: families cite religion, custom and tradition when they want to force girls to toe the line, yet those self-same traditions are abandoned without a moment's hesitation if it suits some other purpose, like getting a relative into the country. So while it is the custom for the girl to join her husband's family, when a British-born Pakistani girl is married off to an imported husband, he invariably comes to England to live. I know of girls who were coached to answer Home Office questions when applying to get husbands and fiancés into Britain, and also some who obtained doctor's certificates to state they had a skin condition that precluded them from living in a hot climate. This was the same hot climate they would subsequently visit regularly, with no adverse medical reactions to the heat, after the husbands were given leave to stay in England.

However, as far as my sisters and I were concerned, having an imported husband would be a most unsatisfactory arrangement. We knew girls who could barely speak the same language as their new husbands. Worse still, they ended up with a husband who depended upon his wife to translate, pay bills, fill in forms and show him his way around because he did not have sufficient command of English and English society.

Employment was a major problem. I knew girls whose families had boasted of marrying their daughter to a teacher or accountant, yet once here those men were not the catch they had been in Pakistan. Their qualifications were not recognised and they found themselves washing dishes in a restaurant or working in a warehouse. The girls ultimately became the breadwinner, translator and nursemaid when what they really wanted was an equal partner.

Matters are not helped by an imported husband's sudden exposure to Western society. For a young man raised in a strict

Islamic state, it comes as something of a culture shock to see, openly on display, things that exist only behind closed doors in Pakistan. Not surprisingly, he begins to wonder exactly how much he can trust his wife, whose values have been corrupted by being brought up among all this Western permissiveness. He starts to question what she gets up to when she is at work, out shopping or simply doing all the day-to-day things that he, as husband, ought to be doing. In a culture where the man expects to be master in his own home, resentment, disappointment or suspicion rears its ugly head, and I know of several cases where a British-born Pakistani wife has been beaten by an insecure imported husband.

Having witnessed these kinds of problems, my sisters and I were adamant that we did not want imported bridegrooms. We were willing to have arranged marriages but on the proviso that the grooms spoke English and were at the very least educated to the same standard as we were. We did not think that we were being at all unreasonable in wanting that. However, my mother seemed to interpret this as our blatant refusal to have any marriage at all, which was not true. But by leaving us unmarried and free to sin, she believed that she would be held responsible for that sin, something that filled her with dread, and it was therefore easier to blame us.

My father, on the other hand, seemed less concerned with spiritual duties than with counting the cost in financial terms. With three daughters to marry off, he had the daunting task of finding three bridegrooms who would take three spirited and outspoken daughters. He also had to find three dowries to pay, as well as the costs of three potentially very expensive weddings which needed to be in keeping with his social standing and *izzat* among family and friends. Faced with such huge obligations, it seemed to us that he actually did very little to fulfil those responsibilities to his faith, his wife or his daughters.

As far as we were concerned, we were in an impossible situation. This was a no-man's land where we were not given a traditional marriage and yet were denied the opportunity to find husbands of our own. We were trapped in a cultural void. It was a no-win situation that was our bad *kismet*, for it was inevitable that whatever path we were to take, it would lead to someone getting very hurt.

I2

The troublemaker

If you can't answer a man's argument, all is not lost;
you can still call him vile names.

Elbert Hubbard (1856–1915)

I knew that if I didn't get away, I'd either murder my father or
be murdered by him. Despite the fact that I was now nineteen,
my father was still hitting me. It could happen at any time and
for any reason. The only thing I was certain of was the fact that,
sooner or later it would happen again.

I recall one morning when I was setting off for college. I
rarely, if ever, asked my father for anything. This was partly to
do with the fact that I considered myself so unimportant in the
pecking order of the family that I never felt I was worth anyone
putting themselves out for me and was used to relying on
myself. It also had a lot to do with the fact that I had as little to
do with my father as possible; I would hastily remove myself
from his presence and scarcely spoke to him unless he spoke to
me first. I often felt a pang of regret at times when he wanted to
share a joke and a laugh, for despite aching to love and be loved
by him and to spend time bonding with him, when the opportunity presented itself I'd always remember my father's unpredictable temperament and impatience where I was concerned,
and would flounder in a wave of panic before hastily construct-
ing an excuse to flee. Afterwards, in the safety of a quiet room,
I'd bitterly regret another missed opportunity.

That particular morning, however, it was cold and raining hard, and as he was around I asked my father for a lift to college. He snapped that he was busy and I'd have to wait. Retorting that I'd walk, I snatched up my bag and began the three-mile walk to college, hurt and resentful that he never put himself out for me.

However, to my dismay, about half a mile along the road my father's car pulled up beside me, and my heart sank as his angry face leaned out of the window.

'Get in!' he barked.

Getting into the car next to him while he was in that belligerent mood was the last thing I wanted to do, but I dared not refuse. To be perfectly honest, I don't have much recollection of what happened in the car other than a hard fist unexpectedly being driven into my face with such force that, from the corner of my eye, I actually watched my mouth swelling up within seconds. It was followed by another blow and then another, leaving me dazed and my vision blurred. As I caught my breath and refocused my eyes, I realised what people meant by seeing stars: that's what I was seeing, with whirly shapes dancing in front of me, making me feel dizzy and disorientated. Hot tears stung my eyes as, with a heart heavy with emotion, I sadly turned away to gaze out of the window at all those people going about their lives unaware of how unhappy my life was. I wondered what it would be like to be someone else.

'I am so ashamed of you,' I thought to my father, touching my battered face. I dared not say the words out loud to him, but I felt the sentiments no less deeply. 'I'm not a child any more. I'm almost grown up but you're still hitting me.'

And my father continued to hit me because there was no one to stop him. My mother had long since given up intervening, and for years she'd pleaded with me to keep the peace, accept what he said and not make him angry. But she could no more stop my father getting angry with me than she could prevent me from answering back and telling him what I felt I had every right to say. It was his will against mine, and neither of us would back down. And although it was not a fair fight, because he was bigger and stronger than me and invariably won every argument by giving me a good hiding, it never stopped me. It never stopped me because my sense of outrage at his unjust treatment of me overcame my fear of him. While I was perfectly willing to accept justified chastisement and appropriate punishment, I would never give in to being verbally abused and beaten unjustly. I'd die first. That, unfortunately, was what the family were afraid of.

Only another male could have stopped him, but there wasn't anyone. For the first time, I found myself thinking about that baby brother who'd died in Pakistan before I was born. His name was Inaam and he'd have been in his twenties now. I wondered if it would have made a difference to my life if he'd been alive. Would the presence and intervention of a grown-up son have made any difference to my father's treatment of me? Would Inaam have stood up to my father, man to man, and persuaded him to be kinder to me?

Sadly, I'd never know. I had one older sister and four brothers who were all younger than me. The eldest, Mohammed, had just turned fifteen. Gentle and easy-going by nature, Mohammed hated any kind of trouble. Not much hope there, I thought. However, I was to be surprised.

One day, not long after the car incident, my father was having a go at me as usual. Mohammed frowned in disapproval as my father unleashed his temper, becoming louder and angrier, and I braced myself for a clout. To my utter amazement, Mohammed stood as a barrier between my father and me.

'Just leave her alone!' he cried. 'You're always picking on her!'

This uncharacteristic outburst from his normally placid eldest son left my father shaken. Uncertain of how to handle this unexpected turn of events, he was suddenly lost for words and left the room in search of my mother, muttering about ungrateful and disrespectful children. I was shaken too, but for quite a different reason.

'At last!' I thought. At last, after all those years of verbal and physical abuse, my eldest brother had grown up and there was a man to defend me.

'But it's too late,' I thought unhappily. 'Too little, too late.' I'd survived a violent, dangerous childhood and I'd grown up. I'd no idea what long-term emotional damage had been caused, knowing only that I was unhappier than any living person I knew.

I was past caring what could happen to me. For some time I'd contemplated suicide because I couldn't see a way out. I felt ashamed and humiliated because my father beat me. I also knew that if I'd been a boy, he'd have stopped years ago. I'd witnessed what had happened the last time he became angry with Shoukat.

Shoukat was fourteen and spent a lot of his time down at the gym, body-building and pulling weights. He also had a hot temper. As my father raised his hand to strike him, Shoukat instinctively squared up to him.

'Don't. Ever. Hit me. Again!' he hissed through his teeth, chest out, fists clenched, face inches from my father's.

My father looked visibly shaken, let his hand fall and walked out of the room. He never hit the boys again. Shoukat, in turn, looked ashamed.

In Asian eyes, it is unforgivable to strike a parent. Had

Shoukat done so, my mother would never have forgiven him. He'd probably never have forgiven himself. This is because respect for elders is deeply rooted in Asian culture. Verbal and physical abuse must be tolerated as rightful correction and accepted with remorse and humility. There is no question of retaliation, whatever the provocation. To do so is a sin that would send them to *jahanum*.

I'd gone past adolescence and the age when brothers and fathers should maintain a respectful physical distance, but my father's violence against me continued nevertheless. This was made worse in light of the fact that he was frustrated now that he could only shout at the boys. However, his temper had no such need of reticence and raged unchecked where I was concerned, because I was a girl and therefore smaller and weaker.

As I grew older, I increasingly stood up for myself as I simply couldn't bring myself to hold my tongue or give up in passive acceptance. I certainly didn't think I ought to apologise to my father for provoking him to beat me. My mother was always telling me that the Koran says it is a sin to defy your parents and that I must accept his treatment placidly and not enrage him further by answering him back. Her pleas fell on outraged ears.

'Bullshit!' I'd cry indignantly, the pain of injustice shaking every fibre of my being. 'How does it become *my* sin? Why does he have the right to bully and beat me? Why do I have to accept responsibility for it? I'm the victim! Why is it my sin and not his? *It's not fair!*' I'd roar.

I had no idea what was written in the Koran other than what my mother told me, but I was outraged that the Koran would allow a father to beat his daughter for no reason. I desperately wanted to respect my parents but I was the victim, not the perpetrator! I burned with a deep sense of outrage and injustice and refused to accept his beatings placidly and submissively as

I was commanded to do by Allah. I was willing to go to hell (where, I was reminded almost on a daily basis, I was heading anyway) so it was inevitable that one day I'd fight back – quite literally.

My parents were on their way out for the evening, when something I'd done or said made my father angry and he turned and stormed back into the room, flinging away his coat.

'*Sali!*' he cried, grabbing me by the throat and pinning me down against the sofa. Something inside me snapped. This was so wrong. I was a girl. He was a grown man, bigger and stronger than me. It wasn't fair. He was wrong to assault me like this. I didn't deserve such treatment and I wouldn't accept it. Not any more! With an anguished cry I mustered all my strength to push him off me, clawing his face with my nails. He staggered back in disbelief. I was horrified and knew I'd pay dearly.

'She laid her hands on me!' he shrieked to my mother. 'The *haramzadi* dared to lay her hands on me!'

My mother silently and resignedly removed her coat. They weren't going anywhere that night. The rest of the family stood petrified. Everyone knew what was coming, but I was no longer afraid of what he could do to me. A lifetime of beatings had taken its toll. Now I was past caring as I passively submitted to the physical onslaught, no longer feeling anything. It became a surreal experience as, through blurred vision, I was strangely aware that in the background the rest of the family looked on in helpless anguish as I was battered around the room. I became an inanimate object, incapable of feeling anything. For the first time I felt a merciful release because my mind was able to detach itself from my physical being and feel no pain, denying him any satisfaction from hearing me screaming. It was not *my* face that was being punched, not *my* throat being choked, nor *my* body being hurled with force against a wall. A part of me wanted him to kill me. Death would be a release. At least I'd be out of his reach if I were dead. It would save me the trouble of killing myself. At least I'd be at peace.

While I have no memory of the rest of the evening, the atmosphere was terrible in the house for many days after. No one spoke or ate very much. I clearly recall that something changed that night. It by-passed the violence that was committed against me and focused on the sense of shock and outrage that I'd dared to lay hands on my father and fight back. Because, in doing so, I'd committed the most reprehensible crime any child can commit against a parent, and my Muslim religion and Pakistani culture permitted no mitigating circumstances in my defence. The crime was mine and the sin was mine. My father was grief-stricken.

The tide of sympathy was beginning to turn against me. My mother was torn between her loyalty to her husband and anxiety for me. But I was aware of her increasing frustration. If only I'd hold my tongue and not answer back, he wouldn't get so mad. The family couldn't understand my refusal to accept my situation, apologise to him and just let him cool down. If I'd just keep silent, the house would not be a battleground.

By this time, my mother's frustration was directed at me and she'd often say, 'The day you leave this house, we will have peace.'

Hearing my mother express those sentiments hurt me deeply and filled me with despair and self-hatred, but I could not deny that she was right. It was my presence that was causing such domestic turmoil and upheaval. It broke my heart to know with certainty that the only way I could bring harmony and peace to my family's home was by leaving it. The problem was, how could I leave?

Respectable Asian girls belonged to their parents until they were married off and handed over to their husbands. They certainly didn't leave home and set up in a flat to live a bachelor-girl lifestyle. Only disreputable girls lived outside the respect and protection of their families. They were no better than prostitutes and were treated as such. Even worse, their reputation would transfer itself to other members of the family, who'd also be shunned by the community for being disreputable and having no *izzat*. And when it came to preserving their *izzat*, for most Pakistanis no price was too high. Any price would be paid, whether that price cost the happiness or even the lives of those involved. So as far as I was concerned, I'd be killed before being allowed to leave home. Aside from simply killing myself, there was really only one way. That was by going into further education.

My mother was totally against it, wanting instead for my father to marry me off. I was also quite happy to be married if it meant escaping. Unfortunately, marriage proposals were rather thin on the ground, and if my parents were looking for a potential husband, I knew nothing about it. My mother warned my father he was setting himself up to be burned again and that I'd do exactly what my elder sister had done and run off to marry a *gora*. Despite being his favourite, she'd broken my father's heart, and according to my mother she wasn't half the *haramin* that I was. But my father wasn't listening.

He enjoyed telling the relatives back in Pakistan how clever I was and how I'd become a lawyer like my Aunt Zainab. He declared that he would let me go away to study because it would not be justice to allow my future to be ruined by what my sister had done to the family. Furthermore, he decreed, I would understand that I'd been given trust, and because I was intelligent and sensible I'd repay that trust by getting my degree, qualifying as a lawyer and returning home with honour.

There was no honour in my Judas's heart, for even while I was promising faithfully to be a good daughter, I knew without remorse or pity that I'd betray their trust because I had no intention of ever returning home if I could help it. In reality, my heart lay in a career in journalism and the media, but I knew that would never satisfy his ambition. It was a lawyer or nothing, and if becoming a lawyer was my exit ticket then I was willing to lie and promise anything. He had his 'King Solomon' head on, and seeing my only chance, I took it.

There was no question of academic ability. With a healthy stash of qualifications I knew I'd easily gain a place at any university of my choice and applied to London colleges. However, for my parents' benefit I applied to universities within and around Lancashire, despite having absolutely no intentions of accepting a place at these. A local college would make no difference whatsoever to my situation as it would entail living at home. Even a live-in situation away from home in a university such as Lancaster, Liverpool or Manchester was no good to me if it was within a couple of hours' drive.

My father would see it as an after-dinner sport to suggest to my mother that they get into the car every evening and take a drive to check up on me. I'd always be anxious about turning a corner and skipping a heartbeat at the sight of his car, never being able to relax and always on my guard. I'd never get any peace because he'd be on the doorstep all the time, parked outside the halls of residence to spy on who was coming and going from my place or who I was sitting with in lectures. Or, which was more likely, parking the car out of sight and spying on me from around corners and through shop windows. Then, when he thought I'd least expect it, he'd suddenly appear in the middle of the day or first thing in the morning to 'catch me out'.

I knew the working of his mind too well. He'd play cat and mouse with me and torment me, and I had absolutely no intention of putting myself in that situation.

I wanted to leave the town, the county and the North West of England altogether and go as far away from him as possible. London was a gratifying five-hour drive away, a ten-hour round trip, which would mean no spur-of-the-moment visits. He'd have to plan at least a day in advance, which meant Farah would be able to warn me he was on his way.

But London would never be permitted if I had even a single offer from a northwestern college and I knew I'd have to be resourceful and deceitful. As my father always opened and read all my letters, I intercepted the mail and carefully destroyed everything that came addressed to me from nearby universities. I told him that everyone had rejected me and the only college to offer me a place was in Ealing, west London. I knew how to play on his ambitions and reminded him of how proud he'd been when he'd opened up my O and A level results; how teachers had always told him how effortlessly I passed exams and that he had an academic genius in the family. So he gave me permission to go to London.

I didn't need telling twice. I flung my bags into the back of his car, trying not to look too happy or excited, and he drove me south to begin my life as a law student in London. I was twenty-one years old and I had taken the first step towards my plan to escape.

Part 3

You can run . . .

13

Freedom

Freedom is what you do with what's been done to you.
                                          Jean-Paul Sartre (1905–80)

My father drove me down and we stayed with one of his old Pakistani friends who used to rent a room in his house years ago. He was now married with a delightful family of his own and living in west London. I remembered him from my childhood and it was like meeting an old uncle again.

Within a day or so, I'd found a room to rent in a lovely big old house in Lammas Park Road, just around the corner from the famous Ealing Film Studios where they'd made those black-and-white comedies years ago.

For someone who'd had a cloistered upbringing, Ealing felt like the most thrilling place on the planet with all its restaurants, wine bars, nightclubs and fabulous quaint little boutiques with clothes and shoes to die for. The people were interesting too. I loved the cosmopolitan feel of London with its fusion of different nationalities, languages, cultures and cuisines represented on almost every corner. You never knew who you would meet and that fact alone thrilled me. I decided London would suit me fine, and without further ado threw myself into a hectic life of parties, concerts, dinner-dances and anything else that sounded like fun. I felt totally at home among the students and young professionals I met and knew from the very beginning that this was where I belonged and that I'd rather die than go home again.

No one knew what kind of home life I'd run away from and, as terrible as it had been and as desperate as I'd been to escape, it never occurred to me for one moment to speak about it with anyone. To confess to being beaten and terrorised at home would be humiliating and simply not done. Furthermore, it would bring shame on my family and that was something I was reluctant to do: despite having run away, now there was distance between us I could finally think fondly of them and feel a sense of duty and loyalty towards them.

On a personal level, even in those early heady days I had boundaries. I'd never indulged in smoking, drugs or alcohol. They'd never interested me before and I didn't see any reason to start now. Being free was intoxicating enough, and I was happy with Perrier and orange juice and simply didn't need other stimulants for confidence. Besides, whenever I required the nerve to face a situation that was new to me (and there were new experiences all the time) I was perfectly capable of manufacturing confidence to order, because no one knew better than I did how to live a lie. All my life I'd had to put on an act, hiding my Eastern culture outside the home and suppressing my Western side in front of my parents. This was no different. I was timid and had no feelings of self-worth and I wasn't really used to being part of a social crowd, but I was a good actress and found it effortless to cover up any self-esteem issues with an act of gregarious bravado. Sometimes I didn't know where my acting ended and my natural personality began, and it would be many years before the layers were stripped away and I could discover the real me underneath.

But right now, I needed to play-act in order to make myself and the rest of the world believe that I was the loudest, funniest and most outrageous person they knew. Regardless of how I was feeling inside, I had the ability to flick an inner switch, and a plain, shy and insignificant girl could suddenly be transformed into the life and soul of the party who was always up for anything. My new friends and I did things my family would have found outrageous. We once dressed up as naughty school-girls in short skirts, stockings, pigtails and painted freckles for a 'St Trinians' themed party, and on another occasion arrived as painted trollops to a Vicars and Tarts bash. We attended every party we were invited to or pouted, giggled and gate-crashed our way into the ones we weren't. We had funny or irreverent nicknames for everyone and made sure we were always in the thick of the action. We didn't need to find the in-crowd because we *were* the in-crowd.

All my life, being Asian had always had negative implica-tions. My experience of being a Muslim had always meant that I'd been forbidden to do many things I'd wanted to do, while duty obliged me to do other things that I didn't want to do. It had set me apart from everyone I wanted to be friends with. I never felt any sense of positivity about my Eastern heritage. Being young and having fun seemed to be frowned upon by the Muslims I knew and gave the impression that 'fun' was something that was only had by other people. I'd come to the conclusion that, as far as my family were concerned, a good girl couldn't have fun, and if she did want to have fun she was morally corrupt.

I had friends of all nationalities, but the Asians I met in London and who became part of my crowd were very different from the ones back home. They were more sophisticated, more integrated into mainstream society and definitely more fun.

It was a new experience to socialise openly with members of the opposite sex without being afraid that some old busybody was going to go running to my parents, accusing me of immoral behaviour. We hung out together, but my friendships with the boys in the group were strictly platonic, which was in itself very liberating. It made me realise that the guilty feeling previously associated with situations like this had been a result of my upbringing and other people's sordid perception of the world, where it was automatically assumed that you could never be friends with a member of the opposite sex, and that if a boy and a girl were seen talking together it was because they were having a sexual relationship. I never had any reason to believe that being Asian could be fun until I met my Asian friends in London.

We went to parties and also organised them. I recall one huge ticketed event that we organised. We booked Alaap, a bhangra band from the Midlands, and put on an impressive dinner-dance for several hundred people. Guests came from all over London and it was an enormous success.

Another time, a group of friends took me to Veeraswamy's in Regent Street, which was, I was told, the most famous Indian restaurant in London, it being one of the first of its kind. I almost keeled over in shock when I saw the prices. In our house, expensive clothes, expensive hobbies and restaurants were the prerogative of the men, not for us girls. It was thrilling beyond words to be suddenly transported to a world where I was driven to a place like Veeraswamy's in a Rolls-Royce. For the first time in my life I owned cocktail dresses and was taken to black tie functions. I felt I'd been reborn and that the life I'd had up until this point belonged to someone else.

Sometimes, my dreams would become mixed up with old fairy stories and I'd wake up with a start, expecting to find myself back at home in my old bedroom, being called by my mother to get into the kitchen and help her cook the dinner. There were other mixed-up dreams, where I was at a party and would suddenly panic in case the magic that had transformed me from a domestic drudge would abruptly reverse itself, leaving me standing in a room of elegant sophisticated people looking curiously at this fat, ugly frump who smelled of onions and garlic.

I'd been a plain and unattractive child and my looks had displayed no promise of improvement when I became a teenager. Beauty had passed me by and left me with a surly, sullen face which had always been quick to display anger and aggression. At home when that happened, my mother would thrust me in front of a mirror and tell me how ugly and scary I looked. Who'd want to marry someone with a face like that, she would ask. Whatever the reason, it was never a face that was attractive to others. On the contrary, most of my life I'd found that it was a face that made people want to punch it. And they frequently had.

I certainly never expected to be attractive to the opposite sex, and it therefore came as a complete shock to suddenly find myself inundated with attention from good-looking, sophisticated men. The saying goes, 'What's in a name?' As far as I was concerned, the names I was being called were a world away from the names I was used to being called. I went from being a 'Paki' to being 'exotic'; from 'ugly' to 'beautiful', and I was no longer 'fat' but 'curvy and voluptuous'. Furthermore, my size 14 figure didn't seem to put men off asking me out. On the contrary, I was pleasantly surprised to learn that the media hype that women had to be thin to be beautiful did not match up to the reality of what real men wanted in a real woman.

I had no patience with all the clap-trap that drove women to starve themselves in order to feel acceptable. I never deluded myself that a man with a taste for willowy gazelle-like creatures would ever be attracted to me. Any man who asked me out would be the type who preferred womanly curves in the first place. It was perfectly obvious that I hadn't got my voluptuous, hourglass figure by nibbling daintily on alfalfa sprouts. If a man asked me out to dinner, he got a date with a girl who actually ordered and ate dinner. And when I found something funny, I didn't smile delicately but threw my head back and roared with laughter. My own friends would comment that there were girls who were so much slimmer than me but who didn't get half the attention that I got. I could have let the compliments and attention go to my head, but when good-looking men said nice things to me I found it hard to believe they were actually talking about me. Nevertheless, it was a very welcome change to be the object of such eligible attention in a positive way.

I'd heard of Asian girls who'd had strict upbringings and then went off the rails as soon as they tasted a bit of freedom. I had no intentions of becoming promiscuous; I just wanted to have fun. I'd never been allowed any freedom at home and suddenly I was free to come and go as I pleased, stay out until late, eat what I liked, wear what I wanted and walk down the street without being afraid of criticism. It was freedom and I breathed it in deeply, drank it in and enjoyed it. For the first time in my life, at the age of twenty-one, I felt happy and free. It was also during this time that I began to learn new things about myself.

I'd had a lifetime of being told what to do and what to think, and of believing that if I wouldn't or couldn't it was because there was something lacking in me. Now that I was living alone, dependent on myself for making decisions, I was surprised to discover that, far from being an idiot, I was actually very intelligent and resourceful. Now that I wasn't being mocked and laughed at and called names by people just waiting for me to drop and break things, I discovered that I wasn't oafish and clumsy but actually very sensible. My nature and character suddenly had the freedom to follow its own course and settle into its real natural shape. It was quite a shock to discover that I was far from being the rebellious and disobedient daughter that I'd always been labelled by others (and also by myself); now that I was far away from my family, I discovered a loyalty that I hadn't known I possessed and genuinely wanted to love my parents and make them proud of me.

And I made an even more shocking discovery. I'd always believed myself to be the most awful liar owing to the fact that I told lies every day of my life. I simply took it for granted that this was down to my born-bad nature and was therefore as inherent in me as being born stupid, clumsy and an idiot. However, away from the restrictions that had been placed upon me at home, I realised that most of my lies were told because I'd led two different lives that had not been compatible: East at home, West outside. I'd told lies about everything, yet now, able to step back and examine this, I realised my lies had simply been my way of surviving. I'd lied to my parents about having late lectures in order to steal an extra hour or so to spend with my friends. I'd lied about being with someone they would approve of in order to be with someone they wouldn't. I'd lied about most things because, being Asian parents, they had to approve of every single aspect of my life. In order to have some semblance of normal teenage life, I'd never been able to be honest with them about the things I wanted to do, the people I wanted to be friends with, the clothes I wanted to wear or even the food I wanted to eat. In my attempts to be a 'normal' young person, honesty and truthfulness had not stood a chance against the dictates of cultural and parental duty. Now, suddenly, I was free to make my own decisions and there was no need to lie as if it was second nature to me.

Learning these new things about myself was like peeling away layers to discover who I really was underneath.

With so many changes to my life, I was totally uninterested in my studies. Not surprisingly, I failed my first year as I'd scarcely opened my books and had done no studying whatsoever. But then, doing a law degree and becoming a lawyer had always been my father's ambition, not mine. I'd learned the hard way that my own ambitions had never really mattered.

I'd always wanted to be a journalist but was told it was not a respectable profession and was out of the question. Any attempts to pursue hobbies or outside interests met with similar opposition. I loved singing and acting and wanted to join a drama group but was told that actresses were prostitutes. Similarly, my attempts to join the Territorial Army at the age of sixteen had ended in tears when my furious parents demanded to know whether I liked the idea of being gang-raped by men in uniform. A sarcastic retort earned me a hard smack across the face which knocked me sideways and sent me sprawling across the floor, leaving me wiping away angry, resentful tears and thinking that any other life was better than the one I had.

It soon became clear that anything I wanted to do would always come second to my father's own ambitions for me and the only way I'd ever escape was to go along with it until I was able to break free. Getting on to a law degree course had simply been a means to an end and in order to achieve that I'd lied and pretended to go along with my father's wishes in order to win my freedom. Now though, I'd got away from home, and the next stage was gaining financial independence.

During that first year it had not been possible to drop out for several reasons. First, belonging to college gave me a sense of security while I became used to being on my own. To go from cloistered domestic drudge to independent single girl had been a huge and sometimes very scary leap. I'd had to deal with homesickness (surprisingly) and getting used to the big wide world with only myself to rely upon.

Second, until I was ready to stand on my own feet and get a job to support myself, I was still dependent on my father signing the grant forms for money to live on. So for the first year I had to continue the pretence of studying and endure a year of law school. The legal stuff was relatively easy but it bored me rigid. By the end of the first year, however, I'd got myself a job and had moved into a shared house, so college had ultimately served its purpose. I informed my parents I'd failed college and been thrown off the course, but that I had to remain here in London because if I worked hard to do re-takes I might be allowed back in again. My father was furious, but I was now financially independent and, with a distance of over two hundred miles between us, there was precious little he could do. There were numerous threats and angry exchanges over the telephone about my treachery and I'd always replace the receiver shaking with dread, but I stood firm. I refused to return home.

14

Farah

Women will be forgotten if they forget about themselves.
Louise Otto (1819–95)

Farah was born five years after me, and while still little more than an infant myself I helped to change her nappies, bottle-feed her, rock her to sleep and care for her.

What I remember most about her as a baby was how incredibly bad-tempered she was. As babies, the boys would wake up beaming irresistibly so you couldn't help but want to pick them up. But woe to anyone who woke Farah from her nap before she was ready to be woken. She was so cantankerous that we used to try to keep her from napping in the daytime. If she did happen to fall asleep in her pram, we'd brace ourselves, knowing with a sense of dread that she'd wake up in a furious temper and give us all a headache by screaming for hours, particularly if her bottle was not immediately to hand as soon as her eyes opened.

Apart from the fact that she was a little girl, there wasn't much else to discern her from the other four younger children whom I also helped to care for, so I have few memories of her until she was about eight or nine years old. Her importance in my life changed when she was old enough to start helping around the house and became an ally and companion in the battle zone that was home.

Once she stopped being a dependant and assumed her role as

fellow skivvy, I saw her differently. She became my friend and confidante and yet, because I'd cared for her as a baby, I never forgot she was my little sister and made up my mind that I'd always look out for her. More importantly, despite being older I treated her as an equal and didn't pull rank on her.

As we grew older, my mother became increasingly unapproachable. She was over-burdened with work and increasingly worried about our lack of religious training and our reluctance to accept a traditional Muslim life. After the age of about five or six, I don't remember receiving any hugs and cuddles in my childhood. It was partly because there were so many younger children competing for the same thing, partly because my father had favourites that he preferred over me. And my mother simply didn't have the time. Nor, I feel, did she have it in her nature to hug or cuddle her children after they had ceased to be babies, this simply not being the Muslim way! So I grew up knowing I had to be emotionally independent with no one to turn to for comfort.

Similarly, there had been no care, no nurturing into adolescence, and I remember how alone and frightened I'd been when I reached puberty with no one to turn to. Of course I'd known about periods from school, but that had been from a clinical point of view; in books and by listening to schoolgirl conversations in the changing room. So I knew about it in theory and waited for the dreadful thing to happen to me too, and when it did happen, at the age of thirteen, I was scared, ashamed and embarrassed. Terrified I'd be in trouble or teased, I kicked my pants under the bed to hide them. My elder sister found them and told my mother, who just remarked, 'Oh, it's happened, has it?' And that was the only discussion I ever had with anyone about puberty and growing up.

I was determined it would be easier for Farah: she'd not feel alone and frightened like I did. I taught her about periods, and when she started it was me she came to, wide-eyed and anxious for advice and reassurance. And I was the one who taught her about other things that a girl needs to know when she is growing up. I taught her about hair, make-up and skin care, advising her to look after her skin, to cleanse and moisturise every night while she was young and assuring her that by the time she was really old, at thirty, she'd thank me for it. I seem to remember that she did in fact thank me many years later, telling me how much she'd squirmed with embarrassment at the time but that she was grateful for all the advice I'd given her.

I looked out for her when she started primary school too. Because I'd been so badly bullied, I made sure no one laid a finger on her. Fortunately for her, when she was at secondary school, she had an older brother and three younger ones, including Lee, the loud, fearless, one-man army, to look after her.

Farah and I shared a bedroom but always slept together in my bed. Nothing was mine; it was ours, and she did not have to covet what little I had, or have to resort to stealing or 'borrowing', as I did with my elder sister. I made up my mind to share everything with her, all my secrets, hopes and dreams, and I'd listen to hers and be her best friend. In return, Farah was the first friend and confidante I ever had. We developed a coded language of our own made up of a mixture of English, Urdu and French, depending on where we were and who could be listening. Even now these words still crop up effortlessly in conversation and make us laugh. In those days, Farah was the only person in my life I was really sure loved me. As worthless as I grew up feeling, she admired me and looked up to me. And I loved and adored her.

She went through a period of hero-worshipping me. In her

fourth year at school, her class were asked to do a project about someone they admired, and to my surprise Farah asked me if she could do her project on me. She took a photo of me into school and showed it to everyone, telling them I was her beautiful older sister. I'd never been called beautiful, having been a very ugly child and a plain teenager. Suddenly at the age of eighteen to be hero-worshipped and thought beautiful by my little sister was a huge compliment and I loved her even more for it.

She copied me in everything and assumed that my opinion was always the correct one to have. For example, when hearing a song for the first time, she wouldn't ask whether I liked it but would instead ask, 'Is that song good?' Her assumption was that if I thought it was good, then it must be good. Such hero-worship was balm to my fragile self-confidence.

Her relationship with my parents was more or less the same as the one that I had, other than the fact that she was never beaten by my father. For many years I envied her that dubious honour, naively thinking it was because she was the youngest girl. However, she too remembers a childhood of violence and abuse, not as a victim, as I was, but as a bystander. Having witnessed my beatings from a very early age, she learned how to survive in our family, later informing me bitterly how she developed the knack of disappearing into the background and never drawing attention to herself. As I grew up and began standing up for myself, she remained silent and passive, never answering back, never being controversial.

It was her good fortune that she possessed qualities that were glaringly lacking in me. When faced with the double standards of the male–female divide in our house, while I would not, could not, hold back in expressing my outrage loudly and forcefully, she, patient, long-suffering and displaying better judgement than me, very sensibly held her tongue. Thus she rarely drew unwanted attention to herself and earned my brothers' affection and gratitude that they had at least one sister who knew her place and duty.

For the sake of a quiet life, Farah did indeed do her duty. She did her utmost to be a perfect Pakistani daughter, cooking, cleaning and – most crucially – keeping her intelligence and opinions to herself.

When I escaped and left home for London it was not without a backward glance and pang of regret for Farah, because I knew I was leaving her to single-handedly carry the domestic burden of helping our mother run the home. But I had no choice. As we whispered together at night, she told me she lived in dread of what might happen to me.

'It's better you leave because at least the fighting will stop and I won't have to go around the house hiding all the knives,' she said matter-of-factly, telling me how for years she'd been hiding the kitchen knives away out of sight because she'd had nightmares about my father stabbing me or cutting my throat one day. We both giggled in the dark as the tragedy of our respective situations sank in.

'You have to get out of here,' she urged. 'Otherwise you'll end up in prison for killing him, or six feet under because he's finally murdered you.'

I knew she was right and so I carried out my plan and finally escaped, but not before promising faithfully that I'd write to her every week and that as soon as I had a place of my own, she too could escape and come to join me in London.

We wrote once, sometimes twice, a week, telling each other about what was happening. She wanted to know every detail about my new life; the people I met and the places and parties I went to. Her own letters to me were sometimes quite heart-breaking to read. I was well aware of the yawning gap in her life after I'd left, but it was still hard to hear about her loneliness. She told me how difficult it was to single-handedly carry the burden of helping our mother run the home, cooking and cleaning up after the men, and how her studies were suffering because she was so exhausted all the time. Burdened with domestic responsibilities and without support at home, she failed most of her exams and sank even deeper into despair. I felt guilty but she never blamed me for leaving, reassuring me that I'd had no choice. Her letters became increasingly desperate as she longed to escape. I did what I could by making regular telephone calls, writing letters and sending money for treats.

She was only sixteen, so there was no question of her simply packing her bags and following me to London. Furthermore, there was the added burden of her duty to help our mother, who had not been well. The sense of guilt and duty was far stronger in her than in me. Having been hardened by years of emotional and physical abuse, I'd never doubted that, when the time came, I'd be able to loosen the iron grip of family ties and make a run for freedom without ever looking back. Farah, on the other hand, could be talked round and made to accept her moral duty and domestic responsibilities, which I knew would end up crushing her spirit. I could see it happening already. She'd write and tell me how lonely and unhappy she was, seeing only a lifetime of drudgery ahead of her.

She needed someone to support and encourage her because the family didn't seem to care about what she wanted or how she felt. Any time she wanted for herself – to study, go shopping or indeed have a life of her own – would always be subject to all the chores being done and meals prepared. Her ambitions for herself would never be allowed to get in the way of a well-run house and three meals a day. Whether she could achieve anything would depend upon her ability to stand up for herself and demand some freedom. But I knew she was not as strong as me. I was hard and had few emotions left, so I was ruthless and I made myself not care where the family was concerned. She, on the other hand, with a stronger sense of duty, would be easier to grind down.

I was glad she'd continued at college and taken some of the same subjects as I'd taken, such as the two-year journalism course, because it encouraged her to take an interest in newspapers and the media generally. She wrote about this dishy reporter called Richard Madeley, one of the presenters of *Granada Reports*, the regional news programme that covered the North West. She'd written to Richard and asked for an interview as part of her journalism course. I smiled as I read this, thinking sceptically, 'Yeah right! Interview my arse! More like an opportunity to get close enough to get a whiff of his aftershave!' That aside, I was actually very grateful to him for taking the time to accommodate her request. Reading through her old letters now makes me laugh because she was still at that stage where she thought any man would be mad not to want to date her older sister. I'd been mortified to read about how, when she met him, she'd tried to set up Richard Madeley on a blind date with me, but he wasn't daft enough to take her up on it.

On the subject of Richard Madeley: over the years I've read articles in newspapers where he has been criticised for being overbearing and over-ambitious. I have no idea of the truth of this and can only judge him by the fact that my sister was not a newsworthy celebrity or someone who could further his career, but just a shy, sixteen-year-old Pakistani girl who wrote asking him for an interview for her college course. Richard took the time out of a clearly busy schedule to send a personal reply inviting her up to Granada Studios, giving her an interview and even showing her around. She wrote that despite being really busy he had treated her with kindness and respect, and she went away with her interview notes, photos and a lot of determination and belief in herself, fired up with the confidence that she too could make something of her life. In my book that definitely qualifies him as a good egg. And apparently he *did* smell nice. Judy's gain and my loss.

In considering my sister's situation at home, I fretted all the more because, with the two elder daughters being allowed to go to college and subsequently absconding, she would never be allowed to leave by a similar route. She didn't even have the prospect of escaping via marriage. I knew there was no more prospect of an arranged marriage for her than there had been for my elder sister and me. My father would fail Farah as he'd failed us. Without me there to help her get up the courage to simply leave, she'd be left in limbo and would remain an unmarried daughter with no status in the eyes of the family: a non-person, defined only by her role as unpaid cook and housekeeper, just as I once was and would still have been had I not escaped. She deserved better than that.

Having cared for her as a baby, despite there being only five years between us I always felt like a mother to her and was sure that no one would ever know or understand her as well as I did. And because I cared about her, I was willing to stick my neck out. I knew they'd blame me and say I'd led her astray, but I was quite happy to accept that if it meant helping my sister escape from her unhappy life. Unlike me, she had somewhere to come to and someone who'd look after her whenever she plucked up the courage to tell my parents she was going. Sure enough, within two years of my leaving, unable to stand it any longer, Farah had packed her bags, left home and come to live with me in London.

I'd just moved into a small flat in Southall, west London. Until then, I'd always shared houses or lived in bed-sits, which meant she was able to visit for only a few days at a time. This was the first time I was able to offer her a permanent home. She was eighteen and had never had a job, but it never occurred to me not to support or take care of her. At the time I had just enough money to pay my rent and cover my living expenses, so making my income stretch for two was challenging, to say the least. We'd grown up in a home where food was available in both quality and quantity. My father had always insisted on the best of everything, and on that score we'd never experienced real want until now. Suddenly we had to rely on our own resources to survive, and it was not easy. At one time Farah and I were so poor we had only 6p left for food that week, so we bought some potatoes. These new potatoes were boiled in their skins and eaten seasoned with lots of salt and pepper, amid a great deal of giggling and merriment. We told each other that we'd look back on these days and laugh, and swore that in future, should we ever feel sorry for ourselves or think we were badly off, we'd always remember this time when freedom meant staving off hunger with 6p's worth of boiled potatoes.

15

Snaring the birds

Understandably, my parents were furious that Farah had left home and they accused me of aiding and abetting her flight, as if I was harbouring a fugitive. Predictably, they also blamed me for what they considered to be her moral demise from quiet, submissive and obedient daughter to the bad lot that they considered me to be. To hear them talk, you could be mistaken for thinking that I'd just recruited her to join me in becoming a prostitute. Their calls became increasingly unpleasant and difficult to endure, to the point where we hated answering the telephone. Aside from the occasional grumble directed at us through our mother, my father took a back seat in dealing with us now. On hearing her dreaded voice at the other end of the line, we'd become frozen to the spot, answering in monosyllables until the call ended and we could breathe a sigh of relief.

Friends advised us to move and not tell the family where we'd gone, but that simply was not an option as we were actually terrified of the consequences of trying to run away permanently. That would simply confirm to the family that we wanted freedom to live a sinful life, and my parents would have searched until they'd found us and dragged us back home. It was a miracle in our eyes that they hadn't already done so, but we certainly didn't dare push our luck. So we had to endure the threat of sudden visits and the difficult telephone calls.

My mother would plead with me to abandon the sinful life I'd chosen, saying I'd exposed the family to the shame of having a daughter who led the life of a prostitute, and she'd beg me to return home into the respectable bosom of the family. When I refused, she'd tell me I'd gone over to the dark side, that I'd become the Devil's creature and would burn in hell for eternity for the sinful life I was leading. One time she begged me to send Farah back, saying, 'You're already going to hell, but if you care about your younger sister then you can still save her from your fate. It isn't too late for her!'

These telephone calls really shook me up. From an early age, I'd accepted that I was not like other Muslim girls who ultimately ended up doing what their parents demanded of them. I had believed what my mother had told me: that I found it hard to be a good Muslim and an obedient daughter because I was born bad. I was the bad gene in our family and was destined to burn in the fires of hell for eternity. I was used to hearing all this and had accepted my fate, yet these telephone calls nevertheless still shook me and gave me terrifying nightmares. In these nightmares I was being chased by demons and would wake up screaming in terror.

To try and placate our parents, Farah and I did go home to visit the family about once every month or so. Inevitably we'd end up in the kitchen helping our mother to prepare the meals and clean up. We were always glad of good home cooking and looked forward to our mother's dinners because she'd often make our favourite meals when she knew we were coming. My father would tell her to cook koftas and rice, which were my favourite meal.

I only realised exactly how much meat was purchased in our

family after I'd left home and had some measure of comparison in other households. Since leaving, I'd perfected my *dhal*-making skills and would frequently make some for myself and anyone else who wanted it. My aversion to meat prompted my mother to look at me doubtfully.

'Pregnant women go off meat,' she'd declare suspiciously, never quite daring to voice the question always forming in her mind about my independent life in London, of which she never approved. Like all Muslims, she was of the opinion that as soon as a girl was out of sight of her family she'd be having sex.

'I'm not surprised I prefer *dhal* and *sabzi* (vegetables),' I'd declare, burning with embarrassment. 'Every time I come home, I open the fridge and find half a sheep staring at me. It's enough to put anyone off meat!'

I recall the first few nervous return visits I made back to the family home following dropping out of university and refusing to give up my flat in London and return home to live as a good obedient Muslim girl. My mother would corner me in the kitchen and tell me I was not living a good life. Only immoral women lived as I was living, and if I were a dutiful daughter I'd come back home.

At first I'd listen in disbelief. For the sake of their *izzat* she was actually asking me to return home, where I could be physically and emotionally abused all over again. After about six months, frustrated by this emotional blackmail, I refused to listen any longer. Previously I'd had no choice, but now I no longer had to put up with any kind of treatment that offended and upset me. I pointed out in no uncertain terms that I had a car parked outside and a home of my own to go to, and if she didn't stop haranguing me I'd simply pack my bags, get in that car and leave! She'd shut up then but I was always left with a sense of guilt at talking to my mother in that disrespectful way.

I ached for her to love me and take an interest in me and ask me about my flat, my friends or my hopes and dreams. Instead, as far as my mother was concerned, there was this unspoken rule that my 'other life' was never to be mentioned. No matter how desperately I wanted to discuss these things with her, my attempts to try to make my mother understand me were futile. I tried to tell her about my wanting to get into journalism, how I longed to be successful and make them proud of me. But she was always too interested in my immortal soul – or perhaps her own. At best I was met with lack of interest; at worst I was coldly told that I was hell-bent on shaming them and robbing them of their *izzat* so they'd never be able to hold their heads up again – I was ruining their lives. Any attempt to chat about personal things was rebuffed as her expression would glaze over or she'd simply cut me short. It always left me feeling utterly dejected and guilty about being a disobedient daughter and a thoroughly bad human being, so it was invariably a relief to get back into the car and start the five-hour journey back home to London.

After I dropped out of college, I'd given myself a year to find my feet and adjust to my new life. While I'd known everything there was to know about housework and cooking, I'd been incredibly naive when it had come to worldly matters. I had to start at the beginning when it came to things like managing money and paying bills, but I didn't care because it was a real joy to be responsible for making decisions that affected my own life.

I wanted diversity and challenge in every area of my life, from the people I met to the jobs that I did. I wanted infinite variety, and in my determination to try everything I worked for a recruitment agency, a law firm and in sales.

One of my favourite jobs was doing promotional work for a small company working in large department stores such as

Harrods and Selfridges. The company was run by a wonderful woman called Charlotte, who really nurtured me and instilled in me a confidence I hadn't hitherto dared to hope that I could possess. I was really good at my job and became her best sales-girl, earning more money than anyone else in the company. More importantly, I earned her admiration and respect. She was beautiful, clever and gregarious, and I couldn't believe that she took an interest in me as a person. If I had a problem she actually seemed to care. I recall how she amazed me once when I discovered she knew I was suffering from PMT. She showed me her diary, telling me she'd worked out my cycle for herself – apparently I became highly strung and temperamental, which could have been a problem at work. However, because Charlotte knew what was causing it, she usually dealt with it by whisking me off to a quiet place for a drink and a chat and a listen, giving me the chance to talk my monthly angst out of my system. No one had ever taken that much trouble with me, certainly not my own mother, and I found myself turning to Charlotte for advice and guidance that went beyond an employer/employee relation-ship. Over our many coffees and lunches together, I found myself wishing I had a mother like her. Charlotte set a pattern for many years to come, because it was not to be the last time that I found myself gravitating towards an older female who would temporarily fill a deep yearning for a mother-figure in my life.

By now I'd decided to follow my dream to become a journalist. Having studied journalism for two years and loved it, I got myself work experience on the *Ealing Gazette* and the *Harrow Observer* while I made applications to the BBC, who had advertised a position to train in broadcasting journalism. I knew that they'd received thousands of applications from hopefuls, all wanting the chance to win this coveted prize. But I had faith in my own abilities. I'd done well on my journalistic

studies course and knew this career would suit my personality
and character. I was confident that I stood as good a chance as
any. After the application stage, I'd just sent in the required
sample broadcast tapes and was waiting to hear the results of
the final interviews. Then fate intervened in a way that would
change my life for ever.

My mother had been in poor health for a year or so and
wanted to make a trip to Pakistan, because it was generally
agreed that she'd improve in a warmer climate. However, there
was a problem because there was no one to accompany her. We
were told that my father had to manage things at home and the
boys were really too busy. Our elder sister was married with a
baby so she was out of the picture, which left just Farah and
me. Despite telephoning a lot, my mother had stopped putting
pressure on us to come back home. This made a welcome
change and meant that we were more inclined to listen and
respond positively to her requests.

My sister and I spent weeks discussing this. It was not
convenient. Both of us were working full time and I was waiting
to hear whether I'd got the job with the BBC. But we were
bombarded with telephone calls appealing to our sense of duty
and compassion towards our sick mother and I began to come
round to considering it. Just by listening to her and giving her
sympathy, we felt closer to her; it was a chance to show her that,
despite wanting to live away from the family, we did love her
and care about her. We both knew what a hard life she'd had
bringing up the seven of us and coping with my father. We also
felt guilty that we'd left home, leaving her alone to carry the
burden of running the home and cooking and cleaning for my
father and four brothers. Our freedom had cost our mother her
health and she implied that we owed it to her – all she was
asking for was two weeks of our time.

I knew that if my mother had really wanted my brothers or my father to go with her, they'd have dropped everything to do so. I knew there was little that my father would not do for her. Deep down, I hoped against hope that the real reason she'd asked us to accompany her was perhaps because she'd begun to understand us and was in her own way trying to reach out to us and build a relationship with Farah and me. I wanted to believe that spending a fortnight in Pakistan together was her way of getting close to us.

She said that she didn't mind which one of us went with her as long as she went soon, because she'd been feeling so ill lately. That was a very shrewd move. We suspected that she really wanted us both to go with her but didn't say as much. But my mother knew us well enough to know that where one went, the other would inevitably follow. All she needed to do was to get one of us to agree to accompany her to Pakistan and the other would soon be packing to go too. It was that simple. She repeatedly promised she'd need only two weeks. That was all, she assured us. Compared to the lifetime of disobedience and emotional pain we felt we had given her, and the guilt that went with this, two weeks did not seem such a long time. I reasoned that we could accompany her to Pakistan and see her health improve, and before long we'd be back home again.

So we booked the time off from work, paid for our own tickets and packed our bags. Everyone joked that we'd be snatched off the plane and married off and we laughed at the very thought. We'd heard about these things happening, but they happened to simple, submissive, uneducated girls who didn't know any better. We were neither stupid nor gullible but feisty and independent and had stood up for ourselves, so our parents knew better than to try and make us do anything we didn't want to do. They wouldn't dare try anything like that with us. As if!

Part 4
Kidnapped

16

Western misfits

As the twig is bent the tree inclines.
Virgil (70–19 BC)

It took almost a week to acclimatise to the culture shock.

Pakistan assaulted all five senses at once. There were the smells of diesel fumes, the heat and dust that mingled with the unmistakable reek of the open sewers that ran alongside the streets. There was the overwhelming sight of so much humanity crammed into one space; the garishly decorated buses, the yellow and black taxis and people – so many people. There were the jostling crowds and men who accidentally-on-purpose knocked into your shoulder, so that for one brief moment they had the satisfaction of touching you, something that was both infuriating and actually hurt. There was the almost deafening sound of buses, cars, rickshaws and motorbikes (sometimes entire families on motorbikes) amid the screeching of brakes, blaring of horns, revving of engines and shouting of destinations by bus owners calling to their customers, women and children in the front portion, men at the back. We couldn't work out whether these people were brave or foolhardy when, unable to cram into these metal deathtraps, they took their lives in their hands by clinging precariously to the outside or perching fearlessly on the roof. Then there was the street food that we never imagined could taste so divine: the just-caught fish, spiced and fried by the beach at Clifton; the pakoras, kebabs and samosas; the corn cobs roasted and sprinkled with salt and lemon juice. When we were thirsty we were offered glass bottles of Fanta, Sprite and Coke or the juice of freshly pressed sugar cane, pomegranate and melon.

Something else that overwhelmed us was the family itself. Only someone who has lived within a nuclear family can appreciate how unreal it feels to be suddenly surrounded by a large extended family. We'd grown up having only siblings and parents. Then suddenly there were aunts, uncles and cousins, once, twice and three times removed, from both sides of the family, and so many that we lost count, all happy to see us and eager to welcome us as one of their own. My parents had both been the second of their siblings to marry and start a family, so there were only two sets of cousins older than us. My parents' other siblings had all married much later and therefore most of my cousins on both sides of the family were far younger than us. I couldn't help thinking that had I been married off at sixteen or eighteen, as my mother had always wanted, my own children would have been the same age as many of these babies and toddlers who were my cousins. What did amuse us was the fact that even some of my *chachis* and *mumanis* were younger than us. However, within the family hierarchy, they were deemed senior to us so we still had to give them respect and call them 'aunt'.

It came as something of a shock to suddenly pick out a pair of eyes, a nose or a smile that reminded us of our siblings or – even more weird – of ourselves. I found myself inexplicably drawn to one particular little girl-cousin whose face seemed strangely familiar and whose eyes seemed to tug at my heart strings. As I let her climb on to my lap I was reminded of a black-and-white picture back home of me as a toddler and realised that this little daughter of one of my *chachas* was the image of me as I had been at her age. Shahnaz Chachi, who was her mother, told me that her nickname was Kakko and she was always crying and eating dirt from the garden. I recalled being told years before by my mother that this was exactly what I'd been like as a child, and again wondered about the nature versus nurture thing.

With so much going on and so much to take in, before we knew it the first week in Pakistan was drawing to a close and we were midway into the second. I began reminding my mother to confirm our return flights. Farah and I would be expected back at work in a few days' time and we were concerned that we'd still not been taken to the airline office to do this. In the beginning she simply brushed us off, saying it would be done. But she seemed to be in no hurry at all, and only after much persistence and badgering from us did she finally show her irritation by curtly informing us that she had no intention of going back yet. Her words shocked me.

'But you promised us we'd be back after two weeks,' I said, an awful sense of foreboding descending. 'We have to go back to work!'

'You have always been a *haramin*,' retorted my mother nastily. 'You've been a *haramin* all your life and now you're teaching her so she can turn out just as much of a *haramin* as you!'

'No more!' she spat. 'From now on, what I say goes!'

We were appalled and could scarcely believe what she was saying or the tone with which she said it. This was my mother speaking and I didn't believe that she could be so spiteful. I'd seen her annoyed and frustrated with my behaviour, I'd had altercations with her when she'd disapproved of me, but I couldn't believe she had it in her to look the way she looked just then. I searched her face for some recognition of the self-sacrificing and yielding mother I'd always known and saw only a stranger glaring angrily back at me.

She'd planned it all. Getting Farah and me on a plane to Pakistan had not been difficult because my mother had used that tried-and-tested weapon that never fails for Asian mothers: emotional blackmail. I didn't know what appalled me more, my mother's deceit or my own stupidity. For months she'd worked on us, appealing to our better nature, to our filial sympathy and compassion, by reminding us how ill she was. We knew she'd been unwell for the past year or so. So seduced had I been by the hope of getting close to our mother that I'd allowed myself to be duped into coming out here. I'd swallowed it hook, line and sinker and had walked straight into the trap.

As the reality of our predicament sank in, I bitterly regretted being such a fool and making it so easy. They hadn't needed to forcibly kidnap us by drugging us and bundling us on to a plane, as we'd heard happened to other Muslim daughters. No, we'd been so gullible that not only had we simply walked on to the plane, but we'd even paid for our own tickets! We'd been so sure that, because we were strong and feisty in England, these characteristics would safeguard us in Pakistan. But this was an Islamic country where unmarried daughters didn't have any rights, and as such we were completely in my mother's power. For that, I could only blame myself. It was my fault! I'd let my guard down and believed that my mother really had been ill. What a fool I'd been! From the moment we stepped on to that plane, we'd relinquished any right to make demands.

To make things even worse, we didn't have the means to escape for we no longer had our return tickets and passports. As soon as we'd arrived at the house from the airport, and before we'd even had a chance to unpack, my Aunt Zainab had persuaded me to hand all our travel documents over to her for safe-keeping, reassuring us that they'd be better locked away in her safe, away from prying eyes and possible theft by the servants.

I'd not been at all happy about relinquishing them because it went against my instincts of self-preservation. Back home, I never left the house without taking my credit cards and some cash. Whoever I was out with, whether male or female, best friend or date, I always ensured that should the worst happen I'd have the means of getting myself home. I considered refusing my aunt but my common sense told me that I had no choice: even if I'd said no, they could have simply taken them anyway. So I'd reluctantly handed over our passports and return tickets.

Now we were trapped, and little did I know what nightmares and traumas my sister and I were to face, the threats to our sanity and our very lives, before we were to see those documents again.

My mother didn't waste much time letting us know that there was nothing we could do about it. This was the first time since I'd left home that she'd been able to detain me in one place. Here, there was no car parked outside to take me back to London if I didn't like what she was saying. Thanks to my own stupidity I was a captive audience with nowhere to storm off to. Thus empowered, my mother suddenly began to display a side to her nature that Farah and I had hitherto never seen.

It seemed that my aunt had been privy to my mother's intentions from the outset. She'd been told what a troublemaker I'd always been, and how my presence had been like a curse on the family, denying any of them peace, turning their lives upside down until the day I'd left. Now I was living an *awara* (loose, wayward) life, bringing shame on them by refusing to get married, which is why our mother had brought us to Pakistan as a last resort in order to save her *izzat*. My mother warned us that we'd already done a good job of taking away her *izzat* in the eyes of the family and that she was determined to make sure we were off her hands before we did any more damage. *Izzat*, that word again! It seemed to me that everything always came back to that.

As I was growing up, I'd figured out that the word *izzat* was intrinsically linked with the word *sharam*, meaning 'shame'. In Asian society the standards of what constitute respect and honour are very different to those in the West. In the Eastern culture *izzat* controls everything we do publicly; to me, *izzat* was not so much about being a better person within yourself but about the way you are perceived by the outside world, meaning less about honesty, integrity and piety and more about the external standards and expectations placed upon us by society. The dread of losing *izzat* also suggested to me that happiness, peace of mind and even lives could be sacrificed, but 'honour' or 'face' must be maintained at all costs.

And yet, despite understanding its harsh standards and being brought up in Western society where the concepts of 'shame' and 'honour' have become almost redundant, I had not completely rejected this ideal, because it is *izzat* that gives you a sense of right and wrong and of belonging to a community. It makes people *salaam* you in public and want to be associated with you. Families are happy for their sons and daughters to marry into a family with *izzat*. For a Pakistani, *izzat* means respectability. It means respect. It means everything. *Bey-izzati* (to be without *izzat*) is something to be avoided at all costs.

What all this means is that there is tremendous pressure in Asian society to conform. Not conforming means being shunned, outcast or treated as dead. To an Asian female, your sense of self depends not upon who or what you are but upon to whom you belong. You are a daughter, a sister or a wife. To leave the sanctity of your family group means you lose all right to respectability. There are few mitigating circumstances in a woman's defence for leaving: not physical violence, threat of death, or divorce. Regardless of the circumstances of her personal life, a woman is expected to remain quiet and stay for the sake of family honour, for even to speak of these things is seen as dishonourable.

For this reason a girl agrees to go through an arranged marriage that is repugnant to her, and a battered wife stays with her violent husband. To leave means to become an outcast, to forfeit any right to respect and honour, leaving a female exposed to public shunning and even the unwelcome attentions of men who now see her as a woman of easy virtue. To sexually harass, molest or even rape a woman who is an outcast is not considered shameful, for in Asian eyes such a woman is stripped of any honour and respectability. She is a non-person and as such is devoid of feeling and unworthy of consideration.

Izzat and *bey-izzati* were words we'd heard all our lives, and we were to hear them almost daily in Pakistan, when they'd be flung at us like weapons, calculated to make us feel guilty that from the moment of our birth we'd deliberately planned to bring misery to our parents. My mother would curse us both for causing her *bey-izzati* and bringing shame and dishonour on our parents by casting aside our own Islamic faith and Pakistani culture and embracing permissive Western ways.

It seemed obvious to us that there would always be differences when moving from one country and culture to another, particularly when those countries and cultures were so vastly different. In Pakistan, these differences were to subject us to a great deal of criticism from the family. We were accused of causing my mother's *bey-izzati* for the most trivial things, such as not walking like a submissive Pakistani daughter should, with eyes down and head bowed modestly, or thirstily drinking a glass of water down in one gulp instead of in the minimum three sips as Pakistani etiquette requires, or behaving immodestly by forgetting to put on the *dupatta*, which we were not used to wearing.

Through things such as these, we subjected my mother to the criticism that during her years in England she'd failed to bring her daughters up to be aware of their Pakistani culture. In fact, from the moment we landed, the criticism and condemnation started. It began with our clothes.

In London, when packing for the trip, we'd taken care to choose clothes that would be deemed 'decent' in Pakistan. We packed trousers with floaty tops that were loose and long enough to cover the curve and shape of the bottom and did not draw attention to our feminine shape. But it wasn't enough. My sister and I were dragged along to a dressmaker to be measured up for *shalwar kameez* outfits of our own. These would take several days to make, so in the meantime my mother angrily flung some borrowed outfits at us, ordering us to put them on and not cause her *bey-izzati* in front of the whole family by dressing like harlots.

To make matters worse we had to endure lies that were told on our behalf. The conspicuous absence from our luggage of any Pakistani clothes of our own gave the lie to my mother's insistence that we always wore traditional clothes at home. Even more obvious was our unfamiliarity and discomfort in the borrowed clothes which we now wore. We struggled with the *shalwar* and the yards of fabric pulled together by a cord tied at the waist which kept coming undone, making us stumble over it. To my mother's disgust and everyone else's amusement, a few times the cord came undone completely and I was only just able to catch the trousers before they fell down. The cords were subsequently removed from all our *shalwars* and replaced with elastic.

However, the item of clothing we detested most of all was the *dupatta*. We had no idea how to wear it and required instruction from amused cousins on how to drape it modestly across our upper body. It fooled no one and told everyone that we'd clearly spent our lives in the immodest Western dress of the *Angrezis*.

To my mother's dismay, even the way we walked, held ourselves and made eye contact with those around us easily identified us as being Western long before we opened our mouths to speak. When we did speak Urdu it was with heavy English accents that caused amusement in the younger relatives and disapproval from the older ones. It was perfectly clear to both my mother and my aunt that, with the best will in the world, we could never be passed off as submissive and biddable Pakistani girls. I couldn't help thinking that it was foolish even to try.

Even more upsetting was the lie about where I lived. Apart from my aunt, no one was allowed to know that I lived in my own flat in London, a long way from my family, because to have a single, unmarried daughter living alone was shameful. Only an immoral woman would live on her own without either a family or parents to give her respectability, and a girl living alone and unchaperoned was automatically deemed to be sexually promiscuous. Telling the family I was studying law and training to be a lawyer had been the explanation given when Burra Mamoo had visited England two years previously. He'd been unimpressed, commenting at the time that it was not right for me to live away from my family, but the explanation had nevertheless sufficed at the time.

But now that the lie of studying could no longer be used,

everyone was told that my sister and I were living in the family home. We were forbidden to mention the flat we shared in London and made to deny a huge part of our lives. This led to inconsistencies in conversations or instances where we'd falter mid-sentence, suddenly remembering that we must pretend we were still living at home, and change the story. I'm certain many of our relations noticed these lies but we had no choice but to go along with it, for not to do so would be to brand our mother a liar, and in those early days we still felt some sense of duty and loyalty to her.

Nevertheless, I was appalled at how easily lies had begun to fall from our mother's lips. When I was a child, my mother had represented to me everything that was good and kind and honest. To my disbelief, within a matter of a few weeks all my life-long illusions about my mother were to be cruelly shattered. But then there were so many different sides to her nature that we were seeing for the first time. I began to wonder if these were new or simply parts of her true nature that had been held in check or suppressed all these years and which circumstances had suddenly awakened.

'They're *kaffirs!* Heathens!' she told my aunt bitterly. 'They dress like *Angrezis* and live and behave like them with no regard for their own culture and *mazhab* (faith). Now everyone is looking at me with mocking eyes because my daughters don't even know how to do *namaz*. They've left me no *izzat*!'

What she was alluding to was the recent incident at Mamoo's house. The early morning rising to observe the Islamic call to prayer was new to us, as at Dadda's house there was a more relaxed attitude towards Muslim duties. Farah and I had grumbled at having our sleep disturbed at daybreak: the Imam's early call of '*Allah hu akbar*' was projected through the sound system of the mosque into everyone's homes for the first of the five daily prayer times, just before sunrise. Robot-like, my Mumani and cousins duly rose and, having performed *wazu*, they prepared their clothing before doing *namaz*. As they wrapped their dupattas around their heads, they threw each other questioning looks before asking us in whispers why we weren't getting ready to do *namaz* ourselves.

'We don't know how to,' we told our astonished relatives, wishing we were invisible. My sister and I waited awkwardly as *namaz* was said. Once over, the *dupattas* were pushed off their heads and repositioned across the chest and shoulders. Then preparation began for breakfast. Farah and I squirmed uncomfortably as we saw them glance at us and then at each other, with the question left hanging in the air as to how we could possibly have been brought up in a Muslim household without knowing how to do *namaz*. Profession of faith and ritual prayer are two of the five pillars of Islam and for anyone not to know how to perform this duty was unheard of. Even in England we knew everyone was taught this. Everyone, that is, except us. No wonder my cousins looked at us in disbelief.

My mother, having completed her own *namaz*, threw us an angry look, letting us know in no uncertain terms how we'd just humiliated her in front of her brother's family.

'What can I do?' she complained unhappily. 'They refused to learn.'

Mumani looked at her sympathetically, but with a look that left my mother in no doubt that we'd been indulged and given far too much freedom in England – what had she been thinking of by not teaching us the basics of being a Muslim? The look on our mother's face left no doubt as to whom she blamed for her humiliation.

The manner of our upbringing was increasingly met with criticism as our lack of proper instruction in our Muslim faith and Pakistani culture became more apparent by the day. The worst of the criticism came from my mother's side of the family, who were poorer, less educated and more fundamental in their Islamic beliefs. They made Farah and me feel that we were not as good as them because we spoke Urdu with a distinct English accent.

Politeness prevented us from pointing out that it took very little skill to be fluent in one's own language, as they were, and that the real accomplishment was in possessing a reasonable enough command of someone else's language in order to understand and be understood. Neither did we tell them that we were far more proficient in languages than all of them put together, because aside from English and Urdu we also spoke French and understood some German and Spanish, and I'd also studied Latin. It was insulting to be mocked by people who thought they were superior to us because they had a better grasp of the culture in which they had been born and brought up.

On the subject of respecting other people's cultures, having absent-mindedly walked out of the house without putting my *dupatta* on, I'd been given a sharp slap by my cousin and dragged back in to retrieve it. I'd felt humiliated at being treated like a naughty child. To hear everyone shout and scold, anyone would think I'd gone out undressed.

'*Yeh humara mazhab hai.* This is our faith,' came the reply. That was my point, I told her. They demanded that we wear traditional Pakistani clothes out of respect for their traditions and culture, because not to do so offended them. Yet would they do the same if they came to my country? Would they respect the customs and values of my society in the same way? Her dismissive shrug told me what I wanted to know.

'Everyone has to pander to you!' I said indignantly, telling her it was wrong to be so judgemental about everyone else's values or to think that her own religion or way of life was superior and so must always be put first. I told her that even American women soldiers stationed in certain Islamic countries were forced to wear the veil, despite the fact that they were Christians. It was done out of respect for the religion of the country they were living in. Yet, I argued, Muslims like her expected to live and dress according to their own religion and way of life whether they lived in their own country or someone else's. Other people's religion and way of life didn't matter to her nor did she seem to care that her religion seemed to take away other people's rights or impinged on their lifestyles. In reply, my cousin said that Islam was the only true religion and the Christians were *kaffirs*, so it was only right that Islamic ways should prevail.

Farah and I felt like foreigners, which in the eyes of our relatives we were. Everything about us was too Western; nothing was Eastern. The only thing that could have given us any *izzat* was the fact that we'd been brought up to be domesticated and could cook and make chapattis. Yet, ironically, we were never given the chance. Everyone was certain that our lives had been spent in idle Western pursuits, fashion and make-up. They laughed at the very suggestion that we could possibly cook. Yet when we offered to show them what we could do, with so many female relatives guarding their domestic domain, we were shooed out of the kitchen and never allowed the opportunity to demonstrate to everyone that we hadn't led pampered and pointless lives.

It offended us that people were given the impression that we were spoiled and over-indulged and had been given far too much freedom. They believed that, having been brought up this way, we'd committed the unforgivable sin of turning our backs on our Islamic faith and Pakistani culture and deserved everything that was coming to us.

In the following weeks we endured a rapidly deteriorating situation in which we were left in no doubt by my mother that we were prisoners. In the beginning, being held captive meant not being allowed to leave Pakistan, because we didn't know where to go or how to get there. We already knew that it was not safe to walk out alone: even being chaperoned didn't stop us being harassed on the street. What I hated even more than the men who deliberately bumped into us were those who'd find themselves 'accidentally' stumbling into us and putting out a groping hand to steady themselves, responding to abuse from my relatives by offering a grovelling apology and begging forgiveness because it was an accident. It happened far too many times to be accidental and led to one incident which escalated out of control.

One of my younger *mamoos* had learned that we were not being allowed to go home, and although he was unable to speak up for us, being my mother's younger brother, he offered to take me out of the house and show me around the city.

In retrospect, this was a really bad idea because he was only a year or so older than me, and walking through the crowded street we discovered that we were attracting some unwelcome attention. I found myself unable to walk in a straight line as I wove through the crowd doing my utmost to avoid being deliberately walked into. Suddenly someone slammed into me with more force than usual, causing me to cry out. As I angrily nursed my sore shoulder, my uncle remonstrated with the perpetrator, only to find himself turned upon by this man and accused of indulging in an illicit relationship by publicly flaunting this girl who was obviously from abroad and quite clearly not his wife or his sister. My uncle's furious assertion that I was not his foreign floozy but his sister's daughter was met with disbelief and derision and, to my dismay, a crowd gathered to give their support to our accuser. They began to shove us, condemning us for offending Islam by our immoral conduct in public. Because Pakistani men wouldn't normally get the chance to openly grope a woman in public, several of these men seized their chance to move in and put their hands on me inappropriately. I protested angrily at being violated like this and struggled to get away, calling out to my uncle to help me, then immediately regretting it because my uncle, outraged at this insult to me, squared up to fight them all. I became afraid, knowing that he could be dragged away and beaten by this crowd of men who felt their religion had been affronted, and I was terrified of what they might do to me, believing that I was an immoral woman. We managed somehow to extricate ourselves from this ugly scene and get back home to Dadda's house where it took me some time to recover from the shock.

The family were clearly also shocked by this incident and decided that, henceforth, I would only go out in a group or with my mother or aunt. It also brought home to my sister and me that it was not safe for us to try to run away and venture out alone. Even in Pakistani clothes, we stood out too much.

While my mother was genuinely shocked at this incident, railing against my uncle for being stupid and taking me out alone, I couldn't help but notice that she looked suspiciously satisfied that I'd been given a fright. I heard her telling my aunt that perhaps it was a good thing that I'd experienced first-hand what an easy target we were for kidnappers or molesters because now we wouldn't try to run away. So without being actually shut up under lock and key, we were practically imprisoned within the walls of my Dadda's house.

17

Hating the West

Moral indignation is jealousy with a halo.

H. G. Wells (1866–1946)

A master tailor by trade, Burra Mamoo had wanted access to the same opportunities that my father enjoyed in England. Two decades after first coming to England, having established himself in business and property, my father was well on his way to achieving every immigrant's dream of prosperity to pass on to the next generation. This was something Mamoo found hard to accept back in Pakistan.

Through letters and telephone calls from Pakistan, my parents had learned that Mamoo accused my father for jeopardising his immortal soul by exposing his family to the evil influences of the decadent West. This contempt for the West was, however, conveniently suspended when, a year after I'd left for London, my father paid for a return ticket for Mamoo to visit England. And while my father did it to make my mother happy, it was an unmitigated disaster.

Mamoo refused to believe that immigration laws did not permit my father simply to pay for tickets to bring his family into the country. Nor would he believe that his visitor's visa forbade him to work. His wish was for my father to set him up in a manufacturing business so he could prosper and offer his own children the same lifestyle opportunities. In this belligerent frame of mind, he complained to a family friend that my father was lying about British laws in order to hold him back from prospering. When this friend confirmed that actually my father was telling the truth, Mamoo saw it as a conspiracy and hated my father even more.

He'd corner my mother and angrily accuse her of disrespecting him. As her elder brother she owed him respect, but we knew she began to dread being alone with him. Witnessing her distress, Dad gave him money to send back to keep his family. It was never enough and Mamoo, knowing Dad always handed family finances over to Mum, frequently cornered her to demand more. When Farah and I came home for a visit, she whispered to us that he'd be happy for her to steal money from her husband to give to him. She used to say she was fortunate that my father tried so hard on her behalf because Mamoo could have caused serious marital problems. I know other Pakistani husbands would not have been so tolerant of the emotional blackmail and demands made by their wife's family.

When he was with his nephews and nieces, Mamoo talked condescendingly to us as if we were babies. But he fooled no one, not least because behind his honeyed, loving words he was a bitter man who never missed an opportunity to criticise my father. I was angry that he dared to bad-mouth my dad to his children behind his back and knew it was because my uncle was eaten up with jealousy. He used to walk around the house taking stock of the material wealth accumulated by the family yet never gave my dad credit for the years of hard work it had taken to earn it.

He found a copy of the Argos catalogue, that bible of Western materialism, and spent hours greedily flicking back and forth through its thousands of products, amazed at the vast choice of consumer goods available to us in this country.

'Look at this!' he'd cry. 'And this and this! Is there anything that you cannot buy in this book?' he'd ask as his eyes glittered covetously.

Something else that he found incredible was the welfare state. Coming from a society where education and healthcare had to be paid for up front and where your family, particularly your sons, were your only policy against illness, old age and unemployment, he could not believe the government actually paid people for having children, and gave you money if you did not work, and paid for your house. Time and time again he'd return to the same subject, checking his facts and committing them to memory, repeatedly stating the fact that in this country you could become rich if you worked, and if you did not, the government would still pay the upkeep of your house and your family. All this on top of free education and free healthcare, he enthused. My father would say that it wasn't free but paid for by the taxes of the people like him who worked hard for a living. He showed Mamoo statements of how much tax he did actually pay, but it served only to convince my uncle that my father was rich. What's more, it provided him with an argument that my father could afford to help him bring across his own family and that, having done so, he would not be burdened with their upkeep as the government would provide for them. Grimly, my father told him that living off benefits was not a path that decent people necessarily wanted to go down.

However, my uncle saw only what he wanted to see and heard only what he wanted to hear. Most of the time we could actually see him bristling with resentment as his anger and hatred of my father ate away at him. He demanded cigarettes every day and began to spend all his time in his room chain-smoking, despite knowing how much the family disliked him filling our non-smoking house with cigarette fumes. He then began to refuse to come down for meals. My mother speculated that his refusal to eat was because he wanted to return to Pakistan thin and gaunt so he could convince everyone that my father had starved and ill-treated him while he was a guest in his home, something that would be seen as shameful in Pakistani eyes.

I remember how happy and relieved the entire family was when his six-month visa expired and he was finally driven to the airport and almost thrown on to the flight back to Pakistan. The relief on the faces of my father and brother Mohammed at Heathrow could barely be concealed. I'd driven over to Heathrow from west London in order to see Mamoo off and couldn't resist winding up my brother.

'There's probably been a military coup in Pakistan this very morning,' I sniggered. 'I'll bet all incoming flights to Karachi have been cancelled and you'll have to keep him for another six months!'

'Don't!' he replied, horrified at the thought. 'That's not very funny!'

We observed Mamoo looking around the airport, taking in his last hour or so of a country that could have offered him so much materially and which he'd probably never have the opportunity to visit again. I searched his face for a trace of regret at the way he had behaved towards my father and saw only the face of a bitterly disappointed man. My father, on the other hand, appeared genuinely upset that his attempts to get on with his wife's older brother had failed so spectacularly and that what had begun as my uncle's simmering resentment towards my father had boiled over into barely concealed hatred of him, his family and his life in England. Mamoo was most definitely not missed.

However, once back in Pakistan, Mamoo no longer held back voicing his hatred of Dad and the West. It was hard to tell which he hated more. It was also not entirely surprising to hear that, as eldest brother and head of my mother's family, he ruled over his brothers, sisters-in-law and their families with an iron will and used his power and influence to discredit my father in the eyes of his in-laws, making things very difficult for my mother. He publicly harangued his only sister's husband and in-laws for selling out their *izzat* and integrity in order to pursue the worship of money and status. His animosity towards my father caused my mother no end of distress.

Now, eighteen months later in Pakistan, I was able to witness with my own eyes the extremes to which his hatred and resentment went. I was dismayed to see him sitting crossed-legged on the floor, cigarette between his fingers, holding court, surrounded by the family and again regaling them with stories of the West: the immodesty of women's dress, immoral public behaviour, the filth on the television, children being born out of wedlock and brought up without fathers, the lack of respect for elders, for authority, for society, for anyone. He told them how pursuit of material riches had distracted people from spiritual pursuits and relieved them of responsibility for their own actions, which now became the responsibility of the govern-ment. His audience would gasp at his account of how the West no longer had any morals and had gone too far to turn back the clock.

I'd listen with rising indignation while he ranted to a captive audience that hung on to his every malice-loaded word as he criticised the society in which I'd been raised.

'And yet,' I thought sadly, 'the West plays into the hands of people like him.'

In the same way that Islam and Pakistani culture are inter-twined, I realised that Muslims would similarly see Christianity and Western decadence as one and the same, so that although most Westerners actually live decent, respectable lives everyone would be tarred with the same brush. I knew – indeed, had seen for myself – that adultery, immorality and sin happened in Pakistan too. The difference is, in the West it is all hanging out, on display for the rest of the world to see and criticise.

Mamoo used Farah and me to discredit my father further by telling everyone how his brother-in-law had neglected his Islamic responsibilities: just look at how his daughters had turned out! The elder one was twenty-four and way past the age when she should have been married off. At her age, he ranted, she should have been a wife and mother of children herself, instead of being given freedom to run around England like an *Angrezi*. Listening to his sanctimonious ravings, I understood why my father had wanted to remove us as far as possible from Pakistan. It was to get away from people like Mamoo. My father had tried his best to be nice to my uncle, and this was how he was repaid. I was furious with Mamoo and angrily cried, 'Don't you *dare* criticise my father when he's not here to defend himself against your lies!'

I got no further as my cousins, horrified at my disrespectful outburst, pounced on me and dragged me from the room, asking me if I was mad. No one ever spoke to the head of the family like that. I was unrepentant and spat that I would *not* remain silent while my father's character was being publicly destroyed by theirs. I told them that, head of the family or not, he was a hypocritical tyrant who attacked a man who wasn't there to defend himself!

But even as I spoke, I knew that all I'd achieved by my angry outburst against an elder and the head of my mother's family was to prove his point far better than he could have done himself. Everyone could see for themselves how my father had spawned a daughter who was disrespectful and argued with menfolk as an equal, and who had not been taught that her rightful place was in the kitchen with the women, her head covered by a *dupatta*, making *rotis*. Pointing to me, he angrily pronounced me a product of the immoral and decadent West.

As every one of her brother's words hit home, my mother's face contorted with pain; she simply hung her head in shame, weeping as if her heart was breaking. I wanted to rush to her and hold her and protect her but didn't dare, knowing she'd only push me away, seeing me as the architect of her shame. I couldn't bear to see the expression I knew I'd see on her face, and not daring to look at her any more I sank into a corner, filled with reproach and self-loathing.

18

Daughters for sale

Martyrdom has always been a proof of the intensity,
never the correctness of a belief.
Arthur Schnitzler (1862–1931)

There was only one reason why my mother had brought us to Pakistan: she wanted to get us married off. She lost no time in telling us as much, assuring us that she had no intentions of returning to England unless and until she'd accomplished what she'd come out here to do. She added unkindly that she needed to do it quickly before word got around that we were *awara* and had been running around England behaving like prostitutes and shaming our parents.

We were not the first women in our family to have married late. My Aunt Zainab had been almost thirty when she finally married. She'd met and fallen in love with a man at college, but she couldn't marry him because our family are Sunni and he was a Shi'ite. I didn't really know the difference but understood that while both groups were factions of the same Islamic faith, Shi'ites and Sunnis clearly mistrusted each other. I assumed Aunt's wish to marry a Shi'ite would have been a similar situation to a Catholic and Protestant wanting to get married in Northern Ireland. Not surprisingly, my grandfather was against the match, so everyone was relieved when the man's family married him off to someone else, leaving Zainab heartbroken and refusing to marry anyone else. This left her with only one alternative and she became his second wife. The family, while not happy, were by this time simply relieved, because being a second wife (albeit to a Shi'ite Muslim) was better than not being a wife at all, especially for a woman approaching her late twenties. Her best friend was also a second wife. Her husband kept both wives in similar lifestyles, and as far as I could see she was very happy with her husband.

Zainab, on the other hand, was not so content, for not only did the majority of her husband's substantial income go to maintaining his first family, but Zainab still lived in her father's house and also supported herself, which was not how it was supposed to be. In Islam, a man may marry up to four wives provided he treats all of them equally in terms of time, finances and accommodation, which clearly was not the case here.

My Aunt Zainab had grown up in an unconventional household where, although she was female and one of the youngest, my grandfather had insisted she was educated beyond her brothers. With a forceful personality of her own as well as a strong, domineering mother as a role model, after my grandmother died she took over as head female of the household, bossing around her older brothers and their wives. She'd always been headstrong, so in the matter of her marriage, as with everything else, no one in the family told her what to do; if they tried, she would bellow at them to mind their own business.

In recent years she'd become a police inspector with author-ity over men, which I thought very unusual in a Muslim country. Zainab was used to having her own way and was always bawling at someone; at work it was the men under her command, at home it was her brothers, their wives or the servants. I always knew when my aunt was around, as small children, servants and anxious sisters-in-law would scatter in all directions as she arrived home from work, hot and dusty and hollering for someone to bring her a cold drink.

But there was always one area where Zainab was vulnerable: her husband. My uncle, however, cleverly secured domestic harmony for himself by long absences working for an oil company in Kuwait, and when he was home in Pakistan he kept both wives under control by playing one off against the other. A complaining, nagging or demanding wife was easily dealt with by simply picking up his car keys and going to the other one. Not surprisingly, both wives hated each other with a passion.

Wife number one had won the first round by being married to him first and producing two little girls. Zainab won round two by becoming wife number two, thus smugly proving to her rival that he still had feelings for her. She then claimed yet another victory by presenting him with his first male child, and further secured her position by giving birth to yet another son. The smile was wiped off her face when, to her utter dismay, wife number one became pregnant again and gave birth to a boy, but despite her disappointment and fury my aunt claimed the upper hand as her own sons were the elder. She eventually went on to have a third son, and having scored three out of three by producing three male offspring, she claimed her victory and had no more children. Nevertheless, while she was devoted to her husband, even he could not completely tame the tigress that he'd married, as my aunt declared that she'd be dependent upon no man and if he refused to provide a house as grand as the one her rival had, she would heap coals upon his head and have one built herself.

Nevertheless, while my aunt's house was being built she remained living in my grandfather's house. It was highly unorthodox for a married woman to be living in her father's house but then my grandfather's family had always been unorthodox on all matters relating to family, whether it was education, upbringing or marriage. That said, it was therefore hardly surprising that my own father had a more casual approach towards the marriages of his daughters.

Whether it was through complacency, indolence or some other reason only to be guessed at, my father had failed to stir himself and arrange marriages for any of his girls. Over the past few years, my mother had watched as, one by one, the daughters of family and friends had been married off and began to produce families of their own. By contrast and to her increasing dismay, her own daughters remained worryingly unmarried.

One had already done the unforgivable and married an *Angrezi*. Now the other two had run away from home, and unless something was done urgently they would do exactly the same, leaving the family unable to hold its head up anywhere. However, in the eyes of others, it was already too late.

I suspect my mother knew this, and with one daughter aged nineteen and the other twenty-four, this was more an exercise in damage limitation than an attempt to find eligible and satisfactory husbands for us. By admitting this to me, she confirmed that our happiness did not figure in the plan at all. My mother was here for the sake of family honour and her fear of eternal damnation for her failure to fulfil her parental duty, as Allah commanded. Therefore, her plan was to get us married off under any circumstances and to anyone.

It is customary to prepare and plan for marriage years ahead, often while the daughters are still children. Frustrated by my father's lack of interest in this matter, my mother had finally taken it upon herself to trick us out here with the sole intention of getting us married off before it was too late. But with no real idea of where to begin, my mother depended almost entirely upon my Aunt Zainab and her connections.

Zainab called my mother Bhabi (Wife of Older Brother). Mum was married to Zainab's favourite brother, and while my aunt was only eight years older than me, both my mother and my aunt were close. Despite Zainab's own unconventional marriage and domestic situation, it was to her that my mother turned concerning private family matters such as two grown-up and unmarried daughters.

But with so little forward planning their subsequent attempts to rectify this state of affairs were hastily contrived and ill-judged. It was a recipe for disaster.

One morning about three weeks after our arrival in Pakistan, my aunt suggested to me that I ought to wear some of the more elaborate new clothes she'd had made for us and perhaps do up my hair and apply my make-up.

'Why, are we going somewhere?' I asked, not unreasonably.

'No, no,' she replied hastily. 'You just never know who might drop by.'

She was not subtle and to Farah and me it was perfectly obvious that they had a potential *rishta* coming around, and to pretend otherwise was downright dishonest. But despite being indignant I didn't want another row so I did as I was told.

'Why won't they just be honest about it and tell us?' I hissed as I pulled on the outfit that had been left out for me. In truth I was cross because this was unfamiliar territory. I'd had no experience of this *rishta* business and was anxious about what was going to happen now that my mother and aunt had lined up some family to come and look at me to see if they wanted to accept me as a potential daughter-in-law.

'I feel like a sodding heifer being prepared for market!' I complained to Farah. 'Except that they haven't actually bothered to prepare me and tell me what is expected of me!'

Neither my aunt nor my mother volunteered any more

information, simply telling me that they were expecting guests and that I'd better not do anything to embarrass them. We were ordered to go and sit patiently in another room. My heart was beating with anxiety as the guests arrived and we heard the usual exchange between hosts and guests. Those people out there had come to see me and would decide on my fate. The Western part of me was resentful at being treated like a commodity, but the Eastern side of me was secretly relieved that at last I was being treated like other Pakistani girls and given the chance to marry.

Since landing in Pakistan, my confidence had been increasingly undermined by comments about our lack of knowledge of our Pakistani religion, culture and traditions. Despite having been brought up thousands of miles away, we were expected to behave as if we'd lived in Pakistan all our lives, and any differences were picked up and criticised. Some comments were very personal and hurt our feelings, although I have to say most of them came from my mother's side of the family, who were very orthodox and had always disapproved of my father's family, and not from my father's side.

One thing people never failed to comment upon was my height. Comparing myself to my *Angrezi* friends, at home I'd always considered myself as being of fairly average height. However, in Pakistan, I discovered that at five foot six I was tall for a Pakistani girl. While my *chachas* were tall, I was as tall as most of the Pakistani men I came across. At five foot four, Farah was more the Pakistani ideal than me. Suddenly I felt huge and ungainly, and as much as my Western side was fighting the embarrassment of being wheeled out for inspection, the Pakistani side of me wanted them to like me and say yes to me.

The new outfit felt itchy and uncomfortable. I was not used to wearing such rich fabrics and had no idea what to do with the *dupatta* that seemed to have developed a life of its own. The day had been hot and the evening seemed to be even hotter. I'd never felt so uncomfortable and awkward in my life, and had it been possible I'd have been tempted to make a run for it.

My aunt breezed in, all smiles and dimples, saying my presence was required in the sitting room because the guests wanted to meet me. She looked me up and down, satisfied at what she saw.

'Whatever Bhabi says about you, she can't deny you're beautiful,' she beamed.

'Maybe she's always been too busy telling me what a troublesome slut I am,' I suggested crossly, thinking how ironic it was that while beauty makes a girl eligible on the marriage market, as far as Muslim parents are concerned a beautiful daughter is considered to be a dangerous and troublesome creature who must be got rid of as soon as possible.

I felt sick to the pit of my stomach because I didn't know what was required of me. Did I sit submissively with my head and eyes lowered and speak when I was spoken to, or, because they'd know I was from England, would they expect me to behave differently? To my dismay, Zainab took my hand as if I were a child and led me to the sitting room.

'Aunt, what am I supposed to do?' I asked desperately as her public smile took shape, just before we went in.

'Just sit and speak when you're spoken to,' she advised. 'You look beautiful. And don't spoil it by opening your mouth and shocking them with your opinions,' she ended as she rearranged the *dupatta* around my face.

As I was led into the sitting room, I saw my mother smiling grimly and chatting as she poured the customary tea and offered round samosas. To my dismay a chair had been put out for me facing them directly. It was like facing a firing squad. I'd never felt so exposed and vulnerable in my life, feeling every bit like the heifer I'd felt earlier, except that now the heifer was on display, being examined by potential customers who might or might not want to purchase. All conversation had stopped as everyone turned their attention to me. In England it is rude to stare, but the East has an entirely different attitude in this situation. I was actually expected to sit and endure half a dozen pairs of eyes critically examining me from head to foot, taking in everything and missing nothing. I sat, eyes lowered, desperate to peek out through the veil-like fabric to see what this potential bridegroom was like. I was relieved to discover that he wasn't repulsive.

He was an army officer in his late twenties, and he was tall and had a pleasant face. Nevertheless, it was most disconcerting to be made to sit there on display, being looked at, and I was furious to see that he didn't appear at all awkward or uncomfortable. I hated it and wished the ordeal could be over.

I have absolutely no recollection of how long it went on for or what was said until I heard my aunt asking me if I wanted to ask anything. I hadn't expected to be allowed to speak and said the first thing that came into my head. Not knowing whether or not I was allowed to look directly at him, I did exactly that and heard myself asking him if he spoke English. He looked startled, glancing across at his family before replying yes, he did speak English. I thought we'd been given permission to talk to each other properly, but to my consternation a few moments later my aunt said goodbye on my behalf and bustled me out of the room, and as the sitting room door closed behind me I went to find my sister, heart sinking without actually knowing why.

After they'd departed, I heard raised voices and picked out my mother's angry voice.

'*Haramin!*' she shouted at me. 'You couldn't help yourself, could you? You had to open your mouth and shame me! You had to let people know how ill-mannered and lacking in *tameez* (etiquette) you are.'

'I don't understand. What did I do? What did they say?' I asked, confused.

'What could they say?' she yelled, smacking me straight across the face. 'Who would want to marry a big fat *bheynse* (buffalo) like you?'

That was the only explanation I ever got. I could only speculate that the army officer's family hadn't wanted to take the *rishta* any further, deeming me unsuitable for reasons that no one would explain. All I knew was that I'd committed some unforgivable faux pas and had somehow humiliated my mother, who was so angry that she couldn't bring herself to even look at me for days.

As I sat alone in a dark room, arms clasped around my knees, pondering over my situation, I tried to make sense of things. My feelings on the matter surprised me. In my mind, having been relieved that the army officer was not short or repulsive, I had in effect decided to accept him as a potential husband. And having decided this, I felt utterly crushed and humiliated that I'd been scrutinised as a potential bride, found unsuitable and rejected for reasons that no one would explain to me and that I could only speculate at.

I was hurt and confused by my mother's constant insistence to the family that I'd refused to get married. That was not true. I'd never been given the chance to refuse because this was the first *rishta* that had ever been brought to me. I'd never refused to submit to an arranged marriage, having always accepted that it would be my fate, as it was ultimately the fate of every Asian girl to be married off by her parents. However I felt about my father and the thought of marrying an Asian man who would behave like the men in my family, I could never subject my parents to the trauma of another daughter marrying an unsuitable boy, and thought that if only obedience were required then I would be obedient and make my parents love me.

Yet, as I'd just learned, willingness to be an obedient Muslim daughter was not enough if I could not be a married Muslim daughter. And as I'd quite clearly been rejected by the one and only *rishta* I'd ever received, it left me in a marital no-man's land, destined never to belong anywhere. There were no more *rishtas* after that for me. But it was another matter for Farah.

I overheard heard my mother and my aunt talking. My mother was saying that I was too old and they'd never get anyone to agree to marry me. My aunt replied that I was beautiful and if they could manage to keep me from talking there was no reason why they couldn't find someone to take me. My mother retorted that even with the lure of a British passport they'd never find anyone who'd accept such a troublesome bitch as me. I'd blacken their faces when it was discovered how difficult I was and that I'd lived like a prostitute in London.

However, my mother had publicly attempted to do her duty by me and, having been seen to do so, had proved to everyone that the fault did not lie with her but with me, so no one could blame her. Therefore, having dealt with me, she turned her attention to my sister.

My mother and my aunt both agreed that it would be easier to marry off Farah because she was younger and easier to handle, and marrying off just one of us was better than nothing.

It didn't take long to find someone. For many Pakistanis, with the promise of entry into Britain up for sale, the lure of a British-born wife is hard to resist. This *rishta* was handled differently. Perhaps having learned the lesson from my own disastrous experience, my mother and aunt took great pains to present my sister to her potential bridegroom in a more subtle way. We were both taken aside and told about the *rishta* that had been brought for my sister. He was twenty-four years old. His family were in manufacturing, his parents had died when he was fourteen and he'd since been brought up by his older brother and his wife, who were now looking for a suitable girl for him. We were told that they were coming to look at Farah.

He was ugly. Of that we were both agreed. Despite being greased back, the kinks in his hair looked as if he had a head of pubic hair so we called him Pube-Head. Farah was appalled.

'How the hell can I marry *that* and introduce him to my friends as my husband?' she gasped in dismay. 'I'll be a laughing stock!' So she point-blank refused to say yes.

This was about four or five weeks into our captivity and it was at this point that things began to get really unpleasant for us. It was the beginning of a battle of wills between us and our mother, who declared that either my sister agreed to marry him or she'd return to England in a coffin and we girls would be responsible for her death. To our horror, our mother began to have episodes where she'd collapse in the grip of an uncontrollable fit. The family would rush to her as she writhed on the ground, her eyes rolling, her body shaking. The family would turn on us, demanding to know what kind of daughters we were to subject our mother to this. If she died it would be our fault!

We'd never seen her have fits like this at home and at first we were scared and concerned by them. As time went on, however, we'd stand by dispassionately, convinced that these fits were either psychosomatic or deliberately brought on in order to turn the family against us and manipulate us. Neither Farah nor I witnessed these fits after this period in Pakistan.

Pube-Head was relentless in his pursuit of his marriage with my sister, with no secret being made of the fact that he was desperate to come to England to study. The violent objections of this potential bride, who glared at him with hatred, did not seem to matter to him at all. In fact, both families appeared unconcerned at her opposition to him, telling each other – and us – that once they were married, everything would be all right. My mother tried to persuade Farah, using the money and status of Pube-Head's family as a bargaining tool.

'His family are wealthy, you'd never want for anything.'

'It's not his money, it's theirs,' she'd reply.

'They live in a beautiful big house.'

'What's he going to do, pick it up and plonk it in the middle of London?' she'd retort angrily. But he and his family continued to visit and the pressure on Farah to agree was increased.

'It's not fair!' she raged to me. 'They're not meant to keep bullying you like this. They're meant to show you someone and if you say no they're supposed to accept it. I'm not rejecting the idea of getting married. Just marriage to *him*!'

But my mother refused to listen, angrily retorting that she would not allow us to go back to England to run around like whores and that we were in no position to turn down good *rishtas*. That only made us even more indignant.

'What do you mean *rishtas*?' I demanded. 'You showed me one person and now you're doing the same with her and forcing her to accept the only one you've brought to her!'

'*Haramin!* That one *rishta* was hard enough to get for a big fat buffalo like you. Now you're trying to ruin it for her,' she cried, as I received yet another slap.

'Why were you sent to plague my life?' she asked. 'Why didn't you drop dead when you were born?' That wish was to mark the beginning of a campaign of blackmail and threats against me that were calculated to force me to use my influence to make my sister change her mind.

19

A little spit in the eye

*Life does not cease to be funny when people die, any
more than it ceases to be serious when people laugh.*
George Bernard Shaw (1856–1950)

One of my aunt's frequent visitors was a senior army officer
who had been at college with her. He became a frequent visitor
to the house, often dropping in unannounced in the evening just
after the servants had left. Probably aged in his early forties, he
was a tall, handsome and cultured man who spoke impeccable
English and who was one of the few visitors who actually went
out of his way to befriend Farah and me and treat us like intelligent human beings. That made a refreshing change, because
most people talked about us or at us as if we were idiots.

As a respected friend of my aunt's, he'd be allowed the
privilege of sitting down and chatting informally with the two
of us, which wouldn't normally have been permitted. Unsure of
how we were supposed to behave, we'd simply sit obediently,
not looking him straight in the eyes or seeming to look too
interested in what he was saying in case we committed some
social faux pas by doing so. He'd always lead the conversation
and chat about our home back in England and the differences
between our two countries. He had a powerful presence and,
compared to any other Pakistani man we'd met, he had
charisma. Back in our room, Farah and I would speculate
disrespectfully that our aunt probably fancied him.

One evening, while my aunt was out of the room, he moved in closer and told us that he was aware of the circumstances of our being in Pakistan. He knew we were being kept there against our will and how unhappy we were, promising to do everything he could to help us get home. I was startled and couldn't believe what he was saying. He told us to trust him and believe that he was a friend who would help us.

After he'd gone, Farah and I could scarcely sleep. We couldn't believe that someone was willing to help us, and because of who he was we dared to believe that he had the power and influence to succeed. He could bring his authority to bear on my aunt and my mother and persuade them to let us go home. After that evening, I decided to trust him and cautiously began to open up during his evening visits. I also noticed my mother and my aunt relaxing around us and not telling us off or putting pressure on us as they usually did, and put it down to his influence. As an educated and cultured man of the world he would have seen how barbaric it was to bring up two girls in the West, trick them into coming to Pakistan and then hold them against their will. I warmed to him and put my faith in him to help us get home.

One night we saw his jeep parked outside and went in search of him, puzzled as to why he hadn't loudly and jovially announced his arrival as he normally did. As we'd not been invited in, we paused outside the sitting room, debating whether or not to simply go in.

'Zainab, listen to me!' we heard him say. 'They're spoilt and wilful and you absolutely must not let them have their own way.'

'What can I do?' my aunt replied. 'The whole household has been turned upside down. My brother and his wife have let them run wild in England and now they've brought them here and lumbered the family with their problem. We've been reasonable but the girls refuse to marry anyone we find.'

'That settles it, then,' he replied. 'You have to stand firm and show them who is in charge and keep those girls here. I'll help you. My younger brother is in his twenties and is ready for marriage. I've already spoken to the family and I'm sure our two families will be able to do business.'

'I'll not say anything to my niece until everything is *pukka*,' agreed my aunt.

'We're really looking at the younger one; the other one is too old. Her sister is much more manageable and has an easier disposition. I'm not sure what anyone can do with the older one,' he added. 'Whatever you do, keep them here until I've arranged matters!'

By this time I'd heard more than enough! I raced outside, wounded with shame and anger, furiously fighting back hot angry tears.

'The lying, perfidious sod!' I cried to Farah. 'He pretended to befriend us. He promised to help us and all the time he's been scheming to get his hands on us for his brother. Well, you anyway,' I cried, 'because apparently I'm too old and past it!'

'It's not true that we keep saying no to anyone they find for us,' protested Farah. 'They've shown you one bloke and I've only had that ugly Pube-headed creature who won't take no for an answer!'

'When has truth ever had anything to do with anything out here?' I asked bitterly. I didn't know what was worse; being forced to marry someone you didn't want to marry or learning that no one wanted to marry you at all! My mother said the same things to me all the time and in much nastier terms. But somehow hearing an outsider say that at twenty-four I was too old, that no one would want to marry me because I was too troublesome, wounded and devastated me far more than my mother had ever done. I could scarcely breathe from the pain of rejection that I felt at that moment.

Then my eyes settled on the jeep which was parked just feet away. It belonged to that treacherous, two-faced weasel who'd told us to trust him. He'd promised to help us get out while all the time plotting to betray us and actually urging my stupid, empty-headed aunt to keep us held here for as long as she could until his own agenda could be served! Smarting from the pain of humiliation and betrayal, I bent down and picked up a piece of broken tile that had a sharp edge and began slashing at the tyres of his precious jeep, becoming even angrier when it scarcely made any impact at all. Determined, I threw away the broken tile and began to unscrew the air valve.

Farah was appalled. 'It's not worth getting a belting for!' she warned, looking about her fearfully in case we were seen.

'Oh but it is!' I replied stubbornly, as I removed the first valve cap and moved on to the second. I had no idea how long it would take for the air to escape, but all the better if he was able to drive home and only realised the next day when he saw four deflated tyres. Or, with a bit of luck, he might even drive into the back of a bus, die and go to hell! Having removed the cap from the fourth tyre I stood up, maliciously contemplating the pristine paintwork and the damage that a sharp stone could inflict.

It was early evening, the family had all gone out and there were no servants about. Just as well, for my sister was right and there would indeed be trouble if I was caught, I thought, as I bent down to pick up a piece of slate. As I straightened up, my heart lurched suddenly as I saw a figure lying on a narrow wall just beyond the iron gates of the house. It was one of the outside servants who, like others of his kind, had this peculiar ability to sleep anywhere, whether it was stretched out on a hot dusty pavement in full glare of the daytime heat with people and traffic rushing by or, as here, perched atop a wall. However, he was not asleep now but stretched out, half-propped up on his right elbow, watching me with calm curiosity.

'Drat these people!' I muttered crossly. 'Why can't they sleep in a proper bed like normal people?'

Farah was more realistic about our situation. 'We're dead!' she wailed.

'You shouldn't be doing that,' he remonstrated quietly.

I was afraid, knowing that if he told on us, I'd be battered. But then I was not a daughter of this house for nothing. I'd seen children and servants scatter in all directions when my aunt was on the rampage. She might have been the only girl in a family of six brothers but her language was no less colourful and she was afraid of no one. I'd seen her roar and bellow and reduce grown men to tears. I'd missed nothing and learned much from her example.

'You'd better not say anything!' I hissed. 'Open your mouth and I'll tell Dadda you've been leering at us and you've been trying to put your filthy hands on us. What do you think he'd do to a *naukar* (servant) who dared to dishonour the *izzat* of his house?' I asked, threateningly close to him by now. 'He'll whip the hide off your bones and throw your remains into a ditch! And I won't even start on what will happen to you if the *chachas* get to hear about it. By the time they've finished with you, there won't be anything left to throw anywhere. Your own mother wouldn't recognise your carcass. So, if you want to keep your job and stay in one piece, I'm warning you, you'd better not tell!'

Then defiantly tossing my head with more courage than I felt, I grabbed my sister and marched back into the house, satisfied that in one evening we'd twice managed to even the score a little.

The scores were inadvertently evened up even more some days later when we were taken out to get some fresh air. For the benefit of neighbours, my aunt occasionally took Farah and me out to buy a Coke from a small ice-cream kiosk nearby. After we had been cooped up for most of the day this brief half-hour outing became something to look forward to.

She engaged in small talk with the old man who ran the kiosk.

'How are these English girls finding our hot Pakistani climate?' he asked.

'*Beycharis*, poor things,' dimpled my aunt, 'the heat is too much for them.' She patted us fondly as we scowled unhelpfully.

'Silly cow! She talks about us as if we're as stupid as she is!' I muttered to my sister as my aunt strained to hear what was said. We smiled back sweetly.

'Cold drink? Ice cream?' he offered, removing two from the freezer.

'No,' I said petulantly, 'I want an iced lolly!'

To our bewilderment, the old man gasped, staggering backwards into the kiosk. I thought he was having a stroke. Blustering that we were children and didn't understand what we were saying, my aunt hastily ushered us out of the kiosk and marched us home, her ample body quivering with indignation, muttering to herself, not trusting herself to speak to us directly.

'Bhabi!' she bellowed as we entered the house, then, discovering my mother in the sitting room, she stormed in, angrily slamming the door behind her, leaving us bemused and still with no idea of what we'd done. A few minutes later my mother came out, trying hard to look stern.

In Pakistan, the word 'lolly' is never used as all frozen ices are called ice cream. There is, however, a word in Urdu that sounds like 'lolly' and means a male appendage. No wonder the old guy looked as if I'd pulled a gun on him.

I'd just asked him for an iced *willy*.

20

Turning the screw

*Fanaticism consists in redoubling your efforts
when you have forgotten your aim.*
George Santayana (1863–1952)

My mother was becoming increasingly angry at my sister's refusal to marry Pube-Head. Even more infuriating for her was the fact that her attempts to bribe Farah with promises of jewellery, cars and a new house were all in vain, as my sister remained adamant that she wanted nothing to do with him. However, when she did finally lose patience at what she saw as my sister's refusal to see sense, her frustration was redirected at me.

My mother resented the fact that, from an early age, Farah had always turned to me for help, advice and support. And while she displayed no inclination to actually step into that role herself, she hated the fact that my sister gave me the unquestioning loyalty and trust that should, of right, automatically have gone to her as mother and matriarch. I was therefore the usurper. During one such tirade she became so angry that she attacked me, 'Who do you think you are?', she screamed, raining down blows on me. *She* was Farah's mother, not me.

It was clear that Farah was seen simply as my puppet while I, the puppet-master, pulled her strings. That was not the case, but from then on the pressure was not on Farah to change her mind but on me to change it for her. I recall conversations I had with one of my older *chachas* who told me it would be better for me if I did as I was being asked to do and ordered Farah to accept Pube-Head. If I did, then it would all be over and we could go back home to England and everything could return to normal.

'Huh! Normal for whom?' I thought, not daring to say it out loud.

Chacha was a big man with a temper, and at that very moment I couldn't help feeling intimidated by him. Every day for the past week he'd come into the room to have a private conversation with me. While these conversations had begun as friendly chats, they'd become increasingly threatening. He told me he wasn't happy that my parents had brought their problem to his home, but my father was his elder brother and therefore he had to respect my parents' wishes in wanting to get us married off. He was shocked at our lack of respect towards our mother and didn't understand it, but supposed that was the English way of doing things. All he wanted to do now was get this wedding over and done with so everyone could get back to their own lives.

'But she doesn't want to marry him,' I told him, not for the first time.

'Tell her to change her mind then,' he replied. 'You seem to be the one with influence over her: tell her to marry him. If you don't, I'll break every bone in your body,' he added. Then without even a backwards glance he left.

Some days later Zainab cornered me when I was alone, for another one of these private chats that were now becoming quite a regular thing. They were all working on me, putting pressure on me as if I was the evil mastermind, hell-bent on thwarting their attempts to arrange a good marriage for my sister. My aunt asked me why I didn't want Farah to marry Pube-head (the family obviously called him by his real name, which I can't even remember now). I replied that it wasn't my decision but Farah's, and she hated him.

'But you could change her mind if you wanted to, couldn't you?' she asked silkily. 'Don't you want to see your little sister settled in a good marriage, have a husband, a home and family of her own?'

'Of course I do,' I replied, resenting the implication that somehow I didn't.

'Then you'll agree it's best for her. Best to get her married before her reputation is ruined,' she said. 'Because once people start talking she'll be ruined, both here and in England.' I didn't understand what she was getting at.

'Bhabi says you don't want her to get married because she'll move on and you'll be left behind. That's why you want to keep her with you.'

'That's not true,' I protested.

'Yes, yes, that's what I told her,' my aunt replied impatiently. 'But that won't stop what they are saying.'

'What are they saying?' I demanded.

'That you won't let her get married because you want to keep her for yourself.' She paused, as if waiting for my reaction before continuing. 'They're saying you're unnatural, that's why you refuse to get married to a man, and they're saying that's why you won't let your sister go.'

At first I didn't understand what she was saying, but as her real meaning became clear I felt tears well up in shock and disbelief. I simply couldn't believe what she was suggesting.

'That's not true!' I gasped. 'She's my little sister! I've always taken care of her ever since she was a baby! How could anyone suggest I have any other reason?'

So these were the depths that they were willing to sink to in order to make me toe the line. They couldn't or wouldn't see things from our point of view. It had nothing to do with them failing to do their duty and arranging a proper marriage for me. It had nothing to do with Farah's refusal to marry that creature because he repulsed her. It had nothing to do with the fact that I was being held imprisoned against my will in this awful place thousands of miles from home, being physically beaten by my own mother and emotionally tormented. No. As far as they were concerned, the only explanation they could come up with for me acting the way I did was because I had this incestuous, lesbian thing going on with my sister! It was sick.

I paced the room, scarcely able to take this in, not knowing whether to laugh out loud like a mad woman or weep for the shame and outrage of our treatment at the hands of these people who should have been caring for us and protecting us. Were they mad? Didn't they know that by saying things like that, they could have us killed? Hadn't they told us innumerable times that in Pakistan the women carried the *izzat* of a family and to damage that honour meant taking away from them the thing that was most precious to them?

I'd heard of men who'd claimed they'd executed their wife or daughter because they suspected her of wrongdoing. She'd been allowed no defence because his *izzat* had already suffered damage. The only way for him to regain that *izzat* was to kill her, so a woman would be put to death at the faint whisper of impropriety. Truth, reality or proof was not necessary. The mere suggestion of an allegation was enough.

Perhaps that was what they wanted me to be afraid of. They knew I'd do anything to protect my sister and, knowing the influence that I did indeed have over her, I'd have no choice but to make her agree to marry and bed with that grotesque creature to save her; to save us both. My head ached trying to make sense of it all and I realised I was afraid. Unable to take all this in properly, I couldn't bring myself to divulge any of it to Farah and cried myself to sleep that night.

A few days after this conversation, my mother came to speak to us. While I acknowledged this person standing in front of me as my mother, since this ordeal had begun I'd found it increasingly difficult to believe that she was the one who'd brought me up. It was as if some evil spirit had somehow taken possession of the mind and body of the gentle, kind, beautiful goddess-mother of my childhood, who'd thrown herself in front of my father begging him not to hurt me and who'd willingly protected me by taking a beating for my sake. I no longer recognised her. Her face was hard and her eyes were cold and bitter. Suddenly, I wondered if she was indeed ill, because the fits had left her gaunt and ugly. And yet, as I looked into her eyes, there was real sorrow behind that coldness. I couldn't bear to look at her because it evoked uncomfortable, painful feelings that I didn't understand. So, averting my gaze away from her face, I listened to what she was telling us.

My mother coldly told us that she'd made up her mind about two things. First, unless we did as we were ordered to do, we'd never see England again. She told us to forget everything we were used to and everyone we'd ever known, because we were never going back. We'd never see our home, our friends or family ever again. It was all in the past because we would never leave Pakistan, so we'd better get used to it. She went on to tell us that she'd come out here determined to do her Muslim duty and marry us off and, unless she was able to accomplish that with at least one of us, she intended to let herself die and the responsibility of her death would be on our heads. Then, as if to show us she meant business, or perhaps it was a sign that her mind or her health really was going, she suddenly seemed to lose consciousness and started to moan and go into some kind of fit.

Farah and I were terrified and stood rooted to the spot even as my aunt, who was seeing to her, shouted for help.

Later, back in our room, we were still in shock.

'Do you think she means it?' Farah asked.

'You heard what she said – you were there yesterday,' I replied.

The day before, other members of the family who were unaware of our situation had come to take us out to the beach. Enjoying the rare feeling of freedom, we hadn't noticed our mother, who was walking close to the water's edge. Suddenly an unusually large wave crashed into her, knocking her off her feet and sweeping her into the water. Amid much shouting the family raced over, catching hold of her to drag her back. She was soaked, and on the way back home told us that she'd been praying to Allah to either save her *izzat* and help her marry us off or else take her, then and there. She told us that she wanted the sea to sweep her away, because if we took her *izzat* away she'd sooner be dead.

Looking at my sister I wondered just how much more we could take. As if reading my thoughts, Farah said that we simply had to get away, and the sooner the better because the situation was getting worse. We began to discuss a plan to run away to the British Embassy and demand our rights as British subjects to sanctuary and help in getting back home to England. There were, however, several problems to be overcome. First, we had no idea where the Embassy was. Second and more important, even if we did know how to get there, how would we escape from the house without being caught and dragged back, as we were never left alone and were watched all the time. Added to that was the danger of being out alone and unprotected, where we could be picked up and abducted by opportunists with rape, ransom or murder on their minds. But having considered the alternatives, we decided to take our chances with the rapists and kidnappers and make a run for the main street, where we would jump on the first bus going in the direction of the city. We knew in which direction the city lay, and once there we'd head straight for the areas where all the big luxury hotels and plazas were, because that was the likeliest place for the British Embassy to be located.

But first we had to get away from the house and try and lose ourselves in the crowds. That was easier said than done because we knew we stood out a mile, but we had to try. It was mid-afternoon and the family were either out or taking their afternoon nap during the hottest part of the day: it was now or never.

Picking up just one bag each, so as not to attract too much attention, we took our first steps out of the courtyard and into the street. The heat and glare of the midday sun seemed to come at us with force, and my heart was beating so fast that I could barely catch my breath to tell my sister to walk casually so as not to attract attention to ourselves. It was a ten-minute walk to the main street, past the houses of neighbours who'd all wonder why we were out alone without a chaperone. However, we'd gone barely a hundred yards before the family appeared out of nowhere. In a panic, we considered trying to make a run for it in an attempt to reach the bus stop, but that would have been no use. We would have attracted too much attention and the resulting hue and cry would have brought out every man, woman and child in the area, to come and gawp at the spectacle of the two girls from England being marched back home.

Not surprisingly, my mother was furious, demanding to know what our game was and whether we were determined to bring shame on the family. Didn't we know, asked my aunt and *chachas*, how dangerous it was for us to be out alone on the streets with no one to protect us?

'Protect us from what?' I demanded. 'Kidnap? Imprisonment? Being beaten and blackmailed? Threatened with murder? Tell me something that couldn't happen to me out there that isn't happening to me in here!'

My mother lunged at me, calling me every bad thing that she could, slapping me around my face, my head and anywhere where it would hurt me, screaming at the others to take me and throw me to the Pathans.

The Pathans were men who came from the Northern Frontier and, we'd been told, regarded women as little more than property. In Karachi many of them drove taxis. No one dared to pick a fight with a Pathan because they were considered dangerous and unpredictable. My mother threatened that if we continued to defy our elders, we'd be given in marriage to a Pathan who'd deal with us in the way we deserved, and they were not strangers to gang-rape and murder.

I angrily defied her to do it. I was a British citizen and she wouldn't dare!

My mother and aunt replied that being a British citizen meant nothing to them in Pakistan. I'd be made to disappear into the mountains where no one would ever hear from me again. They claimed that under Islamic law, they could murder a dishonourable daughter, cut her body up into pieces and bury her. It happened all the time. In fact, I was warned, they could do whatever they liked to us, because as an unmarried daughter I had no rights and the law and Pakistani society would always back them.

Not long after this, my aunt came to tell me that my mother wanted us to be taught a lesson. She wanted Zainab to take us to the police station and throw us in jail for the night. 'These Pakistani jails aren't like your English jails where they give you a television and serve you dinner,' she warned me. They were full of the kind of men who'd throw acid in your face just for looking at them.

'Can you imagine having acid thrown in your face?' she asked. These men would use a girl just because they can, then they'd throw her body away like a piece of discarded rubbish. She went on to tell me that these things happened here in Pakistan because with enough rupees you could do anything, buy anything and arrange anything.

Late that evening, I heard a large vehicle draw up outside. My mother came into our room to order my sister and me to follow her. We were led outside to where a small minibus was parked and ordered to get into the back. There was a man we didn't recognise at the wheel. My mother and aunt got into the row of seats behind him and in front of us, declining to answer our questions as to where we were going.

It was a long, silent drive that took us away from the residential area that we recognised. Throughout the journey, neither my aunt nor my mother spoke a word, either to us or to each other, but sat looking straight ahead. The driver, an unkempt, rough-looking man, kept looking at us through his rear-view mirror, and I waited for the usual outburst from my aunt ordering him to take his eyes off us and keep them on the road. She said nothing. An hour later, buildings began to appear again and I saw that we had come back into the city. The vehicle suddenly stopped outside a police station. The driver got out, followed by my aunt and my mother, who ordered us to stay where we were before they all disappeared into the building. My sister and I sat alone in the dark for what seemed ages but was probably half an hour, during which we had time to convince ourselves that something terrible was going to happen to us and that they'd brought us here to carry out their threat to throw us into a jail full of criminals who would gang-rape and murder us.

'Do you think this is where she works?' my sister asked. I didn't know. I didn't really care because my mind was going back over my conversation with Zainab about Islamic law and how they could do anything to us here. I knew she was right. Being a British citizen meant nothing if you were already dead. We could be murdered and no one would ask questions. If anyone did ask questions, would the British government risk creating a diplomatic incident by accusing the Pakistanis of murdering two Muslim girls, one of whom was actually born in Pakistan? I doubted it. The family would simply tell them that we'd been married and our husbands had taken us away and not told them where. It would be written off as a domestic matter and left at that. We were on our own. There was no one to help us.

Half an hour later, the other three reappeared. This time, despite the ride being just as silent and unsettling, we were driven straight home on a return journey that took half the time. I realised we'd been taken the long way round. We were ordered to get out of the vehicle and to go to bed. No one ever mentioned that journey again, and our only conclusion was that it had been deliberately calculated to frighten us out of our wits.

If that had been the intention then it succeeded. That night had indeed frightened us. It made me wonder what they'd do next and I began to question whether or not there was another way out of this situation. I couldn't stop shaking with fright every time I thought of that long, creepy, silent drive, and I found that I was beginning to lose my ability to think clearly.

My sister and I made a pact that if things began to get out of control, we would take our own lives. Things were bad, but little did we know that they were to get even worse. My father was on his way.

21

From bad to worse

Often the test of courage is not to die but to live.
Conte Vittorio Alfieri (1749–1803)

My mother gave us the news, intending it to be a threat of what was to come. She said that our behaviour had worn her out and she couldn't handle us any more, which was why my father was coming out to deal with us.

However, the news that my father was on his way did not fill me with dismay. On the contrary, I couldn't wait for him to arrive and actually regarded his imminent arrival with relief. This was because my father had never really had much time for religious fanaticism, and had never supported my mother when she voiced her concerns about standing before Allah on Judgement Day to answer to Him as to why they hadn't done their Muslim duty and married off their daughters. The fact that he'd done very little about it over the years proved his disinterest. Added to that was my father's belief that Pakistani customs went too far in the name of religion. He always said that the extremists had got Pakistan in their grip by using religion as a means of gaining political control. If people didn't toe the political line, they'd be accused of being unIslamic. I knew little about Pakistani politics but just looked to my father to save us and take us back home.

When he arrived, it was as I'd guessed. He was not happy about the things that were being said about his daughters. This was because they reflected badly on him and he took this as a criticism of the way he'd brought us up in England. And because I understood him so well, I knew exactly what to say in order to get him on our side and persuade him to take us back home. I told him that Farah hated Pube-head and had said no, but that neither my mother nor Pube-head himself would accept her answer and they'd been bullying her to change her mind.

That was not a hard argument to win, because once he'd met this prospective son-in-law it didn't need me to point out exactly how far down the evolutionary scale Pube-head was.

'I told you he was repulsive. Can you imagine taking him around Preston, introducing him to your friends as your new son-in-law? They'd all laugh at you and feel sorry for you!'

There was another argument. Knowing how much he hated passport bridegrooms, I told my father how his family didn't even bother being subtle about Pube-head's desperation to come to England. That was a real insult to his daughter. And to him. It was disrespectful to my father because he wasn't desperate to marry his daughter off. It wasn't as if he was poor or his daughters were ugly.

My father was appalled. He told my mother that he'd given her the chance to bring us to Pakistan, but since her efforts to marry us off had failed it was time to accept it and book our return flights home. However, my mother had other ideas.

She turned on my father with a fury he'd never seen before, informing him that there were only two ways he would ever get her on that plane: either there would be a wedding or they'd carry her dead body out of Pakistan in a box. It took my father aback to be turned on like that by her, of all people, and it was clear he didn't quite know how to handle it. His confusion turned to real concern when my mother suddenly began to have one of her fits; her eyes rolled and she seemed to be unaware of what was happening around her, while her entire body shook uncontrollably. It had exactly the same effect upon him as it had on my sister and me when it first happened and he stood frozen to the spot, unable to move.

'Zainab! Zainab!' he cried to his sister, who hearing the panic in his voice came running and, throwing herself on the ground next to my mother, cradled her in her arms as she moaned, 'I'll die first.'

I knew then that our hopes of returning home were gone.

Over the next few days, my father learned from Zainab about my mother's declining health, her suicide attempt and her distress because of her worry about us. He turned on us, suddenly seeing us as the two disobedient and insubordinate daughters who were hell-bent on killing their mother.

In a day or so she was up and about but he never left her side, displaying a tenderness towards her that I'd never seen before. As they sat together, we heard her telling him in a weak voice how all she wanted was to see at least one of her daughters respectably married – only when she'd achieved that could she die happy. My father's eyes would mist over and his voice would crack as he'd rebuke her softly for talking like that.

'She's got him exactly where she wants him,' observed my sister in dismay.

'That's what I'm afraid of,' I replied worriedly. We couldn't understand how our mother could have changed so much. We'd believed that our father had the upper hand, that like most Pakistani husbands he did as he pleased and the wife simply went along with him. That had certainly been the case while we children were young. However, I now realised that by the time we were all grown up, my father had become totally dependent upon my mother emotionally, and unless she was in the kitchen preparing his meals, he was restless until she was in the same room as him, giving him her undivided attention.

Back home, he was always very jealous of her attention and would let nothing – not knitting, books, television or children – come between them. She'd often complain that he never let her have any hobbies, to which he'd declare that *he* was her hobby so why would she have need of any other diversion? Therefore, while he still permitted my mother to fetch and carry for him day and night, he was devoted to her. She had become his emotional rock.

At what point did the power shift in my parents' marriage? I'm not entirely certain. Perhaps it was when my brothers grew into men. A young wife tied to a brood of babies becomes a very different creature when she is the mother of strong, grown-up sons. As the mother of men, both in society and within her own home, the status of an Asian woman is unassailable. She becomes a force to be reckoned with. Her will, imposed through these men, gradually over the years becomes the prevailing voice that determines the decisions taken in the family.

This is clearly what had been happening and had come to a head here, in Pakistan. The tables had turned. Now that my father was faced with the unthinkable prospect of losing her and living life without her, the handover of power from husband to wife was complete. He would do anything for her.

I really cannot recollect exactly how it began, but matters deteriorated rapidly. My mother felt that we had robbed her of her *izzat*. We'd brought shame on our parents, and under Islamic law daughters who bring shame upon the family are dealt with severely. It didn't look good for us at all. It was just a matter of time before we would see exactly how far she was willing to go with this newfound power.

My father had been won round to reconsidering Pube-head

as a potential son-in-law. He told my sister, in a voice that clearly conveyed his unwillingness to tolerate any disobedience, that we would be meeting his family for a meal. Her sullenness during the meal and subsequent refusal to agree to marry him enraged him and he turned on her, telling her that she would do as she was told. My mother interjected by telling him that this was what she'd had to put up with for months. Now she'd lost the will to live and was just waiting to die from the shame. My father angrily told her that she was not going to die, because if Farah did not do as she was told he'd beat her until she did. That shocked everyone because my father had never laid a hand on my sister. I'd been used to being beaten all my life, so violence was nothing new to me, but somehow the very thought of him hitting my sister appalled me.

Our lives became a nightmare from then on, with my mother goading my father to turn against us. There would be violent rows during which she'd suddenly become ill and collapse. My father would look frantic and turn on me and hit me. We were forbidden to talk to anyone and confined to our room, which became our prison. We both hated her for what she was doing.

As far as my mother was concerned, my father was paying the price for the irresponsible way in which he'd brought us up. She ranted at him for the way he'd allowed us to run wild, wear *Angrezi* clothes, go to school and mix with *Angrezi* people and learn their ways. He should have allowed her to have a free hand with us and force us to learn our own Pakistani ways. It was all his fault that they could not hold their heads up in their own home with their own family, because everyone was talking about them, criticising them and saying how emigrating to England had backfired on him, because look how his children had turned out. He'd never listened to her and look where that had got him, she nagged. He'd got it all wrong. They had no *izzat* left and it was his fault.

One evening, having been thoroughly wound up, my father snapped, and uttering an expletive lunged at Farah, yelling, '*Haramzadi!* It's all your fault! You've left me nowhere to go! You've shamed me in my own house!'

To my horror, he grabbed her by the throat and started to choke her.

It sounds completely bizarre but I was horrified by the fact that he'd grabbed her and not me and that somehow he'd got the wrong person.

'No!' I cried, hurling myself on his back to get him off her. 'You're not supposed to hurt her! She's not used to it!' He dropped my sister and turned on me, roaring all the names he'd always called me, and let me have it. While it was happening I was vaguely aware of my mother calling him to finish me off, and then I heard no more.

I can't remember anything after that and only recall waking in the dark to find Farah bending over me, urging me in a frightened voice to wake up. She was badly shaken up and terrified that I might not come round.

As we sat together in the dark, our situation was clear to both of us. We were in real danger now. My father didn't handle stress very well. He was being manipulated by our mother and it was simply a matter of time before he snapped. But there was nothing we could do. Farah said she hated her and wished she were dead, and I was shocked to realise that so did I.

There was no one to help us. I'd already pleaded with my aunt to help us, to talk to my father, to help us get back home, to do anything before we were killed. She simply shook her head helplessly, saying that she was powerless to do anything. My father was her elder and she could not defy him. She wasn't happy about what was happening and wished my parents either had never left Pakistan or had stayed in England, because this isn't what my father had wanted for his children. She said that she too was afraid we would end up being killed and she simply didn't know what to do.

We'd hear my parents talking together, but we couldn't hear what was being said. By now most of the family kept well away from this part of the house. Dadda, who could have interceded, suddenly became profoundly deaf and spent most of his time out of the house, while the rest of the family kept to their own rooms.

We spent most of the time in our room, sometimes not daring even to have the light on. There had been a lull for almost a week and we knew that it was simply a matter of time before something happened. Every night we'd scarcely dare to close our eyes for fear of being murdered as we slept. We'd listen hard, straining to catch every sound that could possibly be someone coming to snuff out this shame in the family. In the morning we'd wake, having slept fitfully for only a few hours. My sister looked like an old woman, gaunt from hardly eating and wracked with fatigue through lack of sleep and terror from the strain of staying awake every night. It was hard to believe she was still only in her teens.

'You had another nightmare,' she said matter of factly. I'd forgotten, but suddenly it came back to me, making me shiver. It was a dream I'd been having a lot. I dreamed of a house where there were women sitting cross-legged on the floor, chatting and preparing a meal with children playing around them. It was this house and the people were my family, but somehow I knew they hadn't been born yet because this was in the future. Suddenly there was a frightful sound, a heart-rending wail, and the ghostly apparition of a woman would suddenly appear in the courtyard, crying, 'Why? Why did you let them kill me? I didn't want to die! Let me go home!' Then I'd realise that the ghostly woman was me and would wake up in a cold sweat. This same dream haunted me for days, and I wondered if I was actually losing my mind because I'd have the same disturbing dream even if I only happened to doze off in the middle of the day.

Furthermore, I didn't understand why I was being haunted by a recurring dream about a displaced soul that was not at peace because it wanted to go home. My mother had told me that her labour pains started and I arrived before they could get her to hospital. I'd been born here. This house had once been my home.

But fate had taken me to the other side of the world, where my heart lay and which I was losing hope of ever seeing again. Mist and rain were memories and I'd forgotten what it felt like to be cold, to wake up on a winter morning and snuggle down deep beneath a huge fluffy duvet. With a sinking heart, I realised that we'd never see England again and asked myself how I could bear it. The homesickness I felt was like a physical pain that would only go away when I could see, breathe and feel familiar things. We'd been out here in Pakistan for almost twelve weeks and home was suddenly starting to feel as if it had been something I'd dreamed about once.

I was startled to discover that I'd started to think in Urdu and sometimes dreamed in Urdu. Apart from when I talked with my sister, I never heard English spoken. They'd taken away the English music and magazines we'd brought with us. I couldn't read or write Urdu so had nothing to read. I found myself sinking further into despair.

It was perhaps inevitable that we'd begin to discuss the possibility of giving in and doing whatever they wanted us to do. It would mean accepting whoever they lined up for one or both of us, without question. If we agreed to go through a marriage ceremony we'd be allowed to go home because they'd need us there to apply for a visa to let the husband in. Once we were home, we could secretly write to the Home Office and tell them that we'd been made to do it under duress. That meant that the marriage would be invalid and they'd never let him into the country, so we'd be free.

That part of the plan might work, but there was a price to pay.

Before that happened we'd be made to consummate the marriage first, before they allowed us to leave. The idea appalled us both. I told my sister that if she was willing to go along with the idea of going through a marriage ceremony with Pube-head, she'd also have to face the prospect of being forced to submit to rape on the wedding night.

'If we can buy our freedom by being raped, could you bear it?' I asked her. 'Because if you say you'd rather die first, then that might be the only other way you'll ever leave this place.' That was Plan B.

Plan B was simple and involved an increasing stash of pills that we'd collected over the past few months. My aunt was careless with medication and left it lying all over the house, so it was easy for my sister and me to pick up pills and to add to the hoard at the bottom of my hand-luggage bag. As if she'd read my thoughts, my sister said, 'It's time, isn't it?'

We shut the door and retrieved all the pills from the bottom of the bag and emptied them on to the bed. There were several dozen pills of assorted sizes, colours and shapes which we counted and shared out between us. We had no idea how long the pills would take to work, but as we sat there, a glass of water in one hand and the tablets in the other, I felt calmer than I'd felt in a long time. We were so far away from England, but

From bad to worse

I told my sister that we'd soon be home again because I believed that when a person dies, time and space cease to have meaning and their spirit goes to the place where they want to be the most. And because I knew she was afraid of being left behind and alone, I told her that I'd be there watching out for her right until the end, just as I'd always done since she was a baby. I knew she'd have the courage to take the pills, and my own resolve that this was the right thing to do was clear right up until the point when she was about to take the first handful.

I stopped her. I couldn't let her do it. I knew that however much I despaired and wished to die, whatever decision I made, my sister would follow my example and do the same, and I couldn't let my own despair force my sister to make the same decision. The family were right. I did have influence over her and she would do whatever I did. If I took my own life, she would too.

So, acting more bravely than I felt, I let the pills fall through my fingers.

Not long after, we returned to our room to find that our bags had been searched and the pills were gone. I don't know how they knew; perhaps it had merely been speculation on their part. My aunt and my mother came in and told us they'd found them and disposed of them, asking us what we thought we were playing at. Hadn't we shamed them enough already?

'They want us dead but they object to us depriving them of the pleasure of doing it,' I said bitterly after they'd gone, regretting the loss of the pills.

They watched us closely after that, scarcely letting us out of their sight.

We thought that we'd go mad with the heat and inertia alone. The television was in Urdu, as was the radio. The only papers brought into the house were in Urdu, which we couldn't read, although Farah had learned to pick out simple words from her lessons at the mosque years ago. It felt like another lifetime when we'd been able to pick up a book, newspaper or a magazine that we could read. For these past few months, seeing only Arab script, we'd been starved of any kind of intellectual stimulation. There was nothing to do but wait.

One day my sister came into the room excitedly, closing the door behind her and showing me what had arrived in the delivery of vegetables that morning. The box had been lined with crumpled-up pieces of a glossy colour magazine which was written in English! We carefully smoothed out the creases of each of the dozen or so pages, overjoyed to discover that there was almost a quarter of a magazine. The dollar signs told us it was not English but an American magazine, but that didn't matter. Neither did it matter that most of the pages were adverts, because our eyes devoured the familiar letters that formed the words and were a link to our lives back home. I lovingly ran my fingers over the English script. It felt like a secret visit from an old friend. My heart ached dreadfully with that now accustomed pang of homesickness. Suddenly reminded of where we were, I told my sister that we had to make sure no one knew what we'd found. We smoothed out the precious pages again and folded them in two before hiding them inside our bedding. When we were alone, we'd take out those crumpled pages and read them over and over again, comforted by the familiar words and pictures that came from a society where we belonged.

It must have been a few days later we heard an exchange between my father and my second eldest *chacha*, the one who had encouraged me to change Farah's mind about Pube-head. Although they were clearly making an effort to keep their voices (and, it seemed, their tempers) in check, we managed to catch the gist of what was being said. Chacha was trying to placate my father, telling him they'd all done everything they could but it was clear that the situation had got out of hand. These girls were educated and spirited and had different expectations to those of Pakistani girls. My father asked him angrily if he was disparaging the way he had brought up his daughters, and Chacha quickly assured him that he wasn't criticising him. But people were beginning to ask questions, and the fact was, it wasn't right what was happening to us. If we'd been brought up as Pakistani girls then we'd have grown up knowing exactly what was expected of us. This hadn't happened. But my father was his elder and whatever he did was right, and Chacha said he was simply letting my father know his own feelings on the matter. My father ended the conversation abruptly by telling my uncle that he was right on that score; he was the elder and seeing as this was in fact *his* house, he would do exactly as he thought best where *his* daughters were concerned!

My sister and I listened with dread, knowing what effect it would have on my father to know that Chacha (and therefore probably the rest of the family) thought he was wrong. The idea that he'd lost *izzat* in the eyes of the family would be the worst thing that could happen to him. He'd be smarting with shame and anger, and we knew who would pay. We were right. We cowered as he stood in the doorway of our room, telling us that we'd destroyed his *izzat* and destroyed his life; then, turning off our electric fan, he and my mother went out.

We sat in the dark of our lonely room, not daring to speak, afraid that if we so much as breathed too loudly, something dreadful would happen. We were certain, in fact, that the awful thing we'd dreaded for the past few weeks was about to happen, and there was nothing we could do and no one we could turn to.

'I'm frightened,' my sister whispered.

'Me too,' I replied.

'They're going to murder us, aren't they?' she asked. I shuddered because, despite having dreaded this for weeks, the idea that we might go to sleep and never wake up again terrified me. We sat, holding hands, comforted by the other's presence.

Suddenly I got up and declared that if they were going to try and murder us in our sleep then I intended to put up a fight. Ordering her to help me, I pushed the bed across the room so we were facing the door. Somehow, facing a door through which a murderous intruder would come felt more comforting than falling asleep with your back to it. There was nothing to do now but wait. The unfamiliar position of the bed made us even more nervous and we both knew sleep would not come easily that night. But as we lay in bed, sleep was the last thing we wanted for we were too terrified to close our eyes, afraid that we'd never wake up again. For this could be the night – the night a silent executioner crept into the room and murdered us. There were no other sounds in the house and we guessed that everyone else must have gone out too. That didn't look good. We seemed to lie there for hours, waiting. Not daring to close our eyes, just waiting.

I sat up in bed and a sudden chill gripped my heart as I heard footsteps approaching. A light was snapped on in the courtyard and we heard my father's voice angrily remonstrating with my mother. Suddenly he was talking directly to us as his steps approached our room. I leapt out of bed, frantically turning this way and that in a desperate attempt to find a way out, but the window had bars on it. There was only one way out, and that was where my father stood, banging on the door, angrily asking how dare we try and lock him out! There was no inside lock, but tonight we'd been afraid of leaving it ajar as we'd been ordered to and had disobeyed by closing it shut. I tried to call out and tell him it wasn't locked, just closed, but my voice froze in my throat and no sound would come out. I backed away against the wall facing the door, flattening myself against it with a terrified scream as he hurled himself against the door and it flew open, banging violently as it hit the wall behind.

'*Sali! Haramzadi!* You've destroyed me. Made a mockery of me and shamed me in front of my family! I'm not going to leave you alive after this!' he cried as he lunged at me.

I recall so vividly the seconds that followed as the scene seemed to play itself out in slow motion. The strength in my body just drained away as if a switch had been turned off, shutting me down. I heard a voice inside my head say in English, 'No more,' as I felt myself sinking to the floor, and the last thing I heard just before I lost consciousness was my mother screaming at my father, 'What have you done? You've killed her!'

22

Burri Amma

The hottest places in Hell are reserved for those who in time of great moral crises maintain their neutrality.
Dante Alighieri (1265–1321)

One of the children brought a message from our eldest aunt who lived next door, asking us to come and visit her. My parents were nowhere to be found; therefore, believing it would be OK, we located our *dupattas*, stepped out of the house and walked the few yards next door to see Burri Amma (Elder Mother).

I have no memory of what had happened after I lost consciousness that night or of the days that followed. In retrospect, I think it's fair to assume that I'd had some kind of breakdown, which would explain the lost days. I also have no recollection of my sister and can only speculate what effect my breakdown would have had on her. The first memory I have subsequent to that terrible night was going to Burri Amma's house.

It was a very simple but neat house with white-washed walls and a mango tree in the garden. It was a wonderfully uncluttered and tranquil place. Best of all, while Amma adored her only son, other people's children irritated her, so they were sent away from the gate, making her house one of the few child-free places I knew in Pakistan. The peace was like balm to our shattered nerves.

Amma's history with the family interested me very much. Of the women who'd married into this family, she alone had stood up to her domineering mother-in-law while she'd been alive and refused to allow either herself or her good-natured husband to be bullied by Daddi. Despite suffering the obvious repercussions of being labelled disobedient and disrespectful by her in-laws, she'd always spoken her mind and suffered no fool, gladly or otherwise. She was the wife of the eldest son, and as such refused to allow anyone to browbeat her.

Although my father was the head of the family, he was in fact only the second son. He had an older brother whom we children called Burra Abba (Elder Father) as a term of respect, alluding to the fact that as the eldest brother he was higher in status than our father. However, Burra Abba was seen as slightly 'eccentric' and owing to a peculiarity in his character, which none of his siblings understood, this eldest brother chose to live apart from the rest of the family.

While still attached to the main family house, many years ago his section of the property had been partitioned off by a wall and a separate access was built. There, he lived in a separate family unit with his wife, Burri Amma, and his son, my cousin, Imran. The fact that they had an only child was also seen as a peculiarity, as most Pakistanis aspire to large families with many sons. Some said Burra Abba was simply eccentric. Others put it down to a wife who ruled her husband and didn't like being ruled by her in-laws. What it meant was that, for reasons of his own, Burra Abba 'resigned' from the family, earning his income elsewhere, so it was my father who was acknowledged as the eldest son, and, more importantly, after Dadda as the head of the family.

Over the years, there had been less and less contact between the two houses, to the point where many years had passed since either Burra Abba or Burri Amma had set foot inside Dadda's house next door. From what I'd heard, Imran had not been there since he was a boy, and he was now a man of almost thirty.

When we first arrived, my sister and I had been taken by Zainab to see Burri Amma, who'd welcomed her by reminding her with barely concealed malice of how many years it had been since my aunt had graced her home. My aunt had shifted uncomfortably. Amma's contempt for her husband's family was well known and usually expressed in derogatory terms and through colourful language when alluding to them. She remembered when she'd first come as a new bride to this family many years ago. Zainab had been only a child, but even then, Amma recalled, she'd been very outspoken, precocious and very much her mother's daughter in her personality. There was no love lost between them.

'So?' she said, addressing my sister and me in her distinctive rasping voice. 'Look at the state of you! When you arrived in Pakistan you looked so different. What have those *haramis* next door done to you?'

We must indeed have looked rather different compared to when we'd first arrived all those months ago. Life had seemed very different then. We'd been two strong-willed, spirited, fun-loving girls who took a pride in how we looked, always taking time each morning to style our hair and put on make-up, and carefully choosing what we'd wear that day. We'd felt indestructible.

Twelve weeks later those two girls had gone. I saw my sister's face and knew that I too wore that same sad, haunted expression. There was no fight left in me. I was only twenty-four, yet my hair had turned white at the temples. A heart that had once been full of joy, hope and expectation for the future was now filled with grief and a deep sense of loss that felt like a bereavement. Eyes that once sparkled with mischief now looked dead and filled too easily with tears. I was empty. I was an automaton, barely capable of remembering my own name. My spirit was almost broken.

My sister and I sat quietly, not moving, not speaking but simply watching her tidying her house. Amma didn't expect an answer because she knew. She bustled about, railing against this idiot and that idiot, as was her way, and began to vent spleen on everyone. Her waspish humour did not fool me. Amma was as objectionable as she could possibly be and wished people would leave her in peace and stop coming around and messing up her house. She seemed to be ignoring us, but she missed nothing.

'Why don't you have a sleep?' she suggested unexpectedly, in a softer voice than I'd ever heard her use. 'I've put a fresh sheet on my bed. Come and lie down here and close your eyes.' Then, seeing the sudden panic in our faces as we looked towards the outer door, she told us that she'd lock the gate and no one would be allowed to come in while we slept. She closed the shutters and pulled the door to, before placing her hands on our heads in a motherly gesture and telling us to go to sleep: she would watch over us. We obeyed her without question and, lying down, fell asleep almost instantly.

It was the first unbroken sleep either of us had had in weeks, and although it felt as though we'd only been sleeping for a short while, in reality we'd been fast asleep for many hours. I remember waking up much later in the day, feeling better than I'd felt in a long time. Amma's house was filled with light and a sense of serenity and well being and its tranquillity transferred itself to us, calming our shattered nerves. The doors were all open, letting the sunlight pour into the room, bringing with it the alluring scent of wood smoke. We got up and followed the scent out into the back courtyard where Amma sat, squatting on her hunkers, breaking small pieces of wood and feeding them into a stove.

'You're finally awake then? I thought you'd lie there sleeping all day and all night and make me sleep on the floor,' she grumbled unconvincingly. 'I expect now you'll tell me you're hungry and want me to feed you?'

'Yes please,' we nodded eagerly, thinking that when a person has had the best sleep they've had in a long time, it naturally follows that when they awake, they are hungrier than they've felt in a long time too. We asked her what she was doing and she told us she was lighting the stove to cook, complaining that she wasn't rich like Dadda and *chachas* next door. We'd never seen anyone cook on a wood stove and, fascinated, sat down beside her to watch.

Pakistanis are able to squat on their hunkers for long periods of time while eating or preparing and cooking meals. However, we found, like most Westerners, that our limbs were not used to adopting this essentially Eastern pose, which uses muscles we don't normally use. When we tried it we simply keeled over clumsily, much to Amma's amusement. She brought us a couple of stools that were about six inches off the ground so we could sit and chat with her.

She was cooking *rotis* and *bhindi* (okra), grumbling that we'd probably refuse to eat it because we were used to all that meat and chicken next door. We assured her that we didn't really like eating lots of meat and that *bhindi* was actually one of our favourites.

We stayed at Amma's all day, only returning next door in the evening. The following morning we awoke and, without even waiting to get dressed, picked up our clothes and wash bags and went straight over to Amma's. She was genuinely pleased to see us and cackled with laughter when we asked if we could have a wash and get ready in her house.

The bathroom was an outside room with a large enclosed

water tank and a bucket standing ready to be filled with water from the tap. With a jug, we drew the water from the full bucket and poured the deliciously cold water over ourselves. Even early in the morning the sun felt unbearably hot, making that outside wash one of the most invigorating experiences we'd ever had. We emerged smiling and ready for Amma's breakfast.

My parents had gone away for several days. We weren't told where they'd gone but my sister and I were both relieved by their absence. I dreaded their return: it would be the first time I'd seen them since that dreadful night. Meanwhile, we spent every day at Amma's, bathing, cooking, eating and resting there until it was time to return next door in the evening. Within just a couple of days at Amma's we felt so much better.

On the second morning, we had a visitor. Amma said my cousin Imran had come specially to see us. Because Amma must have told him we girls usually slept and bathed at her house, out of respect he stayed away, and we scarcely saw him as he was usually up and out before we arrived in the morning. From what I gathered, he came and went as he pleased, sometimes disappearing for days at a time. This particular day, Imran had come to eat his lunch with us. As is the custom in many Pakistani homes, we all four sat cross-legged on the floor on the rush mat that Amma had spread out for the meal, eating *rotis*, spicy vegetables and *dhal*.

Amma always complained that we wouldn't like her simple cooking but it was exactly the kind of food we liked. Besides, we told her, Shahnaz Chachi was away and Haseen Chachi was doing the cooking and she was terrible! Amma said that was what you got when you married someone who was more interested in spending her husband's money. Chacha was a fool because he preferred to have a beautiful wife waiting for him when he got home rather than a good meal. We giggled as we described how vain she was (even her name meant 'beautiful'), spending all day shopping, making herself look nice, then shortly before Chacha came home she'd throw together some revolting concoction that even the servants wouldn't eat. He never complained, simply telling her to get herself and the children ready and they'd eat out. Amma uttered a few well-chosen expletives about male vanity. She amused and shocked us by using swear words that we'd only heard men use. Imran told us that our Dadda had bought beautiful women for all his sons.

I liked my cousin, who had us all laughing at stories of when I was little, before my elder sister and I were taken to England. Amma said that he'd always had a soft spot for me because we three had been the only children in those days. I was always crying and eating dirt. I laughed and told her I'd already heard that story. She said I spent a lot of time in their house despite the fact that Daddi objected violently. It was strange to think that I'd spent time playing in this house when I was a toddler. It was stranger still to imagine this house was ever a part of the house next door.

Imran was the closest thing I ever had to an older brother. My own elder brother, had he lived, could have been best friends with him. He spoke to me fondly and indulgently, as an elder brother does to a much-loved sister, and I found myself hanging on to his every word, just as I'd apparently done as a child. I couldn't help wondering what difference it would have made to my life having Imran looking out for me while I was growing up. He told me I used to follow him around like a lost kitten and he always thought of me as his little sister, even after we'd left and gone to live in England.

That evening, back at Dadda's house, my *chachas* warned us that Imran was a thoroughly bad lot and involved in all kinds of things, yet exactly what those things were was not actually divulged.

As the *chachas* hadn't actually forbidden us from going next door, we continued to spend most of our time there. We scarcely saw Burra Abba at all, as he left in the morning and came home only to sleep at night. I got the impression he was a little afraid of Amma, who seemed to regard her husband with the same contempt in which she held the rest of his family. But then it was no surprise that he was wary of her, because everyone seemed to be. She had a vicious tongue and a bad word to say about everyone in the family she'd married into – she didn't single anyone out specially but simply hated everyone with equal venom, telling us that our father was the best of a bad lot. However, her only son, who was himself a product of that family, she loved with a passion. It was while talking of him that Amma told me about the warrior ghost.

Apparently, a great warrior had fallen in battle many centuries ago on the spot where the house now stood. It was his spirit that now watched over my cousin. This Baba, who was supposed to live in a part of her house, always protected Imran as it had done since he was a child.

Suddenly the loneliness and grief of the past few months overwhelmed me as I wished with all my heart that I too had a protector, dead, divine or otherwise. I'd not allowed myself to dwell on it too much, but I knew my parents would be back any day now and it was with a heavy sense of foreboding that I awaited their return, not knowing what would happen next and dreading what I already knew could happen.

It brought home to me how helpless and alone we were. I'd sought help from members of the family but they hadn't dared to intervene. The only one who had the authority was Dadda but he took no part in it, only shuffling around the house grumbling about how 'Acha' had brought this *gurrh burrh* (trouble) to his home. He was out most of the day, and when he was home he turned an extremely deaf ear to what was going on, seeing nothing and hearing nothing. If they didn't help, I thought, perhaps this Baba would.

As the daughter of a Muslim household, I'd grown up with stories of the supernatural world which are an intrinsic part of Eastern folklore and mysticism and a major part of the lives of Muslims. To a Western person, this is perhaps a concept that is difficult to grasp because the West has a very different approach to the idea of demons, ghosts, witches and the supernatural. These things are not embedded into everyday life, so a Westerner might dismiss them as belonging to an earlier pagan age of druids and spirits, or belonging in books or Hollywood films. An Eastern person, however, accepts them without question. To most Easterners, folklore, mystique and the spiritual world pervade every practical and spiritual aspect of their lives.

I thought about the Baba and wondered whether he would help us if I prayed to him. He was Imran's protector, but if Imran was fond of me, surely the Baba would extend his protection to me. I could think of little else and my fear of being murdered by my father overcame my terror of a ghost, so when Amma was busy with visitors I crept into the room where she said his spirit lived, to talk to him. I was so afraid that I couldn't stop shaking as I told him how my sister and I needed a protector because we were all alone with no one to help us. We didn't want to die out here so far from home. The tears began to flow as I pleaded with him, whoever he was, to help us.

I don't know what I expected to happen – whether I expected some supernatural being to appear or perhaps to be filled with some sense of hope or inspiration. What I hadn't expected was to be overcome by an inexplicable terror that suddenly gripped me, causing me to turn and flee.

As I ran from this small room out into the brilliant sunshine, I knew that whether or not the Baba's spirit existed, this was not the answer. I just didn't know where to look for it.

Meanwhile, I sought out the safety of Amma's presence and sat down beside her to help prepare for dinner. The guests had gone and my sister and I quietly sat shelling peas with Amma. As I watched her closely, I realised with a pang that Amma loved me. The love she'd had for me as a little girl had been held in safe-keeping for all these years and was now given to the adult I'd become. I was so much like her, in character, in temperament and far more in shape, colouring and looks than I was like my own mother who'd given birth to me. Beneath that prickly, cantankerous exterior that seemed to dislike everyone, we were very much alike. A thought suddenly struck me.

'Amma, are you my real mother?'

She howled with laughter, asking if that was what I thought or was it what I wished for, adding maliciously that she'd give anything for my *harami* parents to have been here when I'd asked it. She chuckled that the *phaeris* (fairies) had probably brought me because she'd always thought I was too clever and good-looking to belong to that *haramzada* family! We all three laughed. Amma's irreverent way of talking offensively about everyone never failed to entertain us. Suddenly my laughter froze, as my heart lurched at the sight of my father striding grimly across the courtyard. He looked furious.

'Get out!' he ordered, pointing next door. 'Get out and get back!'

My sister and I looked desperately at Amma, who began loudly remonstrating with my father to let us stay because we were doing no harm. He held up his hand to stop her from speaking.

'Bhabi, don't say anything more!' She was his elder but he was respectfully warning her stay out of his business and let him deal with his own daughters. From the dangerous tone in his voice we knew better than to question him and, obeying him, fled. Back next door, he told us we would not be allowed to disrespect him and shame him any more.

'*Bas!* Enough is enough!' he cried, telling us he'd deal with us once and for all. Then pushing us into our room he banged the door shut.

We didn't know what was going to happen to us, but whatever it was we had no strength left to fight any more. Our parents had nothing to lose and everything to gain if we were dead. I told Farah about the Baba but she was scornful, saying they were all as bad as each other. Even if we knew how to pray, there was no point trying to pray to Allah or anyone because no one cared about us. In the eyes of Allah we were bad and deserved to die. No one cared about us, she said bitterly.

She was right. Aside from the people we'd already asked for help, we'd written numerous letters to friends, our brothers, our employers and our sister and brother-in-law Charles, telling them of our plight and begging for help. Charlie's brother was a journalist and we wanted him to contact the media to tell everyone what was happening to us and help us escape. But not one single person had replied. We were to learn later from my father that these letters had all been intercepted and destroyed so they never reached England.

But I needed desperately to believe in Something or Someone. I refused to believe that there was no one. Some hours later, I stopped in the open courtyard, asking myself desperately who we could turn to to beg for help. Who was there left?

Then without warning I clearly heard a voice, saying, 'Ask me.'

For one awful moment I thought I was being asked to go back to the Baba, a prospect that terrified me and which I would have been too scared to do even if I'd been allowed to go back next door to Amma's. I was confused because this voice did not frighten me, it just puzzled me. Like all Muslims I knew that there was only one divine being; the Christians called him God and we called him 'Allah'. It didn't really matter what he was called, because I'd been told he was an all-powerful and fearsome being who demanded obedience and hated those who were disobedient. Why would he speak to a bad lot like me who was destined for hell? I thought I was going mad, wondering if it was Allah speaking to me, but somehow it didn't 'sound' like him. The voice wasn't awesome, mighty or terrifying. Just quiet. But if it wasn't Allah, then whose voice was it?

'Ask me,' the voice said again.

It was a quiet, gentle voice that didn't fill me with terror but made me want to trust and obey. But I didn't know how to obey. The only kind of praying I knew about involved ritual washing, cleansing and chanting verses of the Koran, none of which I knew how to do. Yet, obeying an instinct I didn't know I had, for the first time in my life I went down on my knees, my hand upwards in supplication.

'Help us!' I wept. 'I don't know how to pray and I don't know who you are but we're all alone. No one will stand up to my father, they're all afraid of him. Please send someone to help us. Please send someone!'

I rose and wiped my tears away, overwhelmed with a comforting sense that suddenly I wasn't alone any more and that my prayers had reached Someone, whoever He was. I was so certain that I'd been heard that I returned to Farah to tell her that help was coming and everything would be all right. She just looked at me as though I'd finally lost my mind – which, under the circumstances and after all that had happened, wasn't really too much of a surprise.

We'd heard our parents talking late into the night and knew everything would be coming to a head. They had been shocked by people's feelings that it was their fault we'd turned out the way we had. This was something they hadn't expected and found hardest to accept. Knowing how they felt, we passed a restless night, fearful of every sound, speculating on whether we'd be murdered in our room or taken somewhere.

We both woke early with a heavy heart and a sense of fear and foreboding. No one came to the room where we sat alone, not knowing what to say. There was nothing left to say.

Suddenly, there seemed to be a bustle of activity and excitement outside. The children came running into the house, crying, 'Imran *bhai* is coming, Imran *bhai* is coming!' We rushed to the window and saw it was indeed Imran who was coming through the gate. Everyone was taken aback as it was the first time he'd set foot inside that door for many years. He took a few steps then, venturing no further, began to call loudly: '*Chacha*! England-wallah *Chacha*! Come outside, I want to talk to you!'

My father came out to meet him, but before he had a chance to say anything Imran put up the palm of his hand, preventing him from speaking, saying that it was better they went inside to speak in private. The most private place was in the courtyard just outside our room so we were able to hear everything. And what we heard was beyond belief.

Speaking quietly and respectfully, Imran told my father that he'd heard what had been happening here. He knew everything and had come to tell him that it wasn't right.

'I give you *izzat* because you are my *chacha*,' he said, 'but I'm respectfully warning you that if you lay a hand against my sisters again, if you harm them, I'll hear about it. If that happens I'll forget that you are my elder and that I am younger than you. *Acha nahin hoga!* It won't go well with you!' Then we heard him get up without another word. Pressing our faces against the bars of the window, we saw him cross the yard, throwing a glance in the direction of our room, and then he was gone, leaving everyone in stunned silence.

No one was more stunned than I was. Help had arrived. But it had come from such an unexpected quarter that it was hard to believe. None of those who could have used their authority had dared to help us – not my grandfather, not my uncles nor my aunt. Help had come from a son of the family, a nephew who'd been willing to challenge his own uncle, an elder of the family! It had been done quietly and respectfully, but a threat of repercussion had nevertheless been issued. I had no doubt whatsoever in my mind that now Imran had publicly declared his protection, no one would dare to harm us. To us it was nothing short of a miracle. My prayer had been answered!

Suddenly, things began to happen so fast that the speed with which they took place seemed in itself to be a miracle. It was as if those terrible weeks and months had never happened. My parents knew they'd failed, and a day later my father was on his way back to England, with my mother and us two girls booked on a later flight.

The remaining days passed without incident, our only concern being that our mother would kill herself. She had failed in her mission to get either of us married off and faced the shame and humiliation of having two daughters over whom, everyone had seen, neither parent had any control. The only emotion we saw in her lifeless eyes was hatred. That look frightened us, and even at the airport we never felt safe: anxious for the moment when we'd finally be called to our gate, terrified she'd change her mind and drag us away out of the airport and make us disappear permanently, we sat as near to the gate as possible, to make a run for it as soon as we were called. We jumped every time anyone approached us, in case someone had been paid to kidnap us before we reached the plane.

During that time we could scarcely bear to speak to or even look at our mother. She sat silent and motionless, grief etched deeply into every line of a face that had once been beautiful, and we couldn't bear to be near her. I no longer feared or hated her. I felt nothing.

Finally we were aboard the plane. It seemed like a lifetime since we had arrived in Pakistan, over fourteen long weeks ago. We were finally going home.

Part 5
Living in the void

23

Hendon

True friendship is a plant of slow growth and must undergo and withstand the shocks of adversity before it is entitled to the appellation.

George Washington (1732–99)

Years ago there was an American TV series called *Charlie's Angels*. The title credits always began, 'Once upon a time there were three little girls at the police academy. Their names were . . .'

Perhaps this chapter ought to begin in a similar way, except we girls were not three, but four, and while we joined the police within months of each other, the foundations of our lifelong friendships really began at Goldhawk Road police section house near Shepherds Bush. However, it was at police training school in Hendon, north London, that most of us met.

There were four intakes at Hendon at any one time, with a new intake arriving every month and named according to a different colour: red, green, yellow and blue. Melanie arrived in a red intake; Farah was blue while Susan and I followed in the next red intake. The reason that Farah got in before me was because when it came to the running part of the fitness test, she ran like a gazelle while I ran like a buffalo and had to retake it. (Years later I'd be diagnosed with a congenital heart condition, but no one suspected this at the time.)

When Melanie Elizabeth French was in her teens, her father,

a devastatingly handsome Air Vice Marshall in the RAF, had presented her with a new mother; a charismatic New Zealander called Phillippa, formidable and elegant and a consummate hostess and fitting consort for her high-flying husband. She also taught me how to make the most fabulous sticky spare ribs.

Melanie left home at sixteen to become a nanny before she joined the police. Farah and I first met her when we moved into Goldhawk Road.

The thing we remember best about Melanie in those early days was that her inability to cook her own meals was matched only by her remarkable ability to appear just in the nick of time to help herself to other people's. Furthermore, she never actually showed up when the meal was being prepared. Melanie's radar was far more finely tuned and completely infallible in this respect. Regardless of whether it was day or night, no sooner had a meal been dished up, it was possible to count out the seconds before familiar footsteps could be heard trotting up the corridor and a willowy blonde figure would appear in the doorway.

'Oooh! Food!' she'd squeak, sniffing expectantly.

Then there was Susan, whose middle name was Penelope. I'd never met anyone called Penelope before. In fact there are only two other characters I'd ever come across who were called Penelope. The first was Penelope, the wife of Ulysses, the Greek who went off on a twenty-year-long lads' night out, building Trojan horses, fighting Cyclops and being seduced by Sirens while she stayed home doing tapestry. She was a bit of a door-mat and not very inspiring. The other one was Lady Penelope, the Thunderbirds puppet; aristocrat, spy: feistier, if rather wooden.

Susan Penelope Owers-Parton-Jacob was an altogether less wooden and far more interesting character than either of the two fictional Penelopes. While she was in the same red intake as me, our paths rarely crossed as we were in different classes; we scarcely knew each other well enough even to be on greeting terms. It was when I found her regulation issue handbag in the canteen, where she'd left it, that we almost became friends. Checking inside for identification, I recognised her from the picture on her warrant card and recalled that although she seemed to be really popular, she always stopped to smile and say hello to me. I was late for class but knowing that she'd get into trouble for losing her card, I made an effort to find her and return her handbag. She was charming and thanked me.

'Posh but nice' I thought, thinking what a pity it was that she had so many friends already because I would have liked to have got to know her better. I never imagined at the time how important Susan's friendship would become in my life.

She was engaged at that time and subsequently moved to the other side of London shortly after her wedding, which Farah and Melanie attended. Although I lost touch with her for a while, I heard about her from time to time because she had been posted to Kensington with Melanie. Five years later, she came back into my life when I needed her. Since then she has always been there, giving me friendship and support through some of my darkest moments. It seems hard to imagine a time when Susan and I were not friends.

My sister and I had joined the Met because it gave us a sense of security to belong to the police force, where we thought we'd be safe. In retrospect it was not a good idea, but at the time we could not think rationally. Over a year had elapsed since our escape from Pakistan, most of which had passed in a blur. My sister had been dragged back home with my mother. Because I dared not disobey outright and refuse to come home, I'd bought myself extra time by begging to be allowed to pack up all our things and arrange for them to be transported back home, which of course I had no intention of doing. I'd rather have slashed my wrists and slowly bled to death than go back home again, and desperation had resurrected a lying tongue and scheming heart.

Returning to the empty flat, knowing my father had been there in my absence, was soul-destroying. My landlord had not had any communication from us for months and it was hardly surprising that I came back to discover an eviction notice for non-payment of rent. My father had also had the telephone, gas and electricity disconnected, opened all my mail and had some of my things removed. I stood in the middle of the sitting room staring in despair at my shattered life.

I picked up another pile of letters from the doormat, throwing them on to the table with the others. These were unopened and had obviously arrived after my father had left. A bright yellow envelope caught my eye. My heart sank as I opened it to see that it was a Tele-Message from the BBC. It seemed they were making yet another attempt to get in touch with me, having tried in vain to contact me several times. I frantically searched the pile of opened letters on the table for any earlier correspondence from the BBC, but in vain. Either the letters had not been received or someone had taken them. But what did it matter now? It was too late. The job would have been given to someone else. It was gone, and with it my dreams of a career in broadcasting with the BBC.

I had no money, no job and soon I'd have no home. I sat alone on the floor of that empty flat for hours, my mind and body already so numb with grief and a terrible sense of loss that I never even noticed the dark and chill of the night closing in.

Some days later, I called the BBC to tell them why I'd failed to respond to their Tele-Message. In my heart of hearts I was hoping the job was still mine, but in reality I knew it would have long been offered to the next person eagerly waiting in the wings for an opportunity like this. To my surprise, a short time later I was contacted by journalists who wanted my story. However, I was falling to pieces: I could barely hold myself together to get through each day and was in no state to speak to anyone about what had happened. I'd stay in bed for days at a time, hardly eating or sleeping and crying all the time.

Within a few weeks, to my parents' fury, my sister returned to London and moved back in. We were both in shock and needed to be with each other in order to try and make sense of everything that had happened, but we lived in constant dread of my father turning up at the flat to drag us back home. When it did happen it was no less traumatic because we were expecting it.

Charlotte had given me back my job at the promotion company and that gave me a sense of purpose and reason to get up in the morning. That evening, I'd been persuaded to go out for a meal with Sam, a police-officer friend. I was not good company: even when I could be persuaded to go out I was distracted and anxious, suspicious of doorways and corners, living in a constant state of terror of my father turning up anywhere and at any time. I did not enjoy the evening and couldn't wait to return home. As Sam walked me to the front door, I saw my sister leaning out of the bedroom window, frantically waving her arms. My heart lurched as I heard her call, 'Get away, Dad's here!'

My instinct was to turn tail and run. I wanted to get back into the car and tell Sam to drive, drive anywhere so long as he got me away from my father. But there was no way I could have left my sister to deal with him on her own. Telling Sam to go, I went in to face the music. To my dismay he followed me into the flat, saying that while he had no idea of what was going on, it didn't take a genius to see that I was clearly terrified and he had no intention of leaving until he knew we were both safe.

To be quite honest, had my father walked in on us to discover Farah and me studiously engaged in reading Tolstoy's *War and Peace*, it wouldn't have made a difference. But it was just bad luck that he'd arrived unannounced that evening to discover Farah alone and me out somewhere. It was no more than he expected that when I did eventually return it was to walk in with a six-foot *gora* following just behind me. His cold fury frightened me even more than his rages had done, as he ordered me to pack my bags because he'd come to take us back home. Enough was enough, he declared, looking Sam up and down in disgust, assuming, as I knew he would, that he was one of my many lovers.

My sister and I were rooted to the spot, too terrified even to move. Sam stepped between my father and us, telling him that we girls didn't look very happy at the prospect of going anywhere with him and that if we didn't want to, he couldn't make us. My father snapped that he should mind his own business because we were his daughters and he could do what he liked with us. Sam informed him that this was our home and that unless we gave him permission to be here he was, in fact, trespassing, and ignoring my father's ranting, he turned to both of us and asked whether we wished our father to leave. We were so scared we could barely move our heads, let alone speak, and my father grabbed my sister in an attempt to drag her with him.

At this point Sam informed him that he was a police officer and warned him that if he didn't take his hands off my sister and leave, he'd have no choice but to arrest him. My father continued to rant and threaten us, and next thing we knew, Sam was cautioning him and telephoning for the station to send a vehicle. It was like a bad dream that was becoming a nightmare. My father's anger turned to disbelief, then dismay, calling to each of us in turn. Then, as he was being led away he started to plead with us not to let this happen. I felt sick and wished I was as far away as possible. His voice tormented us all night, calling our names, and we scarcely slept at all.

Sam called us next morning to tell us that he'd asked for my father to be put into a detention room rather than locked up in a cell, which is where he'd spent the night. He'd been no trouble, just very subdued, and had been released without being charged in the morning. We didn't have to worry about him coming back to the flat because he'd gone straight home.

We received an angry telephone call from my brothers later that day, demanding to know what the hell we'd done. My father had come home distraught and had sat down and wept, refusing to talk about what had happened. They asked how we could have had our own father arrested.

That was the question we'd been asking ourselves all day as we woke up to the enormity of it all. We were still numb with shock and could barely speak of it to each other. However, the outcome of that incident was that my family told us we were dead to them and finally left us alone for a long time after.

A year on, and we'd been evicted from the flat. Until we moved into police training school at Hendon we were broke and homeless, staying in one place and then another, with our belongings scattered around London in a variety of friends' spare rooms and garages.

After Pakistan, I'd wanted nothing to do with the Asian side of me and rejected everything that connected me to the culture into which I'd been born. I burned anything that was associated with my Pakistani culture, and rejected the language and the religion; had it been possible, I'd have bleached my skin from brown to white in order to wipe away all visible evidence of my race too.

I was adamant that I'd never marry a Pakistani, even if there was one who'd condescend to think me worthy of him. I was no longer Muslim, nor Pakistani: I was English, and as such would live an English lifestyle and adopt English standards as my own. I'd no longer feel any sense of loyalty towards either my family or the culture into which I'd been born. My Asian culture had treated me abominably and rejected me first, so now I was turning my back on it!

I had this aching emptiness inside me, a lonely, overwhelming sense of grief, loss and pain. But this pain was nothing compared with the rage and fury that stalked me. I'd try as hard as I could to behave normally, but then something innocuous would trigger off a reaction and those feelings would creep up behind me unexpectedly, consuming me, causing me to wail and hurl myself against walls and smash things up. These episodes would leave me utterly drained, and I'd crawl into bed wracked with anguish and filled with self-loathing, despairing at my inability to hold my life together and exhausted by the strain of having to face the world in a dazzling display of bravado and normality that I felt was expected of me. But by now I'd begun to lose any sense of what was normal. Keeping a lid on my feelings in public was hard but, with a few exceptions, I was able to do so. The most memorable episode when I failed to keep my angst in check happened when I started at Hendon.

During one of the first classroom sessions, we had to introduce ourselves, giving a potted history of our lives to date. The class consisted of people from very diverse backgrounds, ranging from police cadets who'd joined straight from school and thought they knew everything there was to know about anything worth knowing, to shop assistants and an ex-Marine who'd served with Prince Edward during his short time with the Marines.

When it was my turn, I didn't have a clue what I was going to say, and the very last thing I expected was to suddenly find myself telling this class of strangers about what had happened to my sister and me in Pakistan. No one spoke and no one looked me in the eye and I knew I'd just made a terrible mistake. The outcome of it was that some days later I was taken aside by the class tutor who told me that my class had collectively decided they didn't feel comfortable with me and believed I was a fantasist, attention-seeker and liar.

In retrospect, at that time of my life I was not emotionally equipped to deal with a career such as the police force. I'd joined for entirely the wrong reasons and had not recovered from the trauma of that experience. Having survived so much, what I really needed was medical help and counselling; I subsequently had a breakdown, which is why I cannot recall much after the night my father was arrested. But I believed that I was doing the right thing by getting on with my life in the best way I could and putting the past firmly behind me.

For its own part, the police force certainly never made any effort to make things easy for either my sister or me. They paid lip service to being ethically-friendly yet in practice placed as many obstacles in our way as they could. I recall being told by one of the officers assigned to oversee me during my street duties period that you should never trust a Pakistani.

'They're dishonest and deceitful and you can't trust them as far as you can throw them!' he declared.

In another incident, we'd arrested a highly emotional black man who'd just been unceremoniously dumped by his white, middle-aged and upper-class boyfriend, at that moment hiding behind the furniture. The prisoner was six foot five tall and it took three officers to hold him down. Under the circumstances I didn't think it was a very good idea for my sergeant to repeatedly prod this distressed and angry young man in the chest and tell him he was a very naughty boy. His size didn't frighten me, and I was easily able to calm him down and talk him into the back of the van, saving *him* from a further charge of assaulting a police officer and my sergeant from the hiding that I privately thought he deserved. He, moron that he was, turned on me, telling me there was no point trying to show him up because I was only there as window-dressing for the politicians.

Nevertheless, I cannot write a story like this without reference to my time in the police force because Hendon training school was an important time in my life, as it was there that friendships and relationships were to be forged that would affect the rest of my life. Things changed from that point on.

Farah had also changed a great deal. Like me, she too had rejected her Asian culture, but we differed in how our experience in Pakistan had affected us. I'd been filled with sadness and a sense of loss, as if something had broken irreparably. For my sister however, outwardly at least, Pakistan and our experiences in the police force had given her character a hard and cynical edge that drew comment from my ex-boss Charlotte, who, observant as always, remarked on how bitter and uncompromising she seemed to have become.

In the years since, Melanie, Susan, Farah and I have collectively shared a close bond that can only be appreciated by a group of women who have supported each other through serious illness, three births, two divorces, five marriages and a death. We first met when we were in our twenties: boyfriends, fiancés and even one or two husbands have come and gone, but we remain. We have disagreed with each other and even fallen out, but now we are in our forties we remain tied by friendships that have carried us through life's pain, joys and grief for almost twenty years. Our friendship is precious, and therefore that time when we first met, all those years ago at Hendon police training school, will remain special and something for which I will always be grateful.

24

To have loved and lost . . .

*No woman ever falls in love with a man unless
she has a better opinion of him than he deserves.*
Ed Howe (1853–1937)

Hendon was also important to me for another life-changing reason.

He arrived in the green intake a month after me. His face was very familiar to me, for it was the very same face that I'd carried in my head since I was in my teens, when I'd daydreamed about the big, handsome husband who would protect me from my father. It was so real to me that I wondered what had taken him so long. The moment he first appeared, carrying the regulation black kit bag issued to all police recruits, I pointed to him and said to my friend, standing on the up-escalator next to me, 'See that guy down there? I'm going to marry him.'

It was love at first sight. He was the most handsome man I'd ever seen. His friend Taffy fancied Farah, so (unbeknown to her) I shamelessly offered Taffy a date with her in exchange for information and discovered that he'd just returned from a six-month trip backpacking round India, where he'd lived on rice and peas and learned only one solitary phrase, '*bahot garam chai*' (very hot tea). However, what made selling my sister worthwhile was learning that he fancied me back. Within five days we were an item.

Two weeks later, we spent Easter bank holiday on a trip to

Snowdonia, staying in a beautiful lakeside village called Llanberis. We climbed Snowdon and were only prevented from reaching the peak by the deep snow that still covered its higher slopes. I was in love and happier than I'd ever been in my life. We spent every free moment together, and within just a short time I couldn't imagine how I'd ever existed without him in my life.

The following year I left the police and was back working for Charlotte and earning a lot of money. He'd also left and by that time we had a flat and were saving to get married. Love blinded me to the warning signs that were so easy to see with hindsight. I recall one bizarre conversation where he'd said that in India, during the days of the Raj, men could have their cake and eat it. They married plain white women who were socially acceptable and indulged their real passions with the Indian women whom they really desired. He'd told me the year before that he loved me but didn't want us to have children. That had devastated me: I felt rejected that he wanted to marry me yet didn't want to have babies, so I packed my suitcase and walked out on him, only for him to run after me begging me to stay. But as much as I loved him, I was adamant that unless he was totally committed to me, it was better to end it now.

'What reason do I have to stay?' I cried at him. 'If you don't want us to have children together, why do you want me?' As I angrily turned away towards the car, dragging my case behind me, he called out, 'Because you're the only woman I've ever loved!'

That stopped me in my tracks. Perhaps I stopped because our private life had suddenly become very public to a small group of passers-by who'd stopped to witness this. But it was more likely because he was not normally a sentimental man given to declaring his feelings loudly in public.

'Go on, love, take him back!' someone called.

So I did go back to him, having been assured by him that we were OK. However, a year later he walked out saying he couldn't go through with it. I was devastated. It felt as though someone had turned out the lights. I couldn't eat or sleep and even breathing took effort. I'd never felt so empty and alone in my entire life.

Losing him had been enough of a blow, without being tortured through my sleeping and waking hours by trying to make sense of the things he'd said to me. I'd turned my back on everything that had been connected with my race, religion and culture. It hadn't been difficult because I'd never felt that I belonged or had been wanted by that side of me. Now I'd been told by the man I loved and wanted to marry that although he loved me he didn't want to marry me. He was English and I was Asian and we were too different. It was so ironic that he couldn't see past the differences in our backgrounds and saw only the part of me that I'd already rejected. Having chosen that Western side of me, I felt that was where I belonged. I felt as English as him. I'd been brought up in the same society as him, had spoken the same language and mixed with the same people, yet he'd told me that despite my Englishness, people would look at me and see only that I was Asian. Now I'd been cruelly thrust into a racial, cultural and spiritual no-man's land. I belonged nowhere and to no one.

Within nine months he'd got married. It had been a big white wedding, and what made it so unbearable was to be told that she was the first girl he went out with after me. What wounded me even more was being told by him that he knew on his wedding day that the marriage wouldn't last; he'd compared the two of us and had asked himself what on earth he'd done. I was beautiful, funny and fun to be with, but ultimately he preferred to marry someone who 'fitted in'. Furthermore, he said it was too late to turn back the clock because she wasn't as strong as me. Whatever happened to me, I had a core of steel running through me and would always land on my feet. Then he was gone.

Losing him felt like bereavement. Indeed, bereavement would have been kinder, for had he simply died I'd have been able to grieve and remember the good times and what we had meant to each other. He'd be in another place with the imprint of my love on his soul, not walking around laughing, eating and sleeping with someone else. I would at least have had the comfort of knowing I'd been the love of his life.

For weeks, I slept on the sofa because it was too painful to lie awake all night in the bed we'd shared missing him next to me. His presence haunted me. Every time I went to the wardrobe, I'd get a waft of his aftershave. Or I'd be in the supermarket and my hand would automatically reach out for his favourite things. Once I woke up and thought I could hear him in the bathroom, humming in that tuneless way of his, tapping his razor against the sink. For a moment I thought the past few months had all been a bad dream and he hadn't really left, and I flew out of bed calling his name, only to reach the bathroom and find it hadn't been a dream and he really was gone.

I never felt that the chapter had closed on our relationship and knew it wouldn't end there. Instinct told me that it was not simply wishful thinking: he was meant to be a part of my life. Meeting him had seemed to be my destiny, yet I did not understand why loving him was so painful. Only years later would I discover the answer.

Despite feeling my heart had been ripped out from inside me, I was determined not to let my life fall apart and for a while at least, I was successful. Few knew the extent of my real inner pain and grief as, outwardly, I was in control. I changed my job, joined a health club, got fit and lost weight. I also changed my hairstyle and my entire wardrobe of clothes, then determinedly accepted every invitation that came my way and pursued a hectic social life. As always, I appeared the life and soul of the party.

But beneath the shallow façade of my loud, extrovert exterior, it wasn't necessary to scratch too deep to discover the insecurity and self-loathing that drove me; I veered from depression to despair, surrounded by people, yet feeling like the loneliest, most unhappy person in the world. I couldn't accept love or kindness, believing these things were for others and not for me, convinced that I deserved to be unhappy because my mother had been right and I was born 'bad'.

I'd been rejected by my family for being Western and now I had been rejected for being Eastern. So I threw myself at men who were demonstrably unsuitable, always pursuing; never allowing myself to be pursued. Jas was one of the good guys. He never failed to be there for me when I needed him, offering me his broad, dependable shoulders to cry on when yet another unsuitable man broke my heart, listening in grim silence, muscles on his jaw tensed as he angrily demanded to know why I hurled myself from one hard place to another, bent upon self-destruction when I knew he loved me. His frustration was plain to see, yet I was afraid to let him get close to me. I could not marry Jas for the same reason that I could not marry anyone who was good and kind. I didn't know how to explain that I was damaged goods and there was something inside me that was broken, a feeling that if I could never be happy, how could I ever make anyone else happy?

One afternoon, alone in my flat, my eyes alighted on the bottles of wine that had been left over from a recent dinner party and suddenly it seemed like a really good idea to drink and take an overdose. Staggering to the bathroom, I suddenly asked myself what on earth I was doing and did I really want to kill myself or was it just a cry for help? I knew I had to stop this before it went any further and called Melanie who drove straight over and let herself into the flat with the spare keys.

'What have you done?' she cried, believing I'd taken an overdose. Discovering the empty wine bottles and realising that I was drunk, she helped me stagger down two flights of stairs, threw me into her mini and practically carried me through the doors of my doctor's surgery, demanding that I get help. Later, after I'd sobered up, I recall sitting in front of my doctor, a stunning Arab lady, who shook her head sadly, asking me why I was doing this to myself. I remember feeling that I'd have quite happily walked into the path of an oncoming bus if only I'd had the courage.

In May 1992, eighteen months after the break up, I was still ignoring my doctor's advice to see a counsellor, making a four hour round trip to work in my job with HM Customs & Excise and generally under immense pressure in a job I hated. The breakdown that followed was inevitable. I was a physical and emotional wreck. I'd lost my job, my periods had stopped and I had a severe eating disorder where frequent binging sessions were swiftly followed by violent bouts of self-induced vomiting. I'd lost all sense of normality. The irony was that, by their own admission, I was envied by many of my friends for the confidence, aggression and the control I had in my personal life over the men who seemed to throw themselves at me. Only Melanie knew that the confidence was sheer bravado, the aggression, a mask for my weakness and that the boyfriends were kept at arms length and I always went home alone.

After the breakdown, I finally saw a counsellor who directed me towards a positive goal. After almost nine years and not without misgivings, I returned to university. I already had an established circle of friends and a life independent of university so I didn't really integrate much. Then the chance came up to go to Denmark to study Public and International Law. While I was reluctant to go, Melanie bullied me into going, saying that it was a good way of breaking out of my safe, comfortable routine. So, with a great deal of apprehension about my ability to cope alone in a foreign country, even more about how the Scandinavians would take to a British Asian like me, I went to Denmark.

Going to Copenhagen Business School was the best decision I could have made. Copenhagen was wonderful. The country breathed new life into me. I loved everything about Denmark. I loved the people. I loved the city; its coffee bars, its sculptures, its shops and its nightlife. I felt myself melt into Copenhagen, letting this new environment transform the wreck I'd been.

Four years after the split, I'd recovered from my breakdown and was happier and more at peace with myself than I'd ever been; fitter, healthier and looking better than I'd done in years. I was happy. Every woman who has had her heart broken needs a passionate, feel-good relationship to heal her shattered confidence. Such a relationship is what helps her make the transition from the despair that she will never love or be loved again, to the hope that one day, perhaps, she just might. I'd had a wonderful passionate affair with a big handsome Belgian that had proved that I was ready and able to sustain a real committed relationship. I knew that Marc was my transitional relationship and expected nothing more. The problem hadn't been me at all and I felt that I needed to tell my ex that, so I wrote to him and told him.

To have loved and lost . . .

Two days later, and totally unexpectedly, his letter arrived. His marriage was over, he was divorced and he'd been trying to find me. I subsequently learned that Melanie and Farah had refused to tell him where I was, deciding I was happy in Copenhagen and if we were meant to be together, fate would step in. Not knowing any of this, I'd set the wheels of fate in motion by sending him that letter. He wrote again telling me he wanted to see me, that he'd never stopped thinking about me and missed me. Now all I could think of was getting on a plane and going back to London to be with him again.

25

Being a single mother

He who has a why to live can bear almost any how.
Friedrich Nietzsche (1844–1900)

Three years had passed since I returned from Copenhagen and my life had taken a very different turn. Melanie and Farah had been dismayed when they learned about that fateful letter, warning me about going back to him. But they couldn't really expect that I'd listen and they wouldn't have concealed things from me if they hadn't already known that I could no more stay away from him than I could stop breathing.

So I'd gone back to my first love and it was as if we'd never been apart. I loved him and couldn't stop loving him even if I tried, so I didn't try. Then out of the blue, four months later I discovered that I was pregnant. He swiftly closed the door to me as did his family. Melanie wanted to apply a blunt object to his head, fuming and calling him all the names she could think of. He promised he'd marry me if I'd have a termination. I never believed I could love anything or anyone as much as I loved him, but now things had changed because I was suddenly overwhelmed with love for this unborn baby and for the first time something meant more to me than he did. So I stood up to him and held my ground. I told him 'no'. He came back when our baby was four months old, then walked out again when she was eighteen months old, telling me that he wanted blonde-haired blue-eyed children. His parting shot had been the cruellest one of all, telling me that as well as being a gold-digger I was the kind of woman a man wanted for a mistress, not a wife, and saying that I should have listened to him – now I'd ruined both my own and the child's life, as no man would want to bring up another man's child, especially one who was half-caste.

I'd worshipped and idolised this man for so long. Now I finally admitted what everyone had been telling me for years – he was nothing more than a control freak, a hypocrite and an emotional bully.

Because of my upbringing, I'd always equated bullying with physical violence and verbal abuse and I'd always been wary of any man who so much as raised his voice to me. As a child and young adult I'd had no choice, but as an independent woman free to make her own choices I refused to allow myself to be terrorised by anyone. I knew the early tell-tale signs of the kind of nature that I wanted nothing to do with, and would simply walk away. Furthermore, I was perfectly ready to punch any man's lights out if he so much as raised his voice to me because never again would I live in terror of any man. I was determined to break the cycle and refused to be a victim of aggression and physical abuse ever again.

However, experience of and vigilance against physical abuse had not prepared me for another characteristic that I did not and could not have known about until it was too late. A busted lip or a black eye is proof of physical abuse and a woman only needs to look in a mirror to see that. Its evidence is objective and irrefutable. Emotional abuse, however, is rather more subjective and takes longer to work out, and even then there is always that element of doubt about its existence. Where I was concerned, it was a long time before I could admit to myself that the man I loved was emotionally cruel and, by his own admission, saw our relationship as a power struggle where he wanted to be the one in control. Increasingly in our relationship he'd played on my insecurities and weaknesses, convincing me that I was unstable, neurotic and hysterical and that all the problems in our relationship were my fault, when really they stemmed from his own insecurities. I'd initially looked up to him and thought that he knew everything and was far cleverer than I could ever be, but going to university had proved that not only was I as clever as him, I was cleverer. My newfound confidence threatened him and he couldn't help wanting to bend my will to his. I realised that we'd never had discussions about decisions: He'd always dictated what I should believe or told me what to do, issuing it in the form of a command. It never occurred to me to refuse. Until the baby came along.

He'd presented me with choices that no woman should have to make. That was when I knew that as passionately as I loved him, it didn't necessarily mean that I had to like him. That realisation told me that the seemingly impossible had happened: I'd fallen in love with my baby and fallen out of like with him. A chapter in my life closed.

After Pakistan, I'd still been able to maintain a kind of uneasy relationship with my parents over the years, although the events that happened there were never mentioned again. I'd had a difficult pregnancy and, regardless of the fact that she'd never been approachable, I'd desperately wanted my mother. I wanted to sit at her feet like I used to as a child, feel her hand on my head and hear her tell me that everything would be all right.

However, understandably reluctant to deal with the inevitable fall-out, my brothers hadn't let me tell my parents that I was pregnant and would block my calls or quickly snatch the telephone from my mother's hands when she started asking about my mysterious illness. At one stage, when I'd come out of hospital after nearly losing the baby, my father had called to say they didn't understand why I was sick but he'd come to London and bring me back home so the family could look after me.

I was afraid to tell them but I couldn't keep the secret for ever. When I was six months pregnant, despite being afraid of their reaction, I needed them desperately. I knew if I went home, it would be in shame and in need and my life would never be mine again. But at that time there were few options left to me. I decided to accept whatever was offered and do whatever they asked of me. I'd hand myself and my baby over to my mother and she'd decide how we'd live, where we'd live and what people would be told about me. I knew she'd insist upon the baby being brought up as a devout Muslim and kept under strict religious and cultural supervision in a way that its mother had never been. I'd fought and lost. I also knew the baby would be made to atone for the sins of the mother.

Two months before the baby was due, I was staying with my older sister. She wasn't happy about the situation but she took me in and took care of me. It was during that time that my parents were told about the baby. There was the inevitable anger and recriminations against me and also my sister, who was made to feel as if she was harbouring a fugitive. I'd cried down the phone when speaking to my mother. For the first time in my life, I told my mother that I needed her. I begged her not to abandon me and promised I'd do anything she wanted me to do. Two weeks later I discovered my parents had gone abroad for the winter, as they always did; they quite clearly felt no compulsion to postpone this year. I was devastated.

While I was still in the care of my older sister, Sophie was born a month premature on 29 December 1995. I left London and moved to Retford permanently a month later. People assured me there was no stigma to being a single parent these days but it made no difference to the way I felt because I didn't know anyone else in my position. My parents had always told me never to mix with the very type of person that I'd become. I remember the names they used to call the *goris* who had children out of wedlock.

One, I recall, after having at least one child before her marriage ended in divorce, later had a half-black child, then a half-Asian child. As she pushed her double buggy down the street, my father would point her out, speculating that all she needed was a half-Chinese one then she'd have the full set.

Being an Asian and a single parent filled me with shame. No one needed to beat me with that stick because I was quite happy to beat myself. Yet, desperate to dispel the stereotype, I discovered another side to being a single parent that I hadn't bargained for.

It happened when I was at a job interview. The interviewer observed that, as a single mother, surely I didn't need to work because I was entitled to state benefits. Perhaps he said this to me because he was black and I was Asian and he felt safe within the ethnic context. I was livid that he dared to intimate that unless I stayed at home receiving state handouts, I was a bad mother. To add insult to injury, he had the audacity to tell me how appalled he'd be if the mother of his children chose to leave them at home with a child-minder and ended up selling herself to an employer as I was doing. Burning with indignation I told him that I was not a single parent through choice and that, having worked all my life, I chose to bring my daughter up with self-respect and dignity, not on state handouts! I left that interview without a job, but even more determined to work for a living as I'd always done.

Nevertheless, I'd begun to wonder whether I'd been wrong after all to have fought so hard against my parents and the role

I'd been born into. By fighting against the traditions and culture that should have been my fate and letting other people decide the course of my life, had I ended up any better off or had I simply made things even worse for myself? Could I honestly say that I was any happier than those Muslim girls who'd been born in the West and had ultimately chosen family over freedom? Had I made any better choices than the ones my parents had offered me? Or had they simply been different choices, ones I'd only thought were better for the simple reason that *I'd* made them? Having made my point, did freedom really taste any better than the cultural enslavement I'd left behind?

From an early age I'd questioned the faith and culture I'd been born into, refusing to accept that in Islam there were different rules for men and women. I'd had two sides to me: my Western life and the Eastern one. I'd grown up frustrated and confused about my identity, not knowing who I was or where I belonged. In a society that demands total obedience, I was labelled a troublemaker for daring to question the East–West anomalies that ruled my life. All my life I'd been different and hadn't minded. But having a baby changed all that and I wanted more for her. I wanted her to belong in a way I'd never belonged. I'd been born into the Muslim religion and Pakistani culture that had brought so much unhappiness into my life, so I'd rejected it. Yet having chosen to do so and completely embrace the Western part of me, I couldn't really say this had made me any happier.

I was still desperately unhappy and very confused. I felt isolated and displaced; belonging nowhere and to no one. My life had been spent outside the boundaries that guide other people. I'd had no nurturing or loving guidance from my parents, only commands, threats and ultimatums. They hadn't even tried to meet me halfway. It had been all or nothing, an ultimatum I knew was given to all Asian daughters who threatened rebellion. Most simply can't face life out in the cold, shunned by those they love and who don't seem to love them enough to take any of their feelings, hopes and desires into consideration.

So, having chosen my freedom, I'd been on my own to do what I'd felt was the right thing, but having no boundaries, no religious or cultural guidelines to trust, I'd floundered. Was it the fault of the society I'd been taken out from, or the one I'd been brought into? Was it my mother's unwillingness to integrate into this society or mine for refusing to segregate myself from it? Whose fault was it? Was it theirs or was it mine?

Sophie was twenty-two months old by now and I'd decided to go back to the only place where things had made sense to me. I'd been happier in Copenhagen than I'd ever been in my life. Of course, things would be different because I now had a baby, but Danish society was far better geared towards working single mothers and I had friends out there. It was the right thing to go to Denmark.

I'd outstayed my welcome at my elder sister's house and was living on my own in Retford with my baby. I missed my friends who still came up regularly to see Sophie and me, but the things I wanted were not to be found in this little rural community. Having been used to a huge cosmopolitan city such as London, I felt that I had nothing in common with the people here. They were friendly enough but I had no special friends and felt no sense of belonging. I began to make plans to leave and try to make a new life in Denmark. I had no job, no home that I could call my own and my friends were miles away. There was nothing for me here. My life had been stripped bare and I was as lonely and alone as I could possibly have been. I belonged nowhere and to no one.

Having searched all my life for something that would fill that empty, yawning ache in my heart, little did I know that the things I most longed for and needed were about to come into my life, and in the most unexpected place I could have imagined.

I was late for a 2.00 p.m. appointment. Despite this however, for reasons I cannot explain, I found myself inside a coffee shop that I'd never been in before.

'Why on earth did I just do that?' I wondered. They were getting ready to close up, I was late for my appointment and I had no idea what I was doing in this coffee shop, which seemed to be full of the sort of people I had nothing in common with. Annoyed with myself and slightly panicked, I turned the pram around to get out as fast as I could, when I suddenly heard something that stopped me dead in my tracks; a Scandinavian accent!

'It couldn't be,' I thought. 'Not out here in this little market town, in the middle of nowhere!' But there was no mistaking that distinctive inflection. Despite being pocket-sized, her voice was such that I heard her in the kitchen before I saw her.

'Excuse me, is that lady Danish?' I asked of someone who looked as though they worked there. I was nearly right: she was Norwegian and her name was Øigund Merrygold.

This meeting proved to be a turning point in my life. Having desperately missed my cosmopolitan circle of friends, I was surprised to discover that not only was there a Norwegian living here in Retford, but this close-knit group of people included a German, a New Zealander, a Greek family and people of various other nationalities. I'd lived in this town for almost two years and had no idea these people had been here.

I'd spent months trying to deal with my own grief and cope with a baby who clung to me and needed the things that I felt emotionally ill-equipped to give her. I had no mother to turn to who would hold me and tell me she'd take care of me, no one who could offer to take care of my baby and give me the space I needed to come to terms with what had happened. Øigund's friendship was a balm to my loneliness and despair. Without being asked, she understood how unhappy I was and how difficult I found being a single mother, alone in a place where I had no friends. Like a whirlwind she swept into my house one morning, barely a week after we'd met, packed up bottles, nappies, baby wipes, a change of clothes, switched the baby seat from my car to hers, then picked up the baby, informing me that she'd bring her back in the evening. Meanwhile, she ordered me to go back to bed, sleep and rest. Then she was gone, leaving me wondering whether I'd been in the company of an angel or a Norwegian lunatic who'd just kidnapped my baby.

The space that Øigund gave me was exactly what I needed. She visited me regularly and would either whisk me off for coffee or lunch or simply take the baby away to give me time and space for myself. On Tuesdays she'd keep the baby overnight. Sophie called her Nanny Øigund, and not surprisingly she became attached to both Øigund and her husband Norman, who'd always greet Sophie by pressing her nose and saying 'beep beep'.

'Don't you let anyone else do that,' Norman told her. 'That's my special hello.'

I remember once someone else tried to beep beep her nose, only to be glared at by an outraged Sophie who snuggled up to Norman, indignantly pushing the interloper away. Another time, she returned from her weekly overnight visit uttering her first complete sentence.

'Midge did that to Thofie'th teddy,' she lisped, happily waving her favourite sailor teddy bear that had been chewed by the Merrygold's little terrier.

Being a single mother

It was my birthday and Susan and Melanie planned a surprise. I'd been doing up the new house and they had the idea of spending a whole weekend decorating Sophie's room for me. They came up from London armed with paint and equipment, then shut themselves in her bedroom. I was ordered to stay out and not allowed near the bedroom at all, which was infuriating as over the next couple of days I opened the door to a stream of helpers and I'd hear laughter and conspiratorial whispering coming from the room from which I'd been banned. I cooked big meals and we all had a fun weekend culminating in my being led blindfolded into Sophie's room, with her in my arms, as we finally got to see the finished room. It looked fabulous, and I knew I had a lot to be grateful for, having friends who were like family to me.

Despite a difficult start in life, I didn't think that my daughter was doing so badly. I'd made a conscious decision to be a working mother for several reasons. First, I knew that I would be happier within myself if I had a sense of purpose outside my role as a mother. Second, I wanted to set an example to my daughter about never allowing yourself to settle for being a victim of circumstances. Working, paying taxes, running a car, keeping up my own home and being independent – all these things gave me dignity and self-respect. The price was that other people were paid to care for my baby, share bath times and put her to bed while I came home from work late, picked her up, put her in the car, drove home and put her to bed before falling into bed myself, exhausted. I was eligible for help towards childcare, but this help was available only if I used a registered childminder, and because I worked a lot of late shifts I was only able to use friends, which meant no help with childcare costs. Childcare, petrol, clothes, make-up and the costs of working ate up a lot of my salary so my independence cost me dearly.

I generally worked between thirty and forty hours a week but grabbed every bit of overtime I could. Sometimes I worked between forty and fifty hours a week, but that took its toll and some months later I collapsed under the strain of exhaustion. I don't really remember much except the afternoon when it happened. I was fortunate in that Annette and Judith, the friends who took care of me, were nurses. Some weeks later Annette told me that they'd not dared to call an ambulance because I'd been in such a state they were worried that I might have been sectioned. What scared me about that story was the fact that I had absolutely no memory of it at all, and it only confirmed to me that, as hard as I strove for dignity and independence, being a single mother was the most difficult thing I had ever done.

I used to bring Sophie into bed with me and prop myself on one elbow and watch her sleeping. During those precious moments, watching her eyelids flicker as she dreamed, breathing in her baby fragrance, all the hardships I endured and sacrifices I'd made for her were worth it. It was during one such night that I made her a promise to find her a new daddy. I'd read somewhere that up to the age of four years children will accept a new man in their life without question. According to this article, after the age of four it becomes progressively more difficult as the child gets older. Believing this to be true, I promised my sleeping baby that I would find a man who not only would want to be a husband to me but would also want her and love her as if she were his own flesh and blood. I promised her that I'd find her a new daddy before she was four years old, and if that was not possible I would devote my life to bringing her up on my own rather than compromise.

Six months later I met the man who was to become my husband.

The life of Riley

He gazed into my eyes, desperately trying not to stare at my cleavage, and uttered the words that no single woman can resist. He offered to do my DIY.

I'd wanted to have my floorboards sanded and received an outrageous quote. Melanie had come up that weekend, and leaving her and Sophie in the garden I announced that I was going to the builder centre to hire a sander and, while I was there, pick up some gullible idiot to do it for me. That was where I met Ion.

I returned home to tell Melanie that I'd found someone who'd practically begged me to let him do the job for me, and if he was stupid enough to spend his August bank holiday weekend sanding my floorboards in return for a curry then it would be rude for me to deprive him of the experience. Mel had thought he sounded too good or too gullible to be true and said he probably wouldn't turn up. A few days later, having returned to London, she rang to warn me that if he did turn up I absolutely must not be alone with him because he was probably a pervert.

On Saturday he did turn up, knocked at the front door and, receiving no reply, went around the back and let himself in through the kitchen. He was dressed in jeans and t-shirt, wearing sunglasses and casually swinging a black leather jacket over his shoulder.

'Great!' I thought. 'He's come dressed for a bloody date, not to sand my floors!' I was wrong: he announced he was ready to start work straight away, so I left him in the sitting room to go and make him a coffee before he started work.

'I'm Thofie,' announced a little voice behind him. He turned and looked scared to death to discover a small child standing in the doorway, beaming up at him.

'Well, he's definitely not The One!' I muttered to myself, handing him a cup of coffee, unimpressed by his reaction to my daughter.

It became a continuing arrangement for him to finish work and come over to my house to do my DIY and share a meal with us afterwards. He asked me out to dinner several times, but although the floors were beautifully sanded there was still an awful lot more to do in the house, and I didn't feel inclined to spoil a perfectly good arrangement by becoming romantically involved with this particular DIY gift horse. Despite this, I enjoyed having him around the place because he was good company, and very soon I began to miss him when he went home to his own flat.

His initial reaction to Sophie had been a mixture of surprise and awkwardness. He hadn't known how to respond to this little girl, but over the next few weeks I saw him relax around her and would watch as they played together. We all began to go out shopping and without even thinking he'd pick her up and carry her in his arms. For her part, Sophie realised that she was on to a good thing and saw no reason whatsoever to use her own legs when this man seemed quite happy to swing her up on to his shoulders or carry her, and she became a decorative fixture around his neck. Having someone beside me to help me with ordinary everyday things such as grocery shopping and childcare was all new to me. Yet while it was seductive, in the beginning I was nevertheless wary and watched him like a hawk, as would any mother.

It mattered to me that my two oldest friends, Sophie's godmothers, approved of any man who had started to spend any significant time around her. Following a personal tragedy, Susan had since resigned from the police force and, having met dashing scientist, Mark Jacob, she moved up to Derbyshire, only an hour's drive away. She had met Ion and liked him, observing how good he was with Sophie.

Melanie had spent years disapproving of every man I'd ever been out with, so it was quite disconcerting to hear her ordering me to marry someone. She'd shriek like a harpy for me not to dare make a decision without telephoning her first so she could talk me out of turning him down, somehow slightly missing the point that, even if I'd wanted to marry him, he hadn't actually proposed. These were strong opinions considering that she hadn't even met him yet. Nevertheless, she was adamant that he was 'The One'. I wasn't so sure.

I hadn't decided whether I wanted that kind of relationship with him, and as much as I'd hated being alone, I'd begun to panic at the thought of him becoming a permanent fixture in our lives. We'd only known each other a few weeks and suddenly I couldn't get rid of him fast enough, picking a fight with him over an innocent remark he made about the meal I'd made that evening.

The next day an Interflora van drew up and delivered an enormous bunch of flowers and a note from Ion apologising for upsetting me. I was not impressed.

'*I* pick a fight with him and *he* apologises!?' I exclaimed to my older sister as I thrust the flowers at her to take home.

'But he sent you those because he likes you,' she said, offering them back to me.

A few hours later, I was upstairs putting up new curtains while Sophie was trampolining on my bed.

'Careful,' I warned the little kangaroo behind me. 'You'll fall off.'

Too late, because she bounced herself off the bed and landed on the bedroom floor with a thud. She whimpered slightly, but once over the shock seemed happy enough. I examined her precious little arm but nothing was sticking out and there didn't appear to be any bruises, so I comforted her and put her to bed as normal. However, at ten o'clock she woke up crying and I knew immediately that something was wrong. Sophie had always been a good baby; she rarely cried, and once in bed she always slept straight through until seven in the morning. She was holding out her arm and I suspected that perhaps she might have sustained a fracture when she landed on it.

It was late and I was distressed by her tears, and my first instinct was to call Ion. I knew I'd treated him badly and had compounded my behaviour by refusing to acknowledge his flowers, so I braced myself to be told to get lost in no uncertain terms. I was wrong, because without any hesitation he told me he was coming around straight away to take us both to Bassetlaw hospital, seven miles away.

Being Friday night it was busy. As we sat waiting to be called, I remember being grateful that Ion was with us. Sophie was whimpering in his arms and I found myself instinctively leaning against his shoulder, comforted by his presence.

'Thank you for the flowers.'

'I wondered if you'd get around to mentioning them,' he replied. 'I waited all day for you to call, and when you didn't I thought that was it.'

'I thought you'd tell me to get lost when I called tonight.'

'I wouldn't do that. You needed me,' came the reply.

It was 2.00 a.m. when we were finally seen and 4.00 a.m. when the test results showed that she had indeed fractured her arm. By now Sophie was hysterical from pain and sheer exhaustion and screamed and kicked at anyone who tried to examine her, and it was decided to keep her in the children's ward for what was left of the night. I was exhausted with worry and fatigue myself – I'd never seen her in such a state – and burst into tears. I felt totally unable to leave my daughter while she was still so distraught, but Ion persuaded me it was best to leave her where she'd be taken care of and promised he'd bring me back the next morning. He drove me home, put me to bed and came upstairs to wake me a couple of hours later to take me to hospital, having scarcely slept himself.

That night at hospital changed my feelings towards him because now I knew he cared about Sophie and me. But that in itself frightened me even more. While I wanted him around, the prospect of letting him get close to me was something I found very difficult, and whenever things began to feel too cosy I'd pick a fight with him and push him away. He'd been spending more and more time with us, sometimes not leaving until the early hours of the morning and going to work straight from my house. I'd justify the way I treated him by telling myself that no one forced him to spend all his time with us and that if he didn't like it he had a perfectly good flat of his own to go home to. But it felt safe and comforting to snuggle up to Sophie at night, knowing that Ion was downstairs.

Nevertheless, it confused me as to why he let me treat him so badly. Over the next couple of weeks I did everything I could to put him down and belittle him, shouting at him that if he was going to leave, it was better he did it sooner rather than later. This state of affairs culminated in a huge row one Sunday evening when he finally turned on me, telling me he knew I didn't care about him, he'd had enough and if I didn't want him I only had to say so and he'd never bother me again. We parted in the certain knowledge that this was finally the end.

Sophie was asleep and I'd had a bath and was ready for bed myself. But I couldn't sleep, pacing the sitting room feeling agitated and disorientated. Ion's quiet presence always filled the whole house and his absence made it feel lonely and empty. I was angry one moment, telling myself that I didn't need him, I didn't need anybody, and it had always been inevitable that he'd leave, then in another moment bereft at the thought of losing him. My heart felt heavy with an emotion that I willed myself not to feel, until I could bear it no longer and, arranging for the lodger to sit with Sophie, I picked up my keys and drove to Ion's flat and rang the doorbell.

It was clear from the expression on his face that I was quite clearly the last person he expected to see. I realised that I must have looked a state. It was raining and I was standing dripping on his doorstep dressed in my nightie and slippers, but I didn't care.

It was the first time I'd set foot inside his flat, and as I looked around me I realised that I'd never given any thought to this private side of him that had nothing to do with Sophie and me. He lived in a very masculine two-bedroomed flat in a big Victorian house with high ceilings and an enormous sitting room. However, what amazed me were the things in the flat that gave an insight to the character of this man, things that hitherto I'd never bothered to find out.

There were huge framed pictures of battle scenes and military aircraft on the walls; on the landing there was a large glass cabinet containing regiments of lead soldiers, all meticulously hand-painted. Then there were the books. His shelves were full of books on military history: many different volumes on the Battle of Waterloo and, in particular, a whole range of material on the First World War, including a complete set of what he told me was the British Official History.

'Have you actually read all these books or do you just collect them?' I asked. He replied that he did like collecting them but he had in fact read every book he owned. He'd been interested in military history since he'd been ten years old and had started collecting books and militaria from about the age of twenty.

As well as his vast collection of military history books, he had all the *Alien* and *Star Wars* films and a lot of comedy videos, including about half a dozen of Ben Elton doing his stand-up act, filmed during his famous *Saturday Night Live* days.

Realising how little I knew about him, I was suddenly in awe of him and the things he knew yet had hitherto never talked about because, I suspected, I'd never shown any interest in finding out anything about him. Yet now I'd finally come to his home and taken an interest, his face lit up as he talked animatedly about the things that made him tick. Possibly for the first time, I noticed how green his eyes were and what a rugged face he had. People were always telling me how handsome he was, but I'd convinced myself that he simply wasn't my type, perhaps for the very same reason that I hadn't allowed myself to get to know him. I realised I'd done everything possible to stop myself having feelings for him. That night I finally admitted to him what I'd been forced to admit to myself: I needed him and wanted him in my life and Sophie's.

Being a single mother had been very difficult. I'd been lonely and had spent the past year or so desperate to find a man who'd care about my daughter and me. Yet when that man had come along, I'd done everything I could to sabotage the relationship and make him leave me. For the first time, I was anxious that I'd pushed him too far and perhaps he'd tell me that it was too late. If he did, I asked myself, would I plead with him to give me another chance? Having let all these thoughts run through my mind as he talked, I realised that perhaps I wasn't taking a chance after all; if I was honest, I'd known all along how he felt and had known deep down that he wouldn't refuse to take me back. Having proved that he wasn't going to leave me, I finally trusted him to stay.

Pulling up outside my house, I handed him the keys and stepped back as he unlocked the front door and let us both in. I was certain I had done the right thing, because now he was back, I knew I couldn't bear to be parted from him again.

Two weeks later and only seven weeks after we first met, he asked me to marry him, saying that he'd wanted to tell me how he felt but held back in case he scared me off. He said I'd been intimidating because I was so aggressive and independent, making it perfectly clear from the beginning that I could cope alone and didn't need anyone. That night at the hospital was the first time the mask had slipped and he'd seen a very different side of me. I'd been vulnerable and had turned to him. According to Ion, that was when he realised he loved me and decided he was going to marry me.

Two years later, in September 2001, Ion and I were married. My parents had not attended the weddings of their other two daughters. They similarly refused to attend mine and it was Norman who gave me away.

One of the deciding factors in my decision to agree to marry Ion was meeting his family. I knew that they wouldn't have known many Asian people, if any at all, and I'd been quite anxious about what they'd think of him marrying a girl who was not only Pakistani but also had a young child. I knew there was a widowed mother and that Ion was third in a family of four, with two sisters, Heather and Catherine, and an older brother,

Andrew. My plan to meet them one by one was thwarted while out shopping in the market place one Saturday when we bumped into his mother and both his sisters. I braced myself for a hostile reception and couldn't quite understand why they seemed so pleased to finally meet me.

'Why wouldn't they be?' Ion replied, as if it was the most natural thing in the world that his family would like the person he chose to marry.

After we announced our engagement, we all met at his mother's house to discuss the implications for Sophie. It was decided by the family that because she was so young, Sophie needed stability, and it was better at the outset for family relationships to be defined straight away. So having called him Ion for seven weeks, she now called him 'Daddy' and also acquired a new nanny and several aunts, uncles and cousins. Catherine's son James is also an only child, and with just eighteen months between them, the two youngest children of the family began as they meant to go on, playing and squabbling like siblings. By the time Ion and I were married, these relationships were an established part of Sophie's life.

I trusted Ion and his family completely. Proof of that came when, six months after Ion and I became engaged, nine of us girls all went off to Amsterdam for Susan's hen weekend. At first I hesitated, but Ion persuaded me to go, saying he was quite capable of looking after Sophie; he assured me, that having made a commitment to be her father, looking after her was something that he undertook willingly. So I went, leaving Sophie in Ion's capable hands, supported by my future mother-in-law. I was genuinely touched by how these people took Sophie into their family and loved her as their own.

I have heard it said on several occasions that Pakistani men don't bring up other men's children. I knew of several men whose wives had died and who within six months had returned from Pakistan with a new wife and mother to bring up the children. Usually she'd be a sixteen-year-old and barely older than the children themselves. However, it is a different matter for a woman widowed or left with children. For the sake of her children, she usually resigns herself to bringing them up alone rather than risk putting them at the mercy of a man who is not their father. In fact the only Pakistani stepfather I know of is my own brother Mohammed. However, he is unusual in this.

It makes me cherish the Riley family's acceptance of Sophie all the more because, having been brought up in a Pakistani family, I found it totally unexpected.

'Uncle Andrew, are you like my daddy?' Sophie asked during one sleepover at Andrew and Tracey's. He replied that they were brothers so he supposed they were alike.

'Yes, but do you *play*?' she wanted to know.

Fortunately for Sophie, Uncle Andrew did play, but that incident is a fairly accurate insight into Ion's relationship with Sophie. From the outset, his role in our lives has never been as a husband who just happened to acquire a step-child when he married the mother; rather, he has been a devoted and adoring father who has always taken an active part in her upbringing. Since she was little they have thundered through the house, chasing each other, playing hide and seek and fighting over sweets.

'Mummy, when you married Daddy, you got a new husband and I got a big brother,' she once declared, confirming what most wives suspect: that when it comes to play, husbands are often the same mental age as their children.

I know I have been unbelievably fortunate. Ion has changed nappies, bathed her, got up in the night if she was unwell, done the school run and generally played an active part in her upbringing, most of it without being asked. During our first family holiday, Susan, Melanie and I were chatting by the pool when we saw Ion coming towards us carrying Sophie in his arms. She'd had an accident and messed herself, and not wanting to disturb our girlie conversation, Ion had taken it on himself to take her away to the showers, clean her up and wash her swimsuit out. He then handed over this little giggling bundle, clean and all wrapped up snug in a big beach towel, before going off for a swim, leaving the three of us staring in disbelief – in a similar situation, most fathers would simply have handed the child over for the mother to deal with.

Being Sophie's godmothers, Susan and Melanie were fiercely protective of Sophie and I always knew they'd be watchful and suspicious of any man who came into our lives. I recall how furious Sue had been when my ex had picked up six-month-old Sophie by the straps of her dungarees. She'd turned purple with indignation and later said it was good riddance to a man who handled his baby like that.

Susan and Mark married in March 2000 and they now live in the picturesque peak district village of Crich. Sophie has adopted Sue's parents, Brian and Margaret, as Grandpa and Nanny Owers, whom she inventively named her 'god-grandparents'. She spends almost every school holiday with Mark and Sue, who have over the years spoiled her with trips to Disneyland Paris and have taken her to the French Alps to teach her to ski. In return, Sophie takes Mark to the cinema so he can watch all the latest kids' movies. In 2002 Susan and Mark were made her legal guardians in the event of our deaths, prompting six-year-old Sophie to declare hopefully, 'I can't wait for you and Daddy to die so I can go and live with Uncle Mark and Auntie SueSue.'

In 1999 Melanie met David Warren, a fellow long-serving police officer. Once she had decided he was not a pervert and courtesy of a bottle of Jack Daniels and a push-up bra, they fell in love and she galloped up the aisle with him in August 2001 in a fairy-tale wedding organised, of course, by the indomitable Phillippa. Dave has since sobered up to discover himself co-mortgagee of a very expensive house in Banstead, Surrey and bewildered father of two pretty little blonde strangers who call him Daddy.

Like most Asian parents, my mother was never required to understand or be understood by her daughters. She simply required unquestioning obedience. Therefore, if obedience is the benchmark as to whether I was a good daughter, then in my mother's eyes I have failed miserably. I am now married to an *Angrezi* husband and mother of a daughter whom she can never permit herself to love as much as she loves her full-blood Pakistani grandchildren. I have shamed and disappointed her.

Over the years I searched my mother's face to rediscover the angel of my early years, but to no avail. She has gone for ever. Or perhaps she never existed and what I saw in Pakistan was the person she truly was all along. Now we rarely have contact. My mother despises everything that I am, and I resent her constant criticism and refusal to meet me even part of the way or try to understand me. She used to telephone once every year or so, although even this has now stopped, which is a relief because when it did happen the conversations were an ordeal for us both. Within a matter of seconds, any resolve at self-restraint on her part dissolved and she would unleash a torrent of painful criticism on me for being a bad, uncaring daughter.

And while able to speak Urdu, I am unable to articulate my mother's tongue well enough to tell her that I was not born 'bad'. I *wanted* to be a good daughter, but it was not my fault I was brought up in a culture that would make me a stranger to my own parents.

Ours is a modern-day tragedy. We have a bond of blood that should have tied us in life and lived on after death for as long as our daughters and their daughters were able to remember us. Instead, we are two protagonists standing on the edge of a huge, yawning chasm that neither of us can breach, divided not only by a generation but by two languages and two conflicting cultures that can never be reconciled in our lifetime.

I'm told my mother hates me. I wish I could love her. But it's hard to love a stranger.

Margaret Riley is the kind of mother-in-law that any wife would choose. Initially she had reservations about Ion marrying me, first because, never really having known any Asian people before, she believed there would be huge cultural differences, and second because there was a young child involved. However, she came to her first Sunday lunch with us with an open mind and told us later that, watching Ion and me cook together and the three of us interacting as a family, she saw with her own eyes that we belonged together and gave us her blessing.

Something that became evident about my husband early on in our relationship was that he was remarkably unburdened by emotional baggage. I put that down to his having had an enviably happy childhood and the relaxed and easy-going relationship he has with his mother. She regularly tells him she loves him as easily and naturally as he accepts it. When Ion completed his Military History degree at Salford University, Mum and Catherine came to the ceremony to see him receive his degree, and I remember how thrilled they were on his behalf; rarely missing an opportunity to tell him. Mum gave Ion a card, reading 'To a much loved son', going on to say how proud he'd made her. It was quite simply outside my experience to know what it would feel like to receive a card like that from my own mother and I became quite tearful. At our wedding she said how fortunate her son had been to marry me.

Since then, she never fails to make me feel special. On birthdays and at Christmas, her gifts are chosen with an enormous amount of thought and care and are always exactly what I would buy for myself, indicating to me that she has taken the time and trouble to find out what makes me tick. I call her Mum and go to her to share my joys and anxieties and receive the love and understanding that I've always craved from my own mother. When Ion and I fall out, it is to her I turn, knowing that despite being his mother, she will never side against me if she feels Ion is in the wrong but will always speak her mind. As mothers-in-law go, I have the good fortune to have one who is there when she is needed and butts out when she isn't.

She has also been a perfect grandmother. She provides child-care for James and has always given that same unwavering support with Sophie over the years, babysitting if Ion and I go out, doing the school run when I worked full time and generally taking an interest in Sophie's development and giving her unfaltering love.

My sister-in-law Catherine is great too, telling me that I'm clever and beautiful and the best thing that ever happened to her brother. I recall on holiday at Center Parcs one year someone had a go at me and Catherine immediately squared up to her. I was concerned that she was about to deck this woman on my behalf and relieved when Ion came over. Actually, I was perfectly capable of punching the woman's lights out by myself, but I was touched that Catherine had jumped to my defence anyway.

Sophie and I have received the same acceptance and affection from all of Ion's family, and for the first time in my life I have a family who loves me and to whom I feel that I belong. That is the one thing I've always searched for. When they close ranks, they take me with them because I belong too. Simply to belong and be accepted into this family would have been enough for me. When I first married Ion, that was all I wanted, and I expected no more.

I approached my marriage with a very Asian attitude. While I wasn't 'in love', I was very much 'in like' with him, knowing he'd be a devoted husband and father who'd bring stability and a sense of belonging into my life and Sophie's. I trusted him and was content to be married to a man I liked and respected and felt it was a sound foundation on which to build a happy marriage and bring up children.

Shortly after our wedding, driving home from work one evening, I was somewhat startled to discover that I'd put my foot down because I couldn't wait to get home to him. Just thinking about seeing him again after being apart for ten hours made my heart lurch in a way that I never expected to feel again, and I knew without a doubt that I'd fallen in love with my husband.

With Ion I have discovered a deep happiness and content-ment that had always been missing. I feel loved and cherished by him. He was the man I'd waited for all my life. Driving home from work that evening, it was as if a veil was suddenly lifted, revealing my own husband to be the tall, handsome, green-eyed, chisel-jawed hero that I'd dreamed of all those years ago. I simply hadn't seen it before because I'd been looking in the wrong place.

For many years I'd been torn by the conflict of my East–West identity, being neither English nor Pakistani, yet at the same time feeling that I was both. I always believed that in order to belong anywhere I'd have to choose one thing at the cost of losing the other. But today, I am happily married to a man who loves me unconditionally, I belong to a family who have accepted me for who I am, and I have friends who have given me unwavering loyalty and friendship over the years. None of these relationships depend upon my being either Eastern or Western.

Out of my Eastern background and Western upbringing, a third person has emerged: a strong, happy, independent British Asian woman who has taken the best of both worlds. I have finally discovered that my true identity lies in the fusion of language, cuisine, ethnicity and heritage that together make me a complete person. This identity has transcended the barriers of race, religion and culture and finally bridged that divide, and through it I have found the peace and sense of belonging that has eluded me all my life. I do not have to choose to be either one or the other because I can embrace both.

All my life I have sought simply to be accepted. I was brought up in a Western society, yet just as important is the acknowledgement of the richness of the Eastern culture into which I was born. The two are inseparable, two halves which together make up the whole of me. I am British and I am Asian.

In the drawer of my bedside cabinet I have a gift tag from a present I received on my birthday. I cherish it. The tag reads simply 'To my exotic daughter-in-law, love from Mum x'. I'm finally home.

Acknowledgements

I would like to thank the other three members of the 'Coven', my sister Farah and friends Susan Jacob and Melanie Warren. We all know what we mean to each other. Thank you also to Ion, Mark, Dave and Michael for the love and support you give to the four of us. You know we're worth it and without us you wouldn't be half the men you are.

Thank you to my beautiful daughter Sophie, the joy of my life. Thank you for being so patient during the twelve months it took me to write this book, when I was locked away in my office, too busy, tired or emotional to give you attention. Apologies most of all for all the times I was busy working or away at meetings in London and left you at the mercy of Daddy's cooking. I hope in years to come, you won't write a book telling the world of the irreparable, long-term emotional trauma those horrible meals must have caused.

Thank you to Lesley Anyon and her gorgeous husband Michael. You both offered friendship and help when I was alone and never expected anything back.

To my dear friend and American Domestic Goddess, Deborah Jenkins. You have seen this project from its inception and with characteristic stubbornness, refused to go away when things became too difficult or emotional for me to handle. Your reactions to the revelations made in this book will be worth paying good money to see.

To Shahenaz, the fifth member of the Hendon Coven. Nothing changes and a true friendship means always picking up where we left off.

To all at New Life in Retford. You know who you are and what you mean to me.

My eternal love and affection to my wonderful Mum-in-Law (dare I call her Mother Riley?) and for the family she has given me.

Lastly, but very importantly, to my husband Ion. You put aside your own projects to support me in mine. You kept the house running, took care of Sophie and helped me by editing this book, letting me get on with the writing of it. Most of all, you have supported me through the emotional upheavals of recalling memories I locked away for years, listening, comforting and never displaying disapproval or judgement about the things you learned about me. All of which showed what jolly good value for money that marriage licence turned out to be.

Glossary

Abba-Ji	Father, with *ji* added for extra respect
Acha Bhai	Good Brother
Acha nahin hoga!	It won't go well with you
Akal	Common sense
Ammi	Mum
Angrezis	The English
Apa	Sis
Awara	Loose, wayward
Bahot garam chai	Very hot tea
Bakri!	Goat
Bas! Bas ho gaya!	Enough! That's enough!
Beta	Darling
Bewakuf!	Idiot!
Bey-izzati	To be without *izzat*
Beycharis	Poor things
Bhahenchode	Sisterf***er
Bhai	Brother
Bheynse	Buffalo
Bhindi	Okra
Biraderi	Brotherhood
Biwi	Wife
Bungla	House
Burra Abba	Elder Father
Burra Mammu	Mother's older brother
Burri Amma	Elder Mother

Chacha	Father's brother
Chachi	Wife of *chacha*
Choti	Younger
Chup!	Be quiet!
Dadda	Paternal grandfather
Daddi	Paternal grandmother
Desi	Native
Dhania	Coriander
Dhoolan	Bride
Dupatta	Scarf
Garam masala	Lit. hot spices
Gora	White person
Gori	White woman
Gurrh Burrh	Trouble, chaos
Habri	Buck-toothed
Haldi	Turmeric
Haramin!	Bastard
Haramzadi!	Bastard
Inki aisi ki taisi!	Lit. up theirs! or to hell with them!
Izzat	Respect
Jahanum	Hell
Kaffirs	Heathens
Kali	Black
Kameeni	Derogatory word for female
Kameez	Shift, tunic

Glossary

Khandani	Family
Kismet	Fate
Kurta	Long white cotton shirt
Maaderchode	Motherf***er
Mamoo	Mother's brother
Mazhab	Faith
Mumani	Wife of Mamoo
Namaz	Prayers
Nanna	Maternal grandfather
Naukar	Servant
Pak	Pure
Pakoras	Gram flour fritters, called 'bhajis' by Westerners
Pattar ka dil	Heart of stone
Phaeris	Fairies
Pukka	Done, cooked
Punkha	Fan
Purdah	Curtain, veil
Quaid-e-Azam	Great leader
Ramzaan	The month of fasting
Rishta	Proposal of marriage
Roti	Unleavened bread also called 'chapatti'
Sabzi	Vegetables
Sali	Derogatory name for a woman
Shaitan ki aulad!	Spawn of Satan!

Shalwar kameez	Traditional dress consisting of baggy trousers and shift
Sharab	Alcohol
Sharabi	Intoxicated
Sharam	Shame
Tameez	Etiquette
Tawa	Flat griddle
Wazu	Ritual washing before prayers

'What Ferzanna endured during her upbringing NO child should have to experience, particularly within the apparent safety of her own family surroundings. Unfortunately, the occurrence of childhood abuse is all too real and sadly cannot be denied. It exists in all societies and cultures thus making child protection a priority for all those who have custody, charge or care of a child whether as a parent/guardian or carer.'

Ali Khan
Chairperson, *roshni

*roshni (meaning 'light' in Urdu) is a Scottish Registered Charity established in 2002. Ferzanna Riley recently joined the Board of Directors and is contributing to the Charity's long-term strategy of raising the awareness of child abuse and empowering young people to challenge the issue. Through its work, roshni ensures that children and young people who are victims of any form of abuse have access to the services they require, which are sensitive to their cultural and religious needs.

For more information please visit www.roshni.org.uk